Wabi 2

Opening Windows

Scott Fordin
Susan Nolin

SunSoft Press
A Prentice Hall Title

SunSoft Press
A Prentice Hall Title

For my wife Paula, whom I love dearly; and for my children, Alyssa, Michaela, and Samuel, who are without a doubt the coolest kids in the universe.

– S.F.

For Eric.

– S.N.

Contents

2 • How Wabi Works   22

6 • Managing Drives   152

7 • Managing Printers

8 • Managing COM Ports

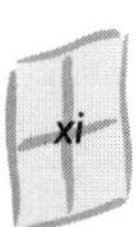

10 • Using DOS Applications   248

11 • Managing Colors   264

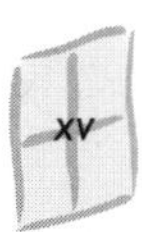

Figures

Wabi 2: Opening Windows

Tables

Wabi 2: Opening Windows

Tables

Preface

This book explains *everything you need to know* about using Wabi™ software... Yes, *everything*, In the process, you may also find some things you don't need to know, some things you thought you knew but didn't, and some things that have nothing to do with Wabi but are interesting nonetheless.

Who Should Read This?

Wabi software lets you run "shrink-wrapped" Microsoft® Windows applications on UNIX®-based computers. If you would like to do such a thing, then this book is for you.

This book, by the way, is intended for *users* of Wabi software—as compared to Windows or UNIX application developers who may wish to run their products under Wabi. While most of the information in this book is technical in nature, all of it has been written with the typical Joe or Josephine User in mind. The information in this book elaborates and expands upon the information in the Wabi user manual, installation instructions, and release notes.

One other note: Wabi software is available from several vendors, including SunSoft, Inc., Hewlett-Packard Company (HP®), the Santa Cruz Operation (SCO®), and International Business Machines Corporation (IBM®) (see page 17). The actual development of Wabi software, however, was done at SunSoft. While some minor desktop integration features may vary in the Wabi packages from other vendors, it is still, underneath it all, SunSoft's Wabi software. For this reason, this book focuses on the Wabi 2.1 package from SunSoft, which was the latest version of Wabi software at the time this book went to press (September, 1995).

Who Shouldn't Read This?

This book is not a programming guide; it does not go into great detail about the Microsoft Windows application programming interface (API). Nor will this book teach you how to use UNIX, the Solaris™ operating environment, or Microsoft Windows—although Chapters 3 and 4 do go into a fair amount of detail about UNIX, DOS, and Microsoft Windows, particularly with regard to the ways they differ from one another.

How This Book Is Organized

This book is divided into fourteen chapters and two appendixes:

- **Chapter 1, "What Is Wabi?,"** explains what Wabi software is, its purpose, features, operating and processor environments, where to get it, and where to find more information about it.

- **Chapter 2, "How Wabi Works,"** provides a technical overview of how Wabi software works.

- **Chapter 3, "Microsoft Windows For UNIX Users,"** explains the various Microsoft Windows interface components, describes how DOS and Windows work together, and how all these things compare to UNIX and the X Window System™. This chapter is intended for people who are familiar with UNIX, but not so familiar with DOS or Microsoft Windows.

- **Chapter 4, "UNIX For Microsoft Windows Users,"** provides basic UNIX information, explains the various UNIX/X Window interface components, and describes how UNIX differs from DOS. This chapter is intended for people who are familiar with DOS and Microsoft Windows, but not so familiar with UNIX.

- **Chapter 5, "Using Wabi Software,"** describes the basics of using Wabi software, including general installation instructions for Wabi software and Microsoft Windows, how to use Wabi

Configuration Manager and Windows Control Panel, different
ways to start Wabi software with command-line options, getting
help in Wabi, and Wabi international settings.

- **Chapter 6, "Managing Drives,"** explains how to connect to
  network-based directories through Wabi, and how to work with
  floppy and CD-ROM drives.

- **Chapter 7, "Managing Printers,"** explains how to install and
  configure printers under Wabi, and includes instructions for
  configuring LPT ports.

- **Chapter 8, "Managing COM Ports,"** explains how to configure
  COM ports under Wabi.

- **Chapter 9, "Using Windows Applications,"** explains how to
  install and use Windows applications under Wabi.

- **Chapter 10, "Using DOS Applications,"** explains how to use
  DOS applications from Wabi. Includes information about DOS
  emulation programs for UNIX.

- **Chapter 11, "Managing Colors,"** provides information about
  the way Wabi works with colors on your UNIX desktop, and
  describes Wabi color customization settings in `WIN.INI`.

- **Chapter 12, "Fonts and Wabi,"** describes how Wabi works
  with display and printer fonts, and explains how to optimize
  your system to work with various types of fonts.

- **Chapter 13, "Network Notes,"** explains various issues relating
  to working with applications in a network environment.

- **Chapter 14, "Tips and Tricks,"** describes specific X Window
  and Microsoft Windows features you can take advantage of
  through Wabi.

- **Appendix A, "Application Notes,"** provides application-specific
  tips for working with various applications under Wabi.

- **Appendix B, "Troubleshooting,"** provides troubleshooting tips
  for Wabi, Windows, and Windows applications.

This book concludes with a glossary of relevant terms, and an index.

Typographic Conventions

Throughout this guide, various typographic conventions are used to convey particular kinds of information. These conventions are described in Table P-1.

Table P-1   Typographic Conventions Used in This Book

Convention	Meaning
`Courier Plain`	File names, commands, or environment variables; UNIX names and commands are case-sensitive; DOS names and commands are not. When they are used in examples of text that should be entered in a file or at a command line, enter the text exactly as shown.
`Courier Bold`	File names and commands you enter, when contrasted with system prompts.
Italics	General emphasis. When used in command examples, denotes a variable string that should be replaced with a command, option, or file name. Variables enclosed in square brackets (that is, [*variable*]) are optional.
Gil Sans Plain	The name of keyboard key, menu command, tool, or dialog box option. In the case of keys, a plus sign between two keys indicates that you hold down the first key while pressing the second key. For example, Alt+F1 means hold down the Alt key while pressing F1. When the keys are separated by a comma, it means they should be pressed sequentially. For example E,Y means press and release the E key, then press and release the Y key.
➢ **Arrow**	Denotes the beginning of a step-by-step procedure.
	Indicates a note of general interest; additional information related to the current topic.
	Indicates a tip, trick, or special *factoid* related (perhaps even loosely) to the current topic.

Convention	Meaning
	Indicates a cautionary note; something about which you should be aware, or which could potentially cause a problem. You will not see these often.
	Indicates a warning; something that will cause problems resulting in data loss. Extremely rare.

Related Reading

Be sure to read the documentation included with Wabi software. In the case of SunSoft's version of Wabi, this documentation is:

- ***Wabi User's Guide*** – General user guide in Sun® AnswerBook® on-line format; there is no printed (hard-copy) user manual

- ***Wabi Installation Instructions*** – Installation and upgrade instructions in the form of CD liner notes

- ***Wabi Release Notes*** – Late-breaking information about Wabi; provided on line in Microsoft Windows Write format and installed as a program item in the Wabi Tools program group

If you are on the Internet, you can also access the Wabi 2.1 ***Frequently Asked Questions (FAQ)*** database, which is a database of questions and answers compiled by Wabi support engineers. You can obtain a current listing of this database by sending e-mail to:

```
wabi2.1-questions@east.sun.com
```

Finally, see "Sources of Information About Wabi" on page 20 to find out where you can get the latest information about Wabi software. Note that other Wabi manufacturers (see page 17) may provide different documentation than is listed here.

Acknowledgments

This book could not have been written without encouragement, technical support, editorial feedback, and general abuse from numerous people. In particular, I'd like to thank Reg Gillmor for selling the idea for this project to the powers-that-be, and for giving me the opportunity to work on it. Thanks also to Greg Doench at Prentice-Hall, and Rachel Borden and Karin Ellison at SunSoft Press (the aforementioned powers-that-be).

Invaluable technical and editorial review was provided by Margaret Riha, Reg Gillmor, Don Dudley, Bob Vandette, Matt Koehler, Tracey Wyatt, Jim Roberts, Charlie Burns, Bruce Murphy, Lorraine Carter, and Susan Cockrell. Maura Burke and Dave Damkoehler provided sage advice on issues regarding grammar and style. Jill Coghlan is the nice lady in the library who helped me track down the answers to so many questions.

Endless appreciation and thanks go to my wife and children, for putting up with a workaholic father in *absentia*—the grumpy guy who's always typing away at his computer. I'd also like to thank Hugh Fordin, who at the outset of this project gave me a huge box of CDs to listen to, and without which my troglodyte existence would have been far less bearable.

Oh, yes: The Wabi engineers also deserve *some* credit for creating a nifty product solely for purpose of giving me something to write about....

– S.F., Hollis, New Hampshire

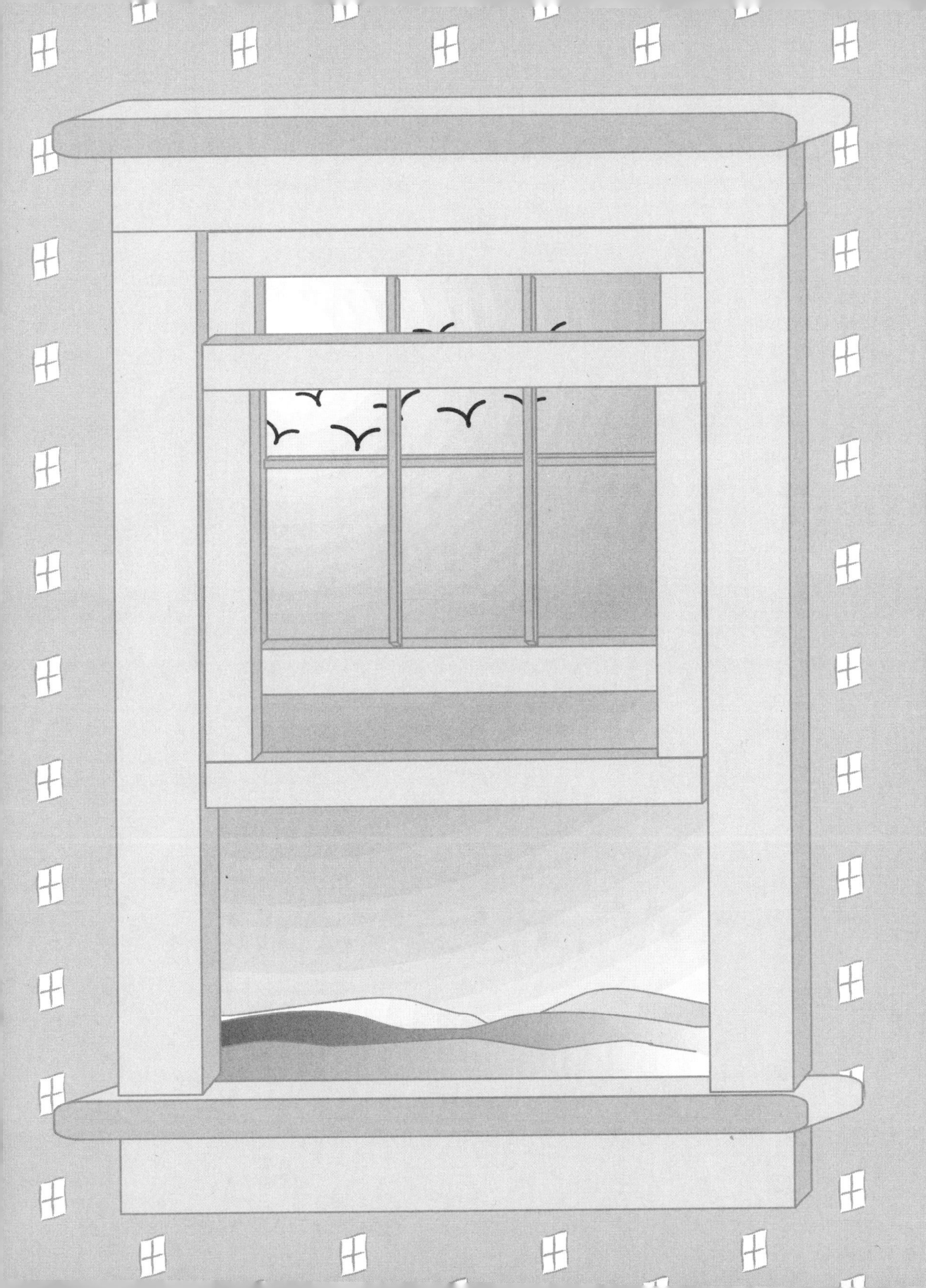

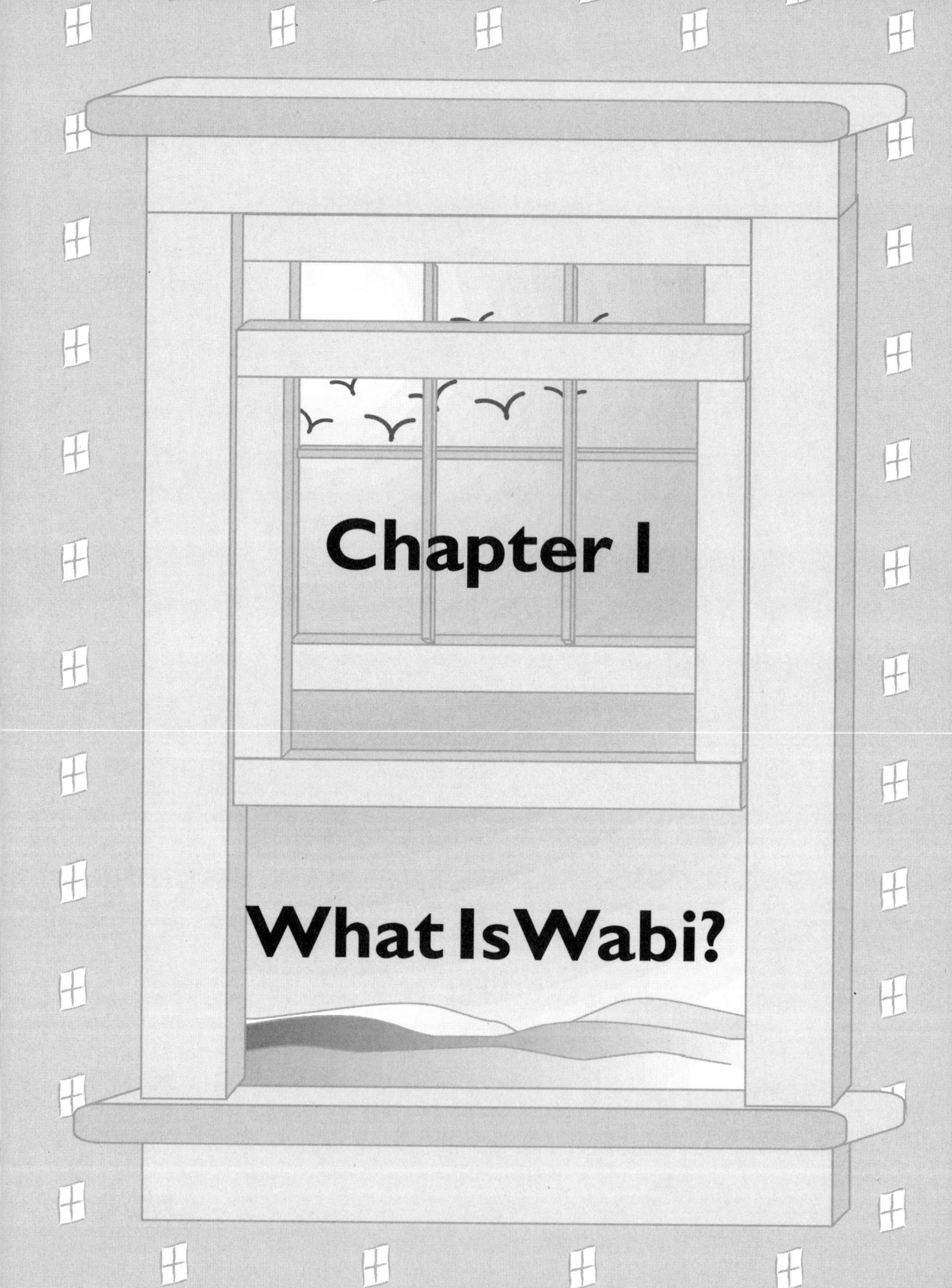

Chapter 1
What Is Wabi?

Wabi (pronounced *wah'-bee*) is a Japanese word (佗) that means, roughly, *quiet taste*. Contrary to popular belief, Wabi does *not* stand for *Windows Application Binary Interface*—though that's a fair description of what Wabi is.

> *You see it's like a portmanteau—there are two meanings packed up into one word.*
>
> – Lewis Carroll, *Through the Looking Glass*, 1872

In This Chapter

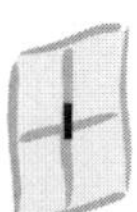

The Thing That Isn't There

Wu Wei doesn't try. It doesn't think about it. It just does it. And when it does, it doesn't appear to do much of anything. But Things Get Done.

– Benjamin Hoff, *The Tao of Pooh (The Pooh Way)*, 1982

The first thing you may notice about Wabi software is that you don't notice it. Without trying to be cryptic, the point is that Wabi is designed to work in the background, silently, without imposing its own interface on you.

You want to run Microsoft Windows-compatible applications on your UNIX desktop, and the Wabi designers—being an exceedingly modest lot—don't want to get in your way. The result is that, after Wabi software has been installed and configured, you are only aware of it in the sense that you now have available to you Windows-compatible applications that used to require a separate PC. Wabi software smoothly integrates unmodified, "shrink-wrapped" Windows 3.1 applications with other applications running under X Window on your UNIX desktop.

For example, you could configure your Solaris Workspace menu to include a command to start Lotus® Notes®; choosing this command would automatically start Wabi, which would then start Notes. Similarly, you could double-click on the name of a Microsoft Word for Windows™ document in the Solaris File Manager to automatically start Wabi and open the document in Word.

Wabi 2: Opening Windows

More importantly, your Windows and UNIX applications run next to each other, side-by-side in separate windows on your Solaris desktop. You can cut and paste between Windows and UNIX applications. You can size and move Wabi windows just like any other Solaris windows. You get the benefits of true multithreading, multitasking, and security provided by UNIX, and the higher-powered graphics and processing capabilities found in most UNIX workstations. Many Windows applications actually perform better under Wabi than they do on the PC for which they were designed!

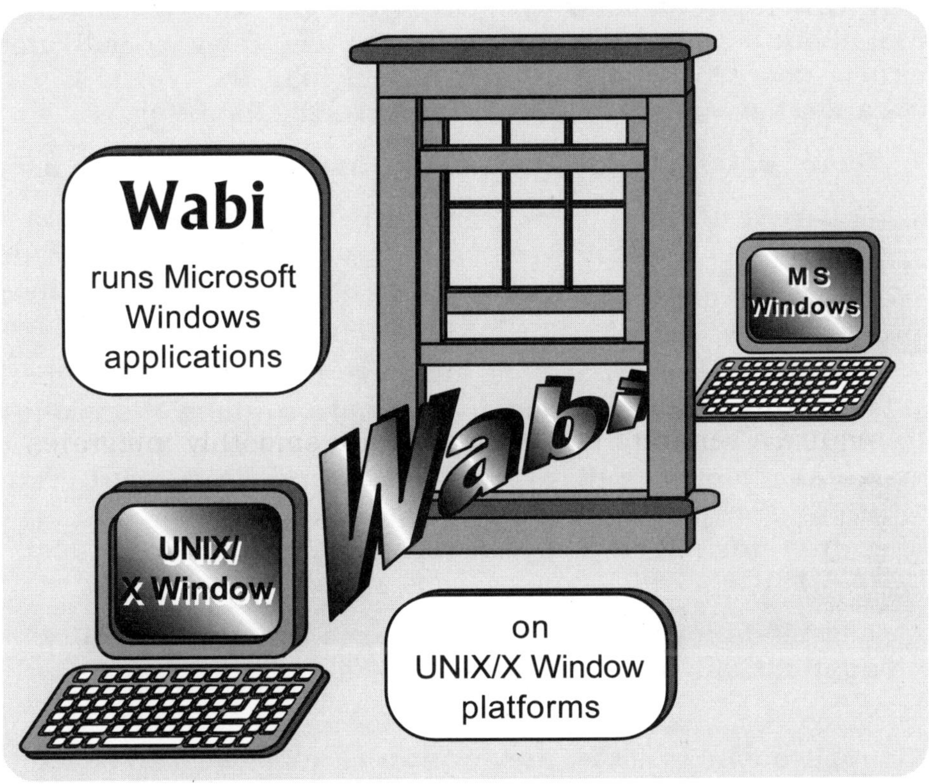

Wabi software doesn't care which UNIX platform you use—in addition to the Wabi software for the Solaris/OpenWindows™ environment (produced by SunSoft, Inc.), Wabi is offered as an OEM product by Hewlett-Packard, IBM, and the Santa Cruz Operation. For most UNIX workstation users, Wabi software makes it unnecessary to incur the cost and hassle of purchasing and configuring a PC just to run a few PC "productivity" applications, such as spreadsheets and word processors.

Who Uses Wabi?

Wabi software is used in large and small corporations, schools, colleges, universities, research organizations, government agencies—anywhere UNIX-based workstations and PCs are used.

Some Wabi users are already familiar with Microsoft Windows, but not with UNIX. Others are familiar with UNIX, but not with Windows. Some know a lot about both environments, while others know virtually nothing about either—you get the idea. In general, though, the typical Wabi user or organization has need to do one or more of the following:

- **Share data between UNIX users and DOS/Windows users.**

  Believe it or not, not everyone runs UNIX. Perhaps more shocking is the fact that not everyone runs Microsoft Windows under DOS. Wabi lets UNIX users share and edit documents and data created by or for Microsoft Windows applications.

  For example, a Lotus Notes document could be shared between two or more users, some of whom are running Microsoft Windows on a PC, and others who are running Wabi on a UNIX workstation. Note that this is true *sharing*—not just working on separate copies of the same document. Wabi's support for UNIX networking allows users to work on the same single document in a single location in a network directory.

- **Establish corporate-wide standards based on popular applications and suites.**

  Many corporations want to standardize on a specific set of applications—that is, they want their employees to be using the same software. Among other benefits, such standardization can reduce software purchase, training, and support costs. Wabi lets UNIX and DOS/Windows users run the same applications, regardless of whether they are using DOS or UNIX.

  For example, Wabi makes it possible for all employees—whether they are running UNIX or DOS machines—to use Microsoft Office™ or Lotus SmartSuite™.

- **Preserve investment in existing data and training while upgrading to more powerful systems.**

  Many growing corporations are moving some or all of their users away from DOS-based PCs to more powerful UNIX workstations. Some benefits of this strategy include faster processor and display subsystems, and more robust networking capabilities. Such corporations, however, may have already invested a significant amount of time and money training users and creating data under DOS/Windows—Wabi makes it unnecessary to throw away that investment.

  For example, suppose your organization has been trained to use Borland® Paradox®, and you have a Paradox database structure containing several years worth of business records. With Wabi, your employees can shift over to their new UNIX-based workstations with virtually no loss in productivity — Paradox is still there, and your database is still there.

- **Eliminate need for two machines.**

  For many users, Wabi software eliminates the need to have both a DOS machine and a UNIX machine—one UNIX machine with Wabi can run all the Windows and UNIX applications needed by *most* users (see the list of "Wabi 2.1 Certified Applications" on page 8).

- **Support mobile users running Microsoft Windows.**

  Nowadays, because of disk space and memory restrictions, most notebook computer users run DOS and Microsoft Windows. In terms of disk space requirements and memory "footprint," the DOS and Windows combination makes for a smaller operating environment than UNIX.

  When mobile users get back to the office, however, they may want to use a more powerful UNIX workstation, with more memory and better networking capabilities. With Wabi, such users can use Windows applications under DOS on their notebooks, upload the files (from diskette, or via a package like PROCOMM PLUS®) to their workstation, and then edit or print the files on their UNIX network.

Supported Applications

Okay, so here's the catch: Wabi runs Windows applications more quickly than any other UNIX-based product today, side-by-side with Solaris applications, with better networking capabilities, and in the more robust UNIX environment—but *it cannot run all Windows applications...* Hence the Wabi concept of *supported* or *certified* applications.

Certified applications are those applications that SunSoft, Inc. *guarantees* will work under its version of Wabi software. This means that each certified application has been thoroughly tested by SunSoft, and each has been found to work correctly—perhaps with some (very few) caveats. If the publisher of a certified application releases a version that does not work under Wabi, SunSoft will, within reason, make changes to Wabi so that the application will work.

Wabi also works with many other *noncertified* applications, but due to the sheer number of Windows applications available, SunSoft can neither test nor make guarantees about their compatibility.

The list of applications that Wabi is certified to run represents roughly 80 percent of the total current market share for Windows applications. To put it another way, 80 percent of all Windows applications sold today are on Wabi's compatibility list. The most popular word processors work, the most popular spreadsheet programs work, the most popular database programs, illustration, and presentation packages work.

Of the remaining 20 percent that are not on Wabi's compatibility list, many will work with Wabi anyway. The difference here is that SunSoft does not guarantee their compatibility. Some applications, unfortunately, will simply not work with Wabi. The next section explains this in more detail.

Why Certified Applications?

There are two primary reasons why the concept of certified applications is integral to Wabi's design:

- **Technical reasons** – Without going into the gory details here, Wabi is a Windows API *translator*, rather than a Windows *emulator*. Briefly, what this means is that Wabi does not try to duplicate the Windows environment in UNIX—with lackluster performance results—but entirely supplants the Windows kernel, and provides instead a true, native UNIX environment in which Windows applications can be run.

  Problems can arise when Windows applications do nonstandard things—like directly address your PC's hardware (which is a no-no under Windows), or use some *virtual device driver*. Well-behaved applications in general work under Wabi; applications that are not so well behaved can cause problems.

- **Too many applications to test** – When SunSoft certifies an application, it is their guarantee that the application will work under Wabi. To be able to make such a guarantee, SunSoft must *thoroughly* test the application with Wabi. This is not a trivial task; the tests are extensive, expensive, and time-consuming. There is simply no way to test carefully and to high standards all the applications on the market.

  You can feel confident, however, that certified applications will run reliably and with good performance under Wabi. Again, many noncertified applications will also run under Wabi, but they have not been as thoroughly tested.

A more detailed explanation of how Wabi works, and how it relates to application certification, is provided in the next chapter, "How Wabi Works," starting on page 22.

Wabi 2.1 Certified Applications

Table 1-1 lists the applications that are certified by SunSoft, Inc. to run under Wabi 2.1 software.

Table 1-1   Wabi 2.1 Certified Applications

Adobe PageMaker 4.0, 5.0	Borland Paradox 4.5, 5.0
CorelDRAW! 3.0, 4.0	Harvard Graphics 2.0, 3.0
Intuit Quicken 3.0, 4.0	Lotus 1-2-3 4.0, 5.0
Lotus Ami Pro 3.01, 3.1	Lotus Approach 2.1, 3.02
Lotus cc:Mail client, 2.0, 2.03	Lotus Freelance Graphics 2.01, 2.1
Lotus Notes client, 3.0c, 3.3	Lotus Organizer 1.1, 2.0
Lotus SmartSuite 2.0, 3.1	Microsoft Access 2.0
Microsoft Excel 4.0, 5.0	Microsoft Mail client, 3.2
Microsoft Office 4.3c	Microsoft PowerPoint 3.0, 4.0
Microsoft Project 3.0, 4.0	Microsoft Windows 3.1, 3.11
Microsoft Windows for Workgroups 3.11[1]	Microsoft Word 2.0, 6.0c
Novell Quattro Pro 5.0, 6.0	Novell WordPerfect 6.0a, 6.1
PROCOMM PLUS 1.0, 1.02	

1. With limited network functionality; some network functions are instead provided by UNIX. Windows for Workgroups™ can be used to satisfy Wabi's Microsoft Windows requirement (see page 25).

This list is subject to change as more Windows applications are tested and certified.

Unsupported Applications

The applications that Wabi does not support can be divided into two general categories: Windows applications and DOS applications.

Windows Applications

In general, Windows applications fail to work under Wabi for at least one of four reasons:

- They use virtual devices drivers.
- They use unsupported APIs.
- They use DOS functions or programs.
- They have special hardware requirements.

The technical details behind these reasons are beyond the scope of this chapter. Refer to "Unsupported Windows Applications" on page 26 for more information about why certain applications will not work with Wabi.

DOS Applications

Wabi does not support DOS applications. One of the major concepts behind Wabi is to avoid DOS entirely; any DOS functions required by Windows applications (for example, file input and output) are translated by Wabi into native UNIX functions.

To run DOS applications from Wabi, you need to use a DOS emulation product, like SunPC™ (for SPARC®/RISC platforms) or Merge® (for *x86* platforms). Both of these products are available from SunSoft, Inc.

You can start such DOS emulation products from within Wabi, and even create program items on which you can double-click in Wabi to start DOS applications. Technically, however, DOS emulators run as separate UNIX processes outside of Wabi, which means that you don't have the same cut-and-paste capabilities or seamless desktop integration.

Using DOS emulators is discussed again briefly later in this chapter, in "Solutions For Running Unsupported Applications." Refer to Chapter 10, "Using DOS Applications," for details about running DOS under Wabi.

Go Ahead...

Experiment! Live a little! There are many Windows applications not on Wabi's certified application list that nonetheless work just fine under Wabi. You should feel free to try them out.

For example, DeLorme Mapping Street Atlas USA™ 2.0 works well under Wabi, as does Shapeware Corporation Visio Pro™ 3.0a, Symantec® TimeLine®, and all games in the Microsoft Entertainment Packs 1 and 2. There are, in fact, more applications that do work under Wabi than don't.

Remember, there is no possible way for SunSoft to test all the Windows applications out there, and SunSoft will not certify an application without rigorously testing it. Just because an application is not certified doesn't mean that it won't work under Wabi.

Solutions For Running Unsupported Applications

For the applications that do not work with Wabi, your only choice for running them under UNIX is to use some sort of DOS/Windows emulator. Such emulators include:

- **SunPC** – From SunSoft; for SPARC/RISC platforms; primarily a DOS emulator. Will run Windows in 386 Enhanced Mode only if a hardware accelerator (the SunPC Coprocessor) is installed (otherwise Windows runs in Standard Mode).

- **Merge** – From SunSoft; for Intel®/*x*86 platforms; primarily a DOS emulator. Version 3.2.2 (not yet released) will run Windows in 386 Enhanced Mode by virtue of the fact that it runs on *x*86-based machines.

- **SoftWindows**™ – From Insignia Solutions, Inc.; for SPARC/RISC platforms; provides IBM® PC/AT-level compatibility, which means it can only run Windows in Standard Mode.

These are just a few of the most popular products available today. In all cases, they use emulation technology, rather than translation, and in all cases, they run Windows applications considerably slower than Wabi.

 SunPC with a SunPC Coprocessor offers similar performance to Wabi (SunPC is just *slightly* slower), but at a greater cost. All other emulation products are *much* slower than Wabi.

Table 1-2 summarizes the strengths and weakness of various combinations of emulation products with Wabi

Table 1-2   DOS/Windows Emulation Products Compared to Wabi

Product	Wabi 2.x	SunPC 4.1	Merge	SoftWindows
Platform	RISC and *x*86	RISC	*x*86	RISC
386 Enhanced?	Yes	Yes[1]	No[2]	No[3]
Standard Mode?	No[4]	Yes	Yes	Yes
Runs DOS?	No	Yes	Yes	Yes
286 Protected?	N/A	Yes	No	Yes
Cut and Paste?[5]	Yes	No	No	No

1. Only with hardware accelerator (SunPC Coprocessor).

2. Version 3.2.2 (not yet released) will support 386 Enhanced Mode.

3. Version 2.0 (not yet released) will support 386 Enhanced Mode

4. Wabi does not run Windows in Standard Mode, but *can* run Windows Standard Mode applications.

5. Between Windows and UNIX applications.

Currently, the best solution is to use Wabi where you can for the fastest application performance and the most stable operating environment. A DOS emulation product like SunPC or Merge should then be used to provide an environment in which you can run DOS applications or the occasional Windows application that is not compatible with Wabi.

It is important to remember that, besides *speed*, stability is a significant issue—after all, the emulation products all run Windows on top of DOS, a combination not noted for being "crash-proof." While Wabi is not crash-proof (nothing is), Wabi can take advantage of file locking, better memory management, and many other UNIX goodies. This means, for example, that if a Windows application crashes under Wabi, it almost never takes down the rest of your system with it. By contrast, when running Windows under DOS, if a Windows application crashes, the crash often brings down the rest of your system as well.

Differences Between Wabi 2.0 and 2.1

If you have been using Wabi 2.0, you should be aware of the enhancements made in version 2.1 (if you are still using Wabi 1.*x*, get off your duff and get the latest version!):

- Updates to the Wabi certified application list
- Changes to Wabi Configuration Manager
- Changes in Wabi font handling
- Different PostScript® printer driver
- Microsoft Windows for Workgroups 3.11 support
- Remote database access support
- Multimedia support

These enhancements are described on the following pages.

Updates to the Wabi Certified Application List

Most of the certified applications for Wabi 2.0 have been revised; the new versions of almost all of these programs have been certified to work with Wabi 2.1. Table 1-1 on page 8 lists the applications and versions certified for Wabi 2.1.

Changes to Wabi Configuration Manager

In all versions of Wabi software through 2.0, the Wabi Configuration Manager has been a separate executable with a Windows program item installed in the Tools program group (although in Wabi 2.0, you could also access the Configuration Manager through the Windows Control Panel). In Wabi 2.1, the Configuration Manager is entirely integrated into the Windows Control Panel—there is no separate executable.

The functions in the Wabi 2.1 Configuration Manager have also been simplified and reduced, and many of its previous functions are now handled directly through standard (non-Wabi) Windows Control Panel applications. Table 1-3 compares Wabi Configuration Manager functions between Wabi 2.0 and 2.1.

Table 1-3   Wabi 2.0 and 2.1 Configuration Manager Functions Compared

Function	Wabi 2.0	Wabi 2.1
Ports	Specify COM port connections and settings.	Specify COM and LPT (printer) port connections and settings.
Printers	Specify LPT (printer) port connections and printer setup.	Removed; specify printer ports with the Wabi Ports tool. Specify printer setup with the standard Control Panel Printers tool.
Drives	Specify network drive connections (mount points).	Specify network drive connections (mount points).
Diskettes	Specify diskette drives.	Specify diskette drives.
DOS	Specify DOS emulator commands.	Specify DOS emulator commands.
Sound Mouse Color International	Specify sound, mouse, color, and international settings.	Removed; use standard Windows Control Panel tools to modify settings for these items.

Changes in Wabi Font Handling

Wabi 2.0 used X Window fonts, which required a special Wabi font cache, and also occasionally caused some differences between what you saw on screen and what you got at the printer.

Wabi 2.1 uses the TrueType™, bitmap, and vector fonts included with Windows itself and some of the Windows applications you may install—X Window fonts are no longer used. While Wabi can still use its own X-based Wabi font server for increased performance, it is not a requirement. Finally, the Wabi font cache of Wabi 2.0 and earlier is no longer used.

Wabi software works with X servers—font or otherwise—running X Window version X11R5.

Refer to Chapter 12, "Fonts and Wabi," for more information about how Wabi works with fonts.

Different Postscript Printer Driver

Wabi 2.1 uses the PostScript printer driver included with Microsoft Windows (`pscript.drv`). Older versions of Wabi used a driver provided by Adobe Systems, Inc. Refer to Chapter 7 for more information.

Microsoft Windows for Workgroups 3.11 Support

Wabi 2.1 provides limited support for Microsoft Windows for Workgroups 3.11 (WFWG). The support limitation comes in the area of functions that require Windows networking, which is not supported. (UNIX provides superior—or at least analogous—networking functions). Table A-1 on page 302 describes Wabi 2.1 support for various WFWG features.

Remote Database Access Support

Wabi 2.1 supports remote database access through Oracle7® and Sybase® SQL Server 10™ database management system (DBMS) servers running on Solaris 2 systems in TCP/IP networks. Several Wabi-certified applications can take advantage of such remote DBMS access; these certified applications are listed in Table 1-4.

Table 1-4   Wabi-Certified Applications Supporting Remote DBMS Access

Lotus 1-2-3 5.0	Microsoft Access 2.0	Novell Paradox 5.0
Lotus Approach 3.0	Microsoft Excel 5.0	Novell Quattro Pro 6.0

These applications can connect through the Wabi Winsock (Windows Sockets) interface by using an Open Database Connectivity (ODBC) driver and appropriate data source software.

- ODBC drivers let applications connect to remote databases. Oracle and Sybase drivers from Intersolv have been tested and determined to be compatible with Wabi 2.1 software. You can purchase these ODBC drivers either individually or as part of a set of drivers in Intersolv's DataDirect ODBC Driver Pack™ 2.0 for Windows.

- Data source software provides TCP/IP connectivity, through Winsock, to a DBMS server. Such software can be obtained from DBMS vendors like Oracle and Sybase. Oracle's data source product is called SQL*Net® TCP/IP 1.1. Sybase's data source product is Open Client Net-Library™ 10.0.2.

For remote database access, Lotus 1-2-3® also requires a proprietary software component, the Lotus DataLens™ driver (DLODBC), to provide an interface to the ODBC driver. The DataLens driver is available on the Lotus Data Access Tools for Windows 2.0 disk set, which can be obtained from Lotus.

See "Using Remote Database Access" on page 238 for more information about ODBC under Wabi. For application-specific information, follow the instructions included with your application.

Multimedia Support

Wabi 2.1 software now supports the playing and recording of waveform (`.WAV`), and playing video files in `.AVI` format. This allows you to take advantage of the multimedia features in supported Windows applications. There are several limitations to this support, however:

- You must be running Solaris version 2.4 or later.

- You must be using a computer with the appropriate hardware:
  - An *x*86-based computer (see page 18) with a Solaris-compatible 16-bit sound card—Creative Labs' SoundBlaster™ and compatible cards will generally work.
  - A workstation with a sound card or chip, like the SPARCstation™ 5, 10, 20, or later. Other models may often be upgraded with an appropriate sound card.

- Software and hardware for Musical Instrument Digital Interface (MIDI) devices, and Audio-Visual Interface (AVI) for video laser disks and audio CD are not yet supported.

Multimedia features are *not* supported under Wabi 2.0 software or on non-Solaris platforms.

Refer to Chapter 9, in the section titled "Using Multimedia Features" on page 235, for more information about using multimedia under Wabi 2.1 software.

Wabi Operating Environments

Wabi software was developed by SunSoft, Inc., initially for the Solaris operating environment. Versions of Wabi software are now available from several other major hardware and software vendors including Hewlett-Packard (HP), International Business Machines Corporation (IBM), and the Santa Cruz Operation (SCO).

Because Wabi software was developed at SunSoft, this book focuses on SunSoft's version of Wabi, which is compiled to run in the Solaris operating environment. In almost all cases, information about Wabi software for the Solaris environment applies to versions produced by other vendors for other environments.

Table 1-5 lists the environments for which versions of Wabi software are currently available.

Table 1-5   SunSoft Wabi Operating Environments

Vendor	Environment	OS Version	Wabi Version
SunSoft, Inc.	Solaris	2.4, 2.5	2.1
Hewlett-Packard	HP/UX	9.x	2.0
Santa Cruz Operation	SCO/OpenServer	Release 5	2.0
IBM	IBM/AIX	3.x, 4.x	2.0

Wabi software is compiled separately for each of these environments. That is, you cannot run the Solaris version of Wabi software on HP/UX, and vice versa.

Wabi Processor Environments

Because Wabi is based on the X Window standard (again, see "Wabi and X Window" on page 30), it can run on hardware platforms that use either RISC processors (like SPARCstations) or Intel *x86* processors (like IBM-compatible PCs).

RISC

Reduced Instruction Set Computer (RISC) microprocessors are used on most UNIX-based workstations, like the Sun SPARCstation line. Microsoft Windows' native processor environment, however, is the Intel *x86* platform. When running Windows applications, Wabi translates *x86* processor instructions as needed into RISC instructions. This process is explained in more detail in the next chapter, in the section "Translation Versus Emulation" on page 28.

Intel

Complex Instruction Set Computer (CISC) microprocessors are used on all IBM-compatible PCs. Specifically, the "IBM-compatible" moniker implies computers based on the Intel *x86* line of microprocessors. Such processors include Intel's 8086™, 8088™, 80286™, 80386™, 80486™, and Pentium™ products. Much to Intel's vexation, there are now also numerous *x86*-compatible processors produced by other vendors, like Advanced Micro Devices (AMD) and Cyrix. In this book, all such products are collectively referred to as *x86* processors.

Because the x86 platform is Windows' native processor environment, Wabi does not need to perform processor-level instruction translation, as is required on the RISC platform. (The process by which Wabi translates processor, DOS, and Windows instructions into UNIX/X Window instructions is described in the next chapter.) A discussion of *x86* processors and their implications in the design of DOS and Windows is provided in "This Thing Called DOS" on page 67.

Where To Get Wabi

Wabi software is available from a variety of sources: some for free, others for varying prices.

SunSoft Solaris

As of Solaris version 2.3, Wabi software is bundled free with Solaris operating environment software. This includes Solaris software that is packaged with Sun SPARCstations and other hardware, and Solaris packages that are sold individually.

Depending on the service contract you have arranged with your Solaris provider, you may or may not automatically receive Solaris upgrades and, hence, Wabi upgrades. The latest version of Solaris software includes the latest version of Wabi. If necessary, you can purchase Wabi upgrades separately or as part of a Solaris upgrade. Ask your Sun service provider for more information.

A demonstration copy of Wabi software can be downloaded from the Wabi World Wide Web site at:

```
http://www.sun.com/sunsoft/Products/PC-Integration-products/
```

Other Wabi Vendors

If you want to get a version of Wabi from a vendor other than SunSoft, contact that vendor directly. See page 17 for a list of Wabi vendors.

Sources of Information About Wabi

SunSoft provides various means by which you can get information about Wabi software. This information ranges from the technical to the sales-oriented:

- **Sun and SunSoft™ resellers and service providers** – Sun and SunSoft resellers and service providers can keep you abreast of the latest versions, sources, and pricing for Wabi software.

- **World Wide Web** – SunSoft maintains a World Wide Web site on the Internet. This site provides information about SunSoft products in general, and not just about Wabi. You can get Wabi software or information about Wabi software at:

  ```
  http://www.sun.com/sunsoft/Products/PC-Integration-products/
  ```

- **Email** – If you are connected to the Internet, you can use the Wabi Frequently Asked Questions (FAQ) by sending e-mail to one of the following email addresses:
  - `wabi2.1-questions@east.sun.com`
    (Wabi 2.1 Knowledge Base FAQ)
  - `wabi2.1-apps@east.sun.com`
    (Wabi 2.1 Knowledge Base App Info)
  - `wabi-query@east.sun.com`
    (auto-search Technical Knowledge Base)

- **Usenet** – The `sun.wabi` usenet news group on the Internet is a forum in which much varied discussion about Wabi takes place.

Chapter 2
How Wabi Works

Wabi software lets you run unmodified, "shrink-wrapped" Microsoft Windows 3.1 and 3.11 applications under X Window on UNIX desktops. In so doing, it combines the strengths of the UNIX/X Window environment with the ease-of-use of the most popular applications for the Microsoft Windows environment.

> *When a cloud reflects the sun, it becomes a colored cloud (hsia), and when a spring gullet flows over a cliff, it becomes a waterfall. By a different association it is given a new name*
>
> – Chang Ch'ao, *Yumengying (Sweet Dream Shadows)*, c.1676

In This Chapter

Wabi Basics

Wabi software is implemented as a UNIX process, and uses a combination of emulation and translation technology to handle program code written for the Microsoft Windows 3.1 environment. Specifically, in most cases, Wabi software *translates* Windows code into native UNIX/X Window-based instructions, making it possible to perform many Windows operations at native UNIX speeds. Moreover, because of the advanced processor and display technology available on many UNIX workstations, graphics operations are often faster running under Wabi than on the PC for which they were originally designed.

When direct translation of instructions is not possible, Wabi *emulates* the Intel $x86$ instruction set (see "Walking Backwards" on page 68) with corresponding RISC instructions. The Windows application is essentially processed as data, with each item of data treated as an $x86$ instruction that needs to be emulated. Emulation is considerably slower than translation, however, and functions that require a high proportion of emulation, relative to translation, can suffer in performance. For example, installing an application from diskette under Wabi can be slower than installing it in the native PC environment, because of disk decompression algorithms that must be emulated at the instruction level. Note, however, that this is only true of Wabi run on RISC-based machines, like SPARCstations. On $x86$-based machines, Wabi can use the native instructions of the $x86$ processor, which means things like disk decompression run at "normal" speed.

Theoretically, the Wabi approach allows any application developed using the Windows *Application Programming Interface* (API)—with some restrictions—to run under Wabi. In reality, implementing emulation and translation technology can be extremely complicated. Windows is a powerful, vast, arcane, and often undocumented API, and includes components that vary from primitive graphics to functions typically provided by a kernel operating system. While Wabi software does not yet support 100 percent of the known Windows API functions, it does support most of them, and most "well-behaved" applications can run well under Wabi.

About Microsoft Windows

Wabi software requires Microsoft Windows in order to run Windows applications. That is, before running any Windows applications under Wabi, you must first use the Wabi Windows Install program (described in Chapter 5, in the section "Installing Microsoft Windows" on page 114) to install Microsoft Windows software.

 The main reason the Wabi designers chose to make Windows a requirement is to avoid having to rewrite the Windows Dynamic-Link Libraries (DLLs), which work just fine—the designers wanted to make the wheel roll more smoothly, not reinvent it.

The Wabi Windows Install program does not install all Windows components—many of them are irrelevant under UNIX, and others are supplanted by UNIX components. For example, the 386 Enhanced tool in Windows Control Panel has no meaning under UNIX.

For the most part, Windows under Wabi behaves just like Windows under DOS. There are some differences, however—and there are actually more differences related to the dissimilarities between UNIX and DOS. To find out more about these differences:

- Read Chapter 3, "Microsoft Windows For UNIX Users," for a detailed explanation of how Microsoft Windows works with Wabi, and how it compares to Windows under DOS. You should also read this chapter if you are a UNIX user who is new to Microsoft Windows.

- Read Chapter 4, "UNIX For Microsoft Windows Users," if you are already familiar with Microsoft Windows, but are not so familiar with UNIX.

About Microsoft Windows Applications

As described in Chapter 1, SunSoft guarantees that its version of Wabi will work with a specific set of *certified applications* (see Table 1-1 on page 8). Wabi will also work with many other applications, but SunSoft does not guarantee it.

The concept of certified applications implies that there are some applications that are *not* certified. Of the applications that are not certified, some will work with Wabi anyway, while others will not.

Unsupported Windows Applications

Without going into excruciating technical detail, Windows applications that don't work under Wabi fail to work for at least one of four reasons:

- They use virtual devices drivers.
- They use unsupported APIs.
- They use DOS functions or programs.
- They have special hardware requirements.

These reasons are explained in more detail below.

- **Virtual device drivers** – Virtual device drivers allow Windows applications to directly access some hardware component, or to intercept a program command that would normally go to a hardware component and redirect it to software. For example, most fax programs use a virtual device driver to emulate a printer in software; when an application prints a file, the fax program's virtual device driver intercepts the call to the printer and instead "prints" the file through the fax software.

  Other programs use virtual device drivers to access "real" hardware, like disk drives. For example, for greater speed, some file backup programs directly access floppy drives, thereby avoiding the overhead of Windows' file services. Theoretically, Windows programs are not allowed to access hardware directly by any means other than a virtual device driver. In reality, some applications break this rule or use device drivers that are not very well behaved in the Windows environment.

Wabi cannot run programs that use virtual device drivers, or that directly access PC hardware. This is because the specific PC hardware components with which the virtual device drivers communicate—and the language used to communicate with them—are handled differently under UNIX.

- **Unsupported APIs** – *API* is an acronym for *application programming interface*, which is a set of functions (sort of like commands) that programmers can use to interact with a given operating system, environment, program, or hardware component. Programmers can use these functions in their program code, and the system or device for which they are programming can understand them. The term API is used to refer to both a collective set of functions (for example, the *Windows API*), and to individual functions within that set.

  As experienced Windows programmers can attest, the Windows API provides an extensive range of programming functions, among which are a significant number of *undocumented functions*. These are functions that exist, but are not "officially" (that is, according to Microsoft) documented or supported.

  Without debating the maintenance issues and general prudence of using such undocumented calls—many applications use them, including (especially?) those from Microsoft—it is important to note that Wabi supports almost all of the Windows APIs, including many of the undocumented ones.

  If, however, a program uses an API that is not supported by Wabi, it will not run under Wabi. There is no easy way to predict which programs use unsupported APIs; hence the reason for extensive testing by SunSoft leading to application certification (explained in "Supported Applications" on page 6).

- **DOS functions or programs** – Wabi doesn't do DOS *at all*. Some Windows programs, however, break Windows' golden rule and perform one or more functions directly in DOS. The most common offenders in this category are installation programs that perform file decompression from DOS, rather than in Windows. Such programs cannot be installed under Wabi.

The Windows setup program has a DOS component. The Wabi Windows Install program, however, neatly bypasses Windows setup, thus avoiding the DOS level entirely.

- **Special hardware requirements** – If a program requires a special type of hardware device that is not physically compatible with your UNIX hardware, it (not surprisingly) will not work under Wabi. Similarly, if your program requires a specific DOS-based device driver, it won't work with Wabi.

See "Windows Interface Objects" on page 42 for more information about hardware and Windows software that will or will not work with Wabi.

Translation Versus Emulation

Perhaps the most significant feature differentiating Wabi software from Windows emulation products is Wabi's translation technology. Whereas *all* other products that run Windows applications in UNIX *emulate* DOS to provide an environment in which unadulterated (but slow) Microsoft Windows runs—usually in Standard Mode only—Wabi entirely supplants DOS, and replaces many core Windows functions with native UNIX/X Window functions. On SPARC and other RISC platforms, Wabi also translates many processor-level instructions (opcodes); such translation is not necessary on *x*86 platforms.

In very general terms, Wabi performs two levels of translation:

- **Windows API** – Wabi can translate almost all Windows APIs, both documented and undocumented, into native RISC/X Window functions. This includes most core Windows functions, as well as many popular support functions. When translation is not possible, Wabi emulates the API at the machine instruction level, processing each API instruction as data. This means that although a specific API may not be explicitly translated by Wabi, it will still work just fine—albeit more slowly—because of Wabi's ability to fall back to emulation technology.

- **Processor opcodes** – Translation of processor opcodes is only necessary on RISC platforms, because the *x*86 platform is native to Windows already. Often, a one-to-one translation of *x*86 instructions is not possible—CISC processors (like the *x*86 line) do things in a different order and via different methods than RISC chips (like SPARC processors). The Wabi 2.1 opcode translator expedites the translation process by fetching instructions in batches; that is, the Wabi opcode translator analyzes multiple instructions at once, figures out what they're trying to do, and then converts them into the appropriate RISC instructions. Wabi also employs instruction caching to further optimize the process.

The advantages provided by Wabi's translation technology, as compared to the emulation techniques used by other products, are fourfold:

- Faster performance in supported applications

- Ability to run 386 Enhanced Mode applications with no additional hardware

- Ability to take advantage of many native UNIX functions, like file locking, multiuser security features, and a flat memory addressing scheme

- Closer integration of Microsoft Windows and UNIX-based applications; for example, cut-and-paste, drag-and-drop, and desktop menu configuration

The primary disadvantage to the Wabi approach is that Wabi cannot run every Windows application—although it can run many of them. Solutions for running unsupported Windows applications side-by-side with Wabi are described in Chapter 1, in the section titled "Solutions For Running Unsupported Applications" on page 10.

Wabi and X Window

Wabi software is based on the X Window System. X Window is a low-level, network client-server-based graphical windowing system that was initially developed at MIT. in 1984. Without going into too much detail here (more information about X Window is provided in Chapter 4), X Window provides the underpinnings on which higher-level UNIX-based window managers can work. For example, Sun's OpenWindows environment commonly uses the OPEN LOOK® Window Manager (`olwm`), which in turn is based on X Window.

One of the biggest advantages offered by X Window is that it is relatively *platform independent*—that is, it can run on a wide range of hardware platforms under a wide variety of UNIX-based operating environments. Applications written to use X Window are therefore comparatively easy to port to different X-compatible hardware platforms and operating systems.

Wabi uses X Window for two categories of services:

- General window display and input/output
- Font display

General X Services

The primary functions performed by X Window for Wabi software are to:

- Manage the display of windows and dialog boxes on screen; for example, sizing and moving windows, displaying dialog boxes, and providing dialog box and window control mechanisms

- Manage input and output (I/O) from keyboards, pointing devices, microphones, and so forth

X Font Services

Font handling under Wabi is a relatively complex process. Detailed information about this process is provided in Chapter 12, "Fonts and Wabi," but for our purposes here, it is only necessary to explain that:

- Wabi 2.1 works with Windows TrueType, vector, and bitmap fonts. Such fonts are included with Microsoft Windows, and are also included with some Windows applications.

- Wabi 2.1 includes an X-based font server executable, called `wabifs`, that runs locally on your workstation, and interacts with a local or remote X server. `wabifs` communicates with the X server via the X11R5 font service protocol, which allows the server to display fonts from the Wabi program (`wabiprog`). If, however, the X server does not support the X11R5 font service protocol, the `wabifs` executable does not run, and Wabi performs all font handling chores within `wabiprog` itself.

Using an X server is optional, but desirable for performance reasons. If an X server is used, and the text to be displayed is in either TrueType or bitmap format, Wabi can simply send text information, via the `wabifs` program, to the X Server. The X server then rasterizes the text information for display. Note that, in all cases, vector fonts are drawn directly by Wabi, bypassing the X server.

Wabi Executables

In the preceding two paragraphs, reference was made to two particular Wabi executable files. These two executables work tightly in conjunction with each other, and are launched by the single invocation of an executable script, which you enter as the `wabi` command (see Chapter 5, "Using Wabi Software"). Table 2-1 synopsizes the purpose of these Wabi executables.

Table 2-1   Primary Wabi Executable Files

Executable	Purpose
`wabi`	A "wrapper" script that determines display type, environment settings, available X servers, etc., and then invokes other Wabi executables as needed.
`wabiprog`	The primary Wabi program executable—the one that always appears in the list of active processes on your system when Wabi is running. Performs the bulk of the interaction with X servers other than font servers.
`wabifs`	The Wabi font server program; intercedes between `wabiprog` and an X server, using the X11R5 font service protocol. If the X server does not support the X11R5 font service protocol, the `wabifs` process is not started.

Desktop Integration

Because Wabi is based on X Window, its window controls and data
functions are closely integrated with the particular UNIX windowing
environment in which it is running. Compared to DOS/Windows
emulation products, which get all their window and data controls from
the Microsoft Windows and/or DOS environment, Wabi's X Window-based
architecture provides several important benefits; for example, in the
Solaris environment:

- Wabi applications can be displayed side-by-side with Solaris
  applications. Emulation products, by contrast, either take over
  the entire screen, or display Windows applications as windows
  within their own process. To put it another way, even if the
  emulator itself can live politely in a Solaris window on your
  desktop, applications running in that emulator are nested at
  least one window deep within the emulator, and have no direct
  contact with Solaris. When you minimize a Windows application
  under Wabi (that is, reduce the running application to an icon),
  its icon sits right on your desktop, next to the icons for any
  Solaris documents or applications.

- You can cut and paste text between Microsoft Windows
  applications and Solaris applications. For example, you could
  cut text from a Microsoft Word document and paste it into a
  FrameMaker® document.

- You can double-click on the name of a document in the Solaris
  File Manager and have it open automatically in a Windows
  application. Similarly, you can double-click on an attachment
  in an e-mail message displayed with the Solaris Mail tool, and
  have that attachment opened automatically in its associated
  Windows application. For example, you could double-click on
  the name of a PowerPoint™ presentation attached to an e-mail
  message to start Wabi and open the presentation in PowerPoint.
  (Similar to the application registry in DOS/Windows, Wabi
  associates files with an executable via the Solaris Binder™
  tool—see page 229 for more information.)

Be sure to read Chapter 14, "Tips and Tricks," for more examples of ways
you can integrate your Solaris and Windows applications under Wabi.

Future Directions

SunSoft, Inc. is continuously expanding and improving upon Wabi software. Three goals are of primary importance to the Wabi developers:

- Increased performance
- 32-bit application support
- A Wabi server product

These goals are explained below.

Increased Performance

Wabi software already runs Windows applications faster than any other UNIX product. This statement is borne out by test results from a wide variety of sources, including manufacturers and independent testing labs. Still, the Wabi engineers want to make it faster. By further optimizing Wabi's translation technology, the engineers hope to take advantage of today's more powerful PCs and workstations. The goal is to keep Wabi a software-only product—and therefore relatively inexpensive.

32-Bit Application Support

As Microsoft Windows moves into the world of true 32-bit application support—either through Windows NT™ or Windows 95™—Wabi will move there also. This goal should be achievable, because UNIX is already a 32-bit operating system, and many of the details required to support 32-bit applications are already in place. Specifically, a Windows 95-compatible version of Wabi software is planned for the near future.

Wabi Server

SunSoft in particular is developing a Wabi Server product, slated for release near the end of 1995 or in early 1996. Wabi Server will take advantage of UNIX client-server techniques to leverage the performance of high-powered servers for running Wabi. Wabi Server will provide the means by which Wabi performance can be boosted significantly, and is targeted to address the needs of demanding "power user" environments. Keep an eye on SunSoft's World Wide Web page for more information about Wabi Server. The SunSoft Web page is at:

```
http://www.sun.com/sunsoft/Products/PC-Integration-products/
```

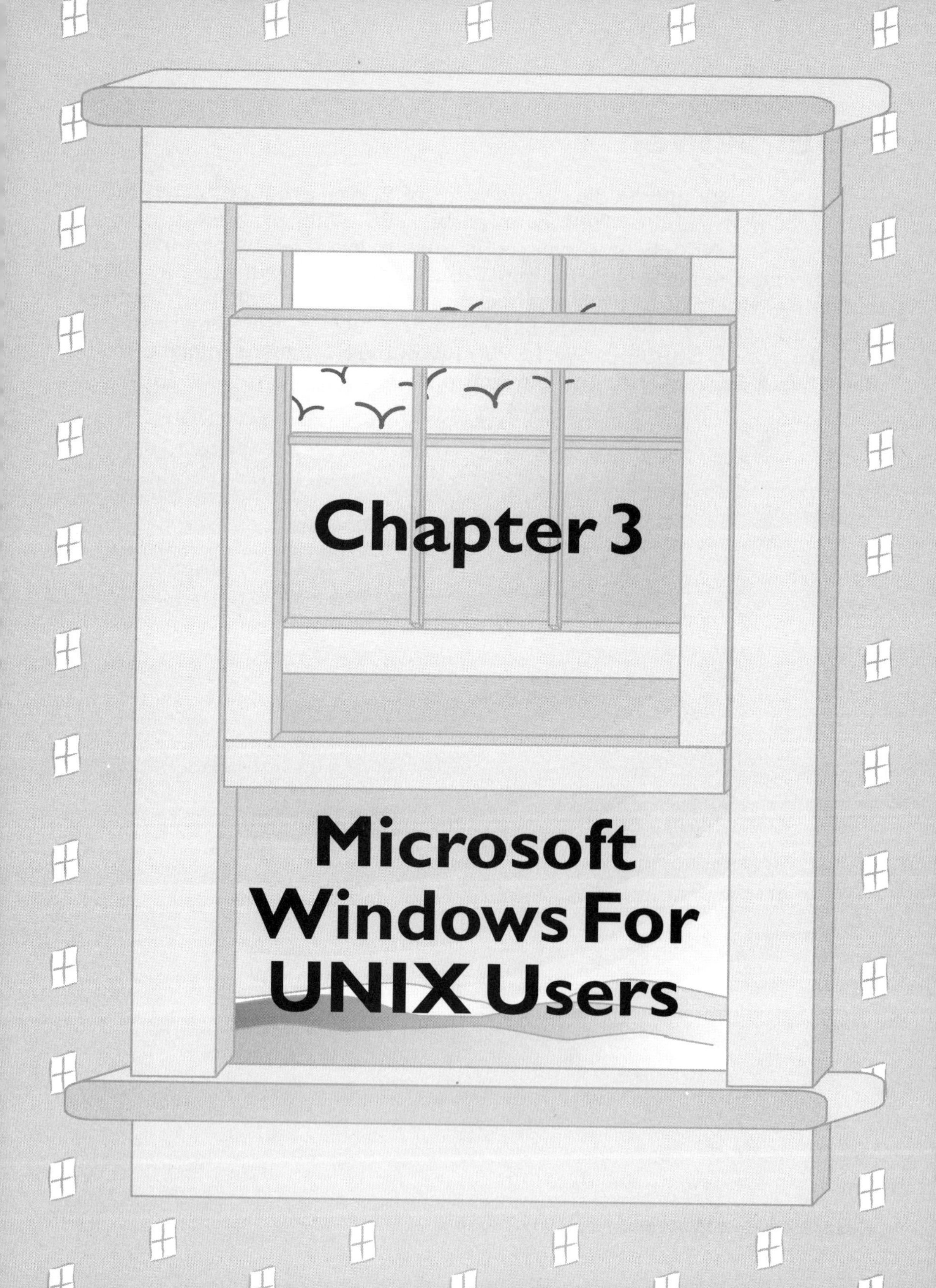
Chapter 3
Microsoft Windows For UNIX Users

Microsoft Windows software is an integral part of the Wabi "experience"—to run Wabi on your workstation, you must also install Microsoft Windows software.

This chapter explains the basics of how Windows works, primarily from the UNIX user's standpoint. It is provided to help folks who were weaned on UNIX get "up to speed" with the Windows environment.

While there are many similarities between Microsoft Windows and some UNIX/X-based windowing environments, such as OpenWindows or Motif®—after all, they all share a common ancestry—there are just enough subtle, *niggling* differences to annoy the unwary.

One man's word is no man's word; we should quietly hear both sides.

– Johann Wolfgang von Goethe

If the blind lead the blind, both shall fall into the ditch.

– Matthew 15:14

In This Chapter

Wabi 2: Opening Windows

About Microsoft Windows

Microsoft Windows 3.1 software is arguably the most popular graphical operating environment used on personal computers today—it is certainly the most popular graphical environment used on DOS-based PCs.

From the user's standpoint, Windows provides a reasonably consistent way to work with different applications. For example:

- Most applications written for the Windows environment provide a similar *menu* structure, through which you can enter commands by "pointing-and-clicking" with a *mouse*.

- Most applications are displayed in *windows* that can be scrolled, moved, resized, and reduced to an icon. Such windows can also be displayed side-by-side with other application windows.

- Many of the activities, other than data entry, that you perform in a Windows application take place in one or more subwindows referred to as *dialog boxes*.

- Certain applications—if they are in a good mood and written politely—can share data dynamically, through mechanisms such as *cut-and-paste*, *Object Linking and Embedding* (OLE), *Dynamic Data Exchange* (DDE), and (less frequently) *object packaging*.

Microsoft Windows also provides an easy means by which users can circumvent (that is, not worry about) the archaic memory restrictions of DOS, the operating system upon which Windows sits. These memory restrictions, by the way, are a moot point in UNIX, under which Wabi software runs. (See "This Thing Called DOS," later in this chapter.)

Finally, Windows versions 3.1 and later include *TrueType* font technology (developed by Apple Computer and Microsoft), which is a portable, outline typeface system for displaying and printing text. TrueType provides similar capabilities to Adobe's PostScript Type 1 format. For Windows users, the most significant difference between PostScript and TrueType is that TrueType is bundled with Windows, whereas displaying PostScript fonts under Windows requires a third-party typeface program, like Adobe Type Manager®.

Wabi software fully supports TrueType font technology. Third-party typeface packages, such as Adobe Type Manager, however, are not supported. While you can print the fonts used by such third-party packages on a PostScript printer, you cannot see those fonts displayed on screen.

Briefly, from the programmer's standpoint, Windows provides a reasonably consistent (and usually documented) way for applications to work with hardware, such as display adapters, input devices, COM ports, and printers. Windows also provides programming functions that make it easier to create the graphical user interface—windows, menus, dialog boxes, and so forth—so the programmer does not need, unlike DOS, to recreate the interface for each application.

Applications written for the Microsoft Windows environment represent the fastest-growing segment of the software industry today. This has resulted in a kind of "snowball" effect, in which PC application developers are shifting their focus to Windows, which leads to more Windows applications, which leads to a larger market segment, which encourages still more programmers to write for Windows.

The catch here is that Windows is still based on DOS, which is generally regarded as a technical dead-end. Let's be blunt: DOS pales in comparison to UNIX. For example, UNIX is a multiuser, multithreaded, high-capacity, distributed-yet-secure operating system. In contrast, DOS is a single-user, single-tasking system, hobbled by a 15-year-old 640K memory restriction. DOS is enormously popular, however—it's cheap, runs on minimal hardware, and works just fine for many basic PC users—and on these merits alone, it deserves the attention it gets.

Enter Wabi: by letting Windows applications run under UNIX—truly under UNIX, not just Windows on top of emulated DOS under UNIX—you get the best of both operating systems. The most popular Windows applications can run on top of the most robust operating system.

Wabi 2: Opening Windows

Windows Versions

Microsoft Windows software is available in several different versions. The most ubiquitous—the version bundled with almost every new DOS-based PC over the past three years—is Windows 3.1. An incremental release, version 3.11, fixes some bugs and provides a few performance boosts over Windows 3.1.

Other versions of Windows include Windows for Workgroups 3.11, which is regular Windows plus built-in, peer-to-peer, networking capabilities. Like Windows 3.1, Windows for Workgroups sits on top of DOS.

Windows NT is a 32-bit, multiuser, multithreaded *operating system*, rather than just an operating environment; unlike the other versions of Windows, Windows NT entirely supplants DOS. You can choose to keep DOS on your system, but NT does not need it to run. Unfortunately, there are currently few Windows applications written to take advantage of Windows NT features; indeed, many applications written for regular ol' 16-bit Windows 3.1 run slower on Windows NT than on 3.1 or 3.11.

Finally, there is Windows 95, a hybrid 16/32-bit, "object-oriented" operating system that, like Windows NT, supplants DOS. Unlike Windows NT, however, Windows 95 still retains many core architectural features of DOS. At the present time, Windows NT is positioned by Microsoft as a product for "advanced users" and server environments. By contrast, Windows 95 is intended for "general users," and offers a radically different—and ostensibly easier to use—interface than any of the other versions of Microsoft Windows to date.

Wabi software is compatible with Microsoft Windows versions 3.1 and 3.11. Wabi 2.1 (but not Wabi 2.0) is also compatible with Windows for Workgroups 3.11 (WFWG), but is not compatible with WFWG network features. (This is mostly irrelevant, however, because UNIX already provides robust networking.) Finally, Wabi software is currently not compatible with any 32-bit version of Microsoft Windows, such as Windows NT or Windows 95, although such support is planned for future versions of Wabi software (see "Future Directions" on page 34).

Windows Interface Objects

Microsoft Windows comprises numerous *interface objects*—that is, the stuff you use to communicate with your computer, and the language used by your computer to communicate with you. For example, you communicate with your computer by typing on the keyboard and clicking on menu commands with the mouse; your computer communicates with you by crashing and displaying Unrecoverable Application Error messages.... No, seriously, your computer communicates with you by displaying beautifully laid-out pages of terse prose and glorious full-color graphs charting all the money you made last year, while politely asking you if it's time yet to send off that postponed fax to your theatrical agent.

The interface objects in Microsoft Windows can be divided into six general categories, three each for hardware and software:

Hardware

- Input devices (*page 42*)
- Output devices (*page 47*)
- Communications equipment (*page 49*)

Software

- Windows (*page 49*)
- Menus (*page 57*)
- Dialog Boxes (*page 59*)
- Dialog Box Controls (*page 63*)

Input Devices

Input devices refer primarily to keyboards and mice (an acceptable, albeit quasi-illiterate, alternate plural is *mouses*—eek!), but also to things like digitizing tablets, stylus pens, scanners, microphones, and so forth.

One of the *joys* of Microsoft Windows is that it provides consistent support for input devices via a standard set of programming functions. What this means is that each individual application does not have to provide, say, its own mouse driver—it simply makes calls to a common mouse driver configured under Windows for your particular mouse.

In general, Wabi software supports common input devices like mice, keyboards, and (Wabi 2.1 only) microphones. Support for less common devices, like digitizing tablets and pressure pens varies according to the device, your hardware configuration, and the software required to use the device with your Windows applications. Some specific tips regarding various input devices are as follows:

- **Mice** – Users of UNIX-based windowing environments should already be familiar with *Mus musculus*—the common mouse. The most obvious difference between the Microsoft mouse and most UNIX mice (like the Solaris mouse) is that the former has two buttons whereas the latter has three, as shown in Figure 3-1.

  It seems that the more complex the interface, the more mouse buttons you have: Apple® Macintosh® (reputedly the simplest) uses a one-button mouse; PCs running Windows use two buttons; UNIX uses three. Some DOS-based CAD programs use pointing devices with 16 or more buttons!

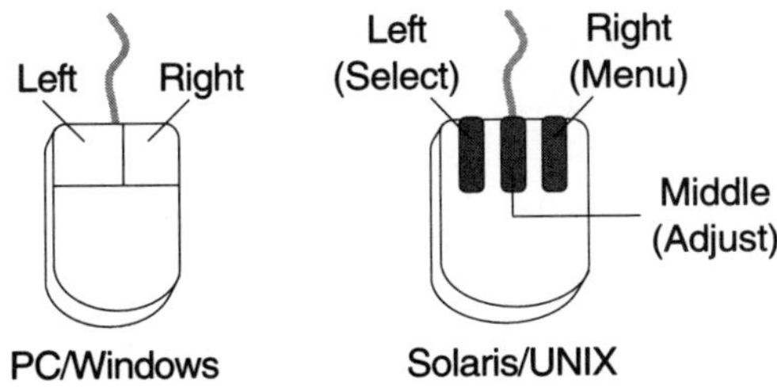

Figure 3-1   Two-Button PC Mouse and Three-Button Solaris Mouse

For UNIX users, using a three-button mouse with Microsoft Windows applications is generally not a problem. The leftmost button on the three-button mouse corresponds to the left button on the two-button mouse, and the rightmost button corresponds to the right button. Some Windows applications let you program the middle button for some custom purpose, but in general that extra button is unused.

Note that Wabi supports only pointing devices that attach to a serial (COM) port. This means that pointing devices that attach to a game port, although similar in some ways to mice, are not supported.

- **Keyboards** – UNIX keyboards, like the ones included with Sun SPARCstations, differ in several ways from the standard AT style keyboard. For example, the Meta key (◆) on the Sun keyboard serves no "native" function in Windows, although it can be used to eject diskettes under Wabi. Table 3-1 describes how various "special" keys on the Sun keyboard work (or don't work) with Windows applications under Wabi software.

- **Digitizing tablets** – Digitizing tablets are generally not supported under Wabi software, although there are exceptions. Unfortunately, there are so many configuration factors that can limit compatibility that it is impossible to simply list the devices that will or won't work. A few factors immediately rule out a given device, however:
  - If it requires any DOS-based device drivers or TSRs (as might be loaded in `CONFIG.SYS` or `AUTOEXEC.BAT` files)
  - If it requires a special interface card that cannot be installed in your UNIX workstation
  - If it requires a virtual device driver or "impolite" DLL that directly accesses hardware

  If your tablet does not require any of the above components, there is a fighting chance that it will work under Wabi software.

- **Stylus pens/pressure pens** – Stylus pens and pressure pens are supported under Wabi as long as they can be connected, like a mouse, to a serial port. If a pen requires an interface card, it is not supported. As with digitizing tablets, stylus pens and pressure pens are not supported if they require any special DOS-based device drivers or TSRs, or if they require DLLs that directly access the serial port. Also note that:
  - Pressure and angle sensitivity is not supported; the pen can only act as a simple, mouse-like input and pointing device.
  - Microsoft Windows for Pen Computing is not supported.

Wabi 2: Opening Windows

- **Scanners** – Most scanners require some sort of hardware interface card, either SCSI or proprietary (or both, with some weird implementations of SCSI), and also require a DOS-based device driver and/or TSR. Because of these conditions, Wabi generally does not support scanners, even if you have a scanner connected to your workstation. The workaround is to use your scanner with a UNIX-based program and then cut and paste or open the scanned file in your Windows application under Wabi.

- **Microphones, MIDI** – Wabi 2.1 supports microphones and similar analog devices. Musical Instrument Digital Interface (MIDI) devices, like MIDI keyboards, are not supported. See "Multimedia Support" on page 16 and "Using Multimedia Features" on page 235 for more information about using various multimedia devices under Wabi.

Table 3-1   Different Keystrokes for Different Folks

Key[1]	Function Under Windows
Alt	Same as AT keyboard, although Sun Alt keys are smaller.
Alt Graph	The Graph portion has no effect; AT keyboards have no equivalent key. Alt portion behaves the same as AT key.
Compose	None; there is no equivalent on AT keyboards. Refer to the Windows Character Map program for a list of special characters that can be accessed by using Alt+Numeric Keypad combinations.
Control (Ctrl)	Same as AT keyboard, although Sun keyboards have only one Control key.
Cut/Paste/Copy	These keys do not work within Windows applications; use the equivalent commands from the application's Edit menu. Many applications provide Control key shortcuts —for example, Ctrl+C for copy—that do work from within Wabi. See "Cut, Copy, and Paste" on page 290 for instructions on using cut and paste under Wabi.
F1 – F12	Same as AT keyboard.
Find	None; use the equivalent command—sometimes called Search—in the Windows application.

Key[1]	Function Under Windows
Front	Works mostly the same as with other UNIX windows, although some flakiness may occur if the Wabi window you want to bring to foreground on your X desktop is not already on top of other Wabi windows. See "Window Focus and Raising" on page 292 for more details.
Help	None; press F1 from within most Windows application to display on-line help. In some Windows applications, Shift+F1 displays context-sensitive help.
Meta (◆)	There is no native equivalent on AT keyboards, although ◆+E can be used to eject diskettes under Wabi.
Open	None; press Enter (or Return) in Windows Program Manager or File Manager to open the selected item.
Pause Break	Same as AT keyboard.
Print Screen	Same as AT keyboard.
Props	None; press Alt+Enter (or Alt+Return) in Windows Program Manager or File Manager to display Properties for the selected item.
Scroll Lock	Same as AT keyboard.
Stop	Same as with other UNIX applications—pressing Stop+A halts your system (an action generally to be avoided).
Undo/Again	None; use the equivalent commands in the Windows application, if available.

1. On a typical Sun keyboard.

Wabi 2: Opening Windows

Output Devices

Output devices most commonly refer to video displays and printers, but also include sound cards, pen plotters, and suchlike. As with input devices, Windows provides a common means by which all Windows applications can use the given output device.

For example, every Windows application in your particular Windows configuration can use the same printer driver. Similarly, every Windows application in your environment uses the same display driver. The benefit of this arrangement is that individual applications do not need to provide their own custom interface to the output device.

As with input devices, any output device you can connect to your UNIX workstation will generally work under Wabi. Of course, there are always exceptions to this rule. Some special considerations regarding output devices under Wabi are as follows:

- **Printers** – Indeed, it is true: just about any printer you can use with your UNIX workstation will work under Wabi. The trick is to make sure that you have the correct Windows printer driver for the printer to which you want to connect. This is rarely a problem, however, because Windows includes a substantial array of printer drivers. Even if you cannot find an exact match, there is usually a close enough approximation available to make things work okay.

  For example, a PostScript-based SPARCprinter™ works just fine with the Apple LaserWriter® IINTX printer driver. Refer to Chapter 7, "Managing Printers," starting on page 178, for complete information about using printers with Windows applications under Wabi.

- **Video displays** – Wabi software is designed to work with any video display and display adapter you can run on your UNIX workstation. This does not mean, however, that every Windows application can actually use that display driver. Some rude programs or functions within programs (we won't name names, they know who they are) require displays of a specific size—usually a PC-standard 640 x 480 pixel VGA (the lowest common denominator in the Windows world). Such programs, by the way, also do not run correctly on "real" PCs with, say, a 1024 x 768 pixel display. The most frequent offenders here are self-running tutorials and demos, which must know the exact size of the screen so they can accurately control the position of the mouse pointer.

Microsoft Windows itself works just fine with the Wabi display driver. This means that almost every Windows application can use this driver as well. On the flip side, the Wabi display adapter is the *only* display adapter with which Windows can work under Wabi software—you don't get a choice in the matter.

On DOS-based PCs, the choice of display adapter, along with a few other settings, is controlled through the Microsoft Windows `SETUP.EXE` program; this program is not installed with the Wabi Windows install routine (see page 114).

- **Sound cards** – Wabi 2.1 software supports the use of sound cards with Windows applications, provided you have suitable UNIX sound card drivers. See "Multimedia Support" on page 16 and "Using Multimedia Features" on page 235 for more information about using various multimedia devices under Wabi.

- **Pen plotters** – You may think that pen plotters are basically the same as other types of printers but, of course, they're not. Pen plotters are a rarified variant used by architects, engineers, draftspersons, and their ilk. The salient difference between a regular printer and a plotter is that the former rasterizes page images (that is, turns page images into bunches of dots) before printing, whereas the latter turns the page image into a series of vectors (mathematical equations representing individual lines, curves, crosshatch patterns, and so forth).

Wabi software supports over 200 different printers. The plot thickens, however; none of those currently supported printers includes a pen plotter, and you cannot add other printer drivers.

Wabi 2: Opening Windows

Communications Equipment

For the most part, communications equipment refers to modems and their ubiquitous variant, fax/modems. Wabi software supports any communications device that uses a serial (COM) port.

In the PC world, COM ports almost universally use the RS-232 asynchronous protocol (Macintosh computers use RS-234). Wabi software uses whatever COM port protocol is native to your UNIX system.

As far as Windows applications are concerned, Wabi software provides an environment in which those applications can use the COM ports on your UNIX system, whether those ports are local or out on a network. Windows itself, however, is not terribly clever at handling device contention—that is, when two devices are competing for the same port. The bottom line is, only one device can use the port at a time if one of the competing devices is a Windows application.

Complete information about using COM ports and managing device contention under Wabi is provided in Chapter 8, "Managing COM Ports," starting on page 196.

Windows in Windows

Okay, enough about that hardware stuff, you say; Windows is, after all, a *software* environment. And what's the most important component of the Windows interface? Why, the windows of course.

The Microsoft Windows software interface is explained here in terms of how various interface components differ from UNIX-based windowing environments, in particular Solaris OpenWindows. It is *not* the intention here to provide a primer on how to use Microsoft Windows itself—such information can be obtained from the *Microsoft Windows User's Guide*, included with your Microsoft Windows software.

The windows in Microsoft Windows (Windows windows?) are movable, sizable display regions on screen, which display one or more interface elements of a running application or process.

The whole point of a windowing environment like Microsoft Windows is to provide a means by which multiple windows, each running a different application or portion of an application, can be displayed side-by-side or overlapping on screen. For example, Figure 3-2 shows two overlapping windows, one for the Windows Write program, and the other for Windows Control Panel.

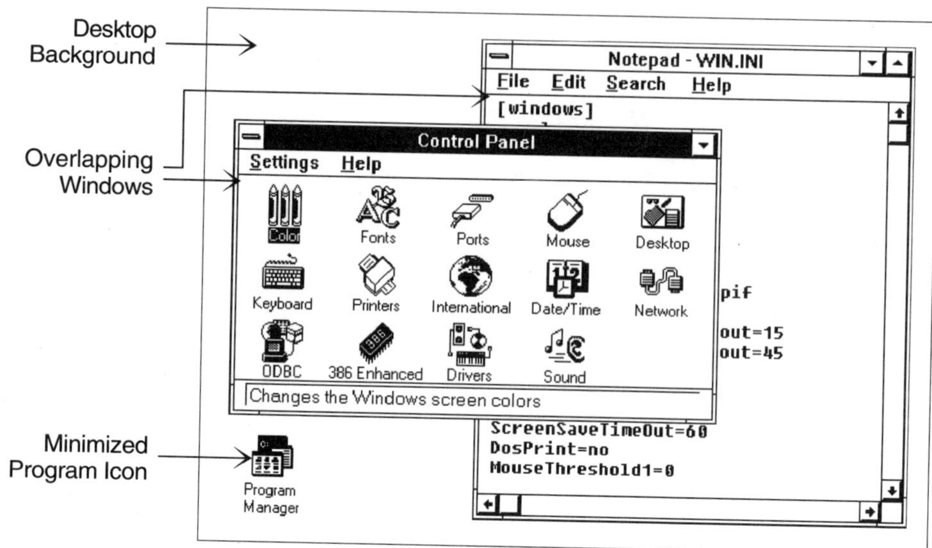

Figure 3-2   Windows in the Microsoft Windows Environment

Clicking anywhere in a Windows window activates it and brings it to the foreground. This is different from, say, a Solaris Window, which can be configured to be brought into the foreground only when you click on the window's title bar or when you press the Front button on your Sun keyboard. Moreover, a Solaris window can be active—that is, it can accept input from you—even if it is in the background; Microsoft Windows windows must be in the foreground to accept your input.

Also notice that, in the lower-left corner of Figure 3-2, is an icon for the *minimized* Program Manager program. In the Windows environment, a minimized program is one whose window has been reduced to an icon, although the program continues to run in the background. The process of restoring a minimized window to the size and position it was in before it was minimized is called, in Windows parlance, *restoring* the window. Sizing the window so it fills up the entire screen is called *maximizing* the window.

Wabi 2: Opening Windows

Closing a window in the Solaris environment is analogous to *minimizing* it in Microsoft Windows. Moreover, in Microsoft Windows, *closing* a window is analogous to the Quit command in Solaris—that is, it shuts down the application or window. To continue on a related note, *maximizing* a window in Microsoft Windows is similar to the Full Size command in Solaris. Note, however, that Maximize causes the window to fill the entire screen, whereas Full Size only fills the screen vertically—the window's width remains unchanged. Finally, *restoring* a window in Microsoft Windows is analogous to *opening* the window in Solaris. To confuse things further, the Restore Size command in Solaris windows, which returns a window to its original size after it has been full-sized, is analogous to the Restore command in Microsoft Windows when (and only when) applied to a maximized window. Bewildered yet? Table 3-2 summarizes these differences in terminology.

Table 3-2   Different Things You Can Do to Windows

Windows Command	Solaris Command	Explanation
Minimize	Close	Reduces the window to an icon; the program continues to run in the background.
Close/Exit	Quit	Shuts down (ends) the program or document.
Restore (1)	Open	Only for windows that are currently minimized; returns the window to the size and position it was in before being minimized.
Restore (2)	Restore Size	Only for windows that are currently maximized; returns the window to the size and position it was in before being maximized.
Maximize	Full Size	Maximize causes the window to fill the entire screen. Full Size causes the window to fill the screen vertically, but the width remains unchanged.

There are two general types of windows in the Microsoft Windows environment:

- **Application windows** – The main window in which programs run. Such windows usually contain:
  - Vertical and/or horizontal scroll bars
  - Four window borders
  - An application workspace
  - A title bar
  - A Control-menu box
  - Minimize and Maximize buttons
  - A menu bar

  In addition, application windows often contain a *status bar* along the bottom edge. A typical application window, in this case for Windows File Manager, is shown in Figure 3-3.

- **Document windows** – Some applications provide windows within windows. For example, Microsoft Word can display one or more document windows within its main application window. Similarly, Windows File Manager can display multiple drive windows—representing disk drives or network directories—within the File Manager application window.

  Document windows are displayed only by applications that provide a *multiple document interface* (MDI). Such applications are capable of displaying one or more documents (or drive windows, or whatever) at a time. Applications that can display only one document at a time are referred to, not surprisingly, as having a *single document interface* (SDI). For example, Microsoft Word for Windows provides a multiple document interface—you can open up a bunch of documents at once. In contrast, Windows Notepad™ has a single document interface; you can only open one document at a time.

  As with applications windows, you can do all the things described in Table 3-2 to document windows. Unlike application windows, document windows usually do not have a menu bar, a status bar, or other such amenities. A typical document window, in this case from Microsoft Word for Windows, is shown in Figure 3-4.

Table 3-3, on page 54, describes the purpose of each of element in a typical Windows application window and document window.

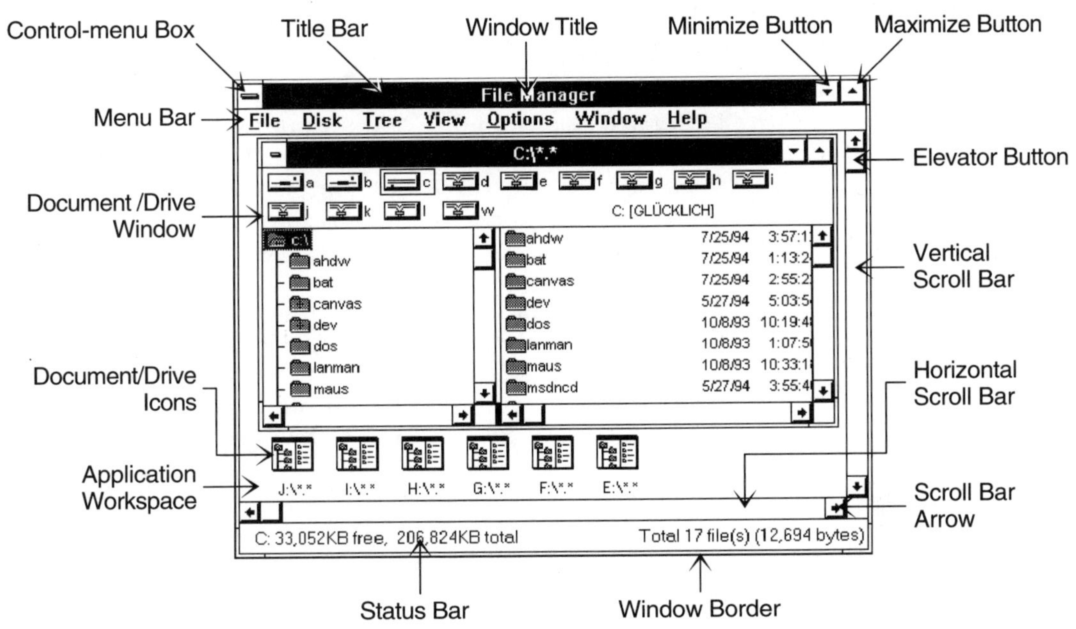

Figure 3-3   Parts of a Windows Application Window

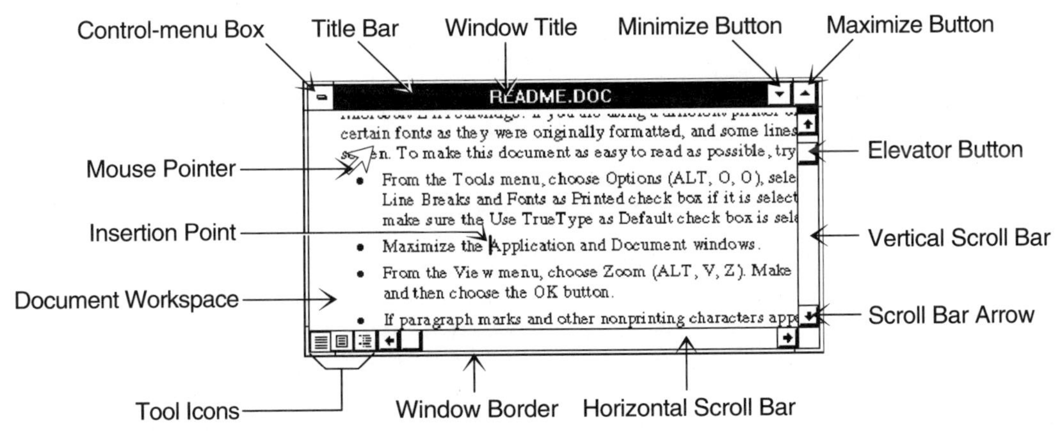

Figure 3-4   Parts of a Windows Document Window

Table 3-3   Elements of Windows Windows

Window Element	Purpose
Application Workspace	The background of the application window; the area in which document windows and document window icons are positioned. This is usually the largest portion of the application window. Note that this area does *not* include the menu bar, status bar, scroll bars, window borders, title bar, maximize/minimize buttons, or the Control-menu box.
Control-menu Box	Provides access to Control menu commands (such as Close, Minimize, Maximize, Restore, Move, and Size). Click once with the left mouse button on this box to display the Control menu. Double-click to close (quit) the application or document window.
Document Workspace	Similar to the application workspace; the portion of a document window in which the document text or other window content is displayed.
Elevator Button	Drag with the left mouse button to move horizontally or vertically through the window contents. The position of the elevator button in the scroll bar indicates the relative position in the window. Note that, unlike Solaris elevator buttons, the elevators in Windows do not include scroll bar arrows (see below).
Horizontal Scroll Bar	Allows you to move horizontally through the window; lets you see contents that are currently not in view.
Insertion Point	The position at which the next input in the window will be inserted, for example, when you type text. Note that this differs from the mouse pointer position.
Maximize Button	Click once to expand the window so it fills the entire screen (for application windows) or the application workspace (for document windows). Same as choosing Maximize from the Control menu.
Menu Bar	Provides access to pull-down menu commands for the application; menu bars are usually not present in document windows.

54

Table 3-3   Elements of Windows Windows (Continued)

Window Element	Purpose
Minimize Button	Click once to minimize the window (that is, reduce it to an icon). Same as choosing Minimize from the Control menu. Double-click on the icon to restore it to its original size and position.
Mouse Pointer	Indicates the current screen position of the mouse.
Scroll Bar Arrow	Click with the left mouse button to scroll through the window contents in the direction indicated. Unlike Solaris, Windows scroll bar arrows are located at the ends of the bars, rather than on the elevator buttons.
Status Bar	The status bar at the bottom of most application windows and some document windows provides (usually) relevant information about the current document or task. For example, the status bar may provide a quick explanation of the menu or button over which the mouse pointer is currently positioned.
Title Bar	The horizontal bar at the top of all application and document windows; displays the name of the current application of document. Also provides a "handle" by which you can drag the window to a new location. Double-clicking the title bar maximizes the window.
Tool Icons	Collectively referred to as a *toolbar*. Sometimes displayed near the top, bottom, or edges of document or application windows; provide point-and-click access to some common application commands. Not all windows have toolbars.
Vertical Scroll Bar	Allows you to move vertically through the window; lets you see contents that are currently not in view.
Window Border	Drag document or application window borders to resize the window horizontally or vertically. Drag on a window corner to resize the window horizontally and vertically at the same time.
Window Title	Displays the application name (in application windows), document name (in document windows), or both (in SDI application windows).

The Control-menu box and Minimize and Maximize buttons for Windows and Windows applications look slightly different under Wabi than they do under Windows running on a DOS-based PC. These differences are shown in Figure 3-5.

	Wabi	Windows
Minimize/Maximize		
Control-menu Box		

Figure 3-5   Windows and Wabi Buttons Compared

As indicated in Table 3-3, starting on page 54, there are also a few differences between scroll bars in the Microsoft Windows environment and the Solaris/OPEN LOOK environment. These differences are illustrated in Figure 3-6. Remember, Windows applications running under Wabi use Windows-style scroll bars.

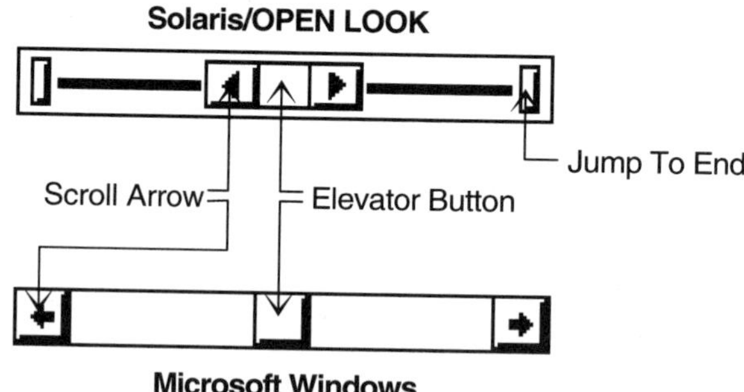

Figure 3-6   Windows and Solaris Scroll Bars Compared

Notice that Windows scroll bars do not have the OPEN LOOK "jump to end" buttons at the ends of the scroll bar. You must either drag the elevator or press the scroll arrow as long as required to get to the end of the scrolling region. Also notice that, on the Solaris scroll bar, the scroll arrows and elevator button are integrated into a single, multifunction button. By contrast, Windows scroll arrows are separate from the elevator button, and are always located at each end of the scroll bar. Finally, unlike the elevator buttons in OPEN LOOK or Motif, Windows elevator buttons do not vary in appearance based on document size. For example, in Motif, the longer the document, the smaller the elevator button.

Wabi 2: Opening Windows

Menus

After the windows themselves, the next most obvious software interface elements in the Microsoft Windows environment are the ubiquitous *pull-down menus* (Figure 3-7). These menus are generally (or should be, according to the *Microsoft Windows Interface Style Guidelines*) organized on a *menu bar* arrayed across the upper portion of application windows.

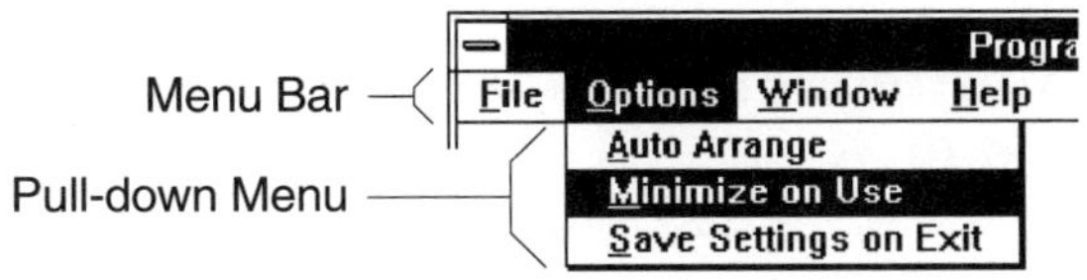

Figure 3-7   Typical Windows Pull-down Menu

Menu bars are generally not displayed in document windows, although the menu names and/or available commands in a given application may vary according to the status or contents of the document window. For example, in Microsoft Word 6.0 for Windows, the commands available to you vary depending on whether you are viewing a document in Normal, Outline, or Print Preview mode.

Cascading menus (Figure 3-8) are a subset of the standard pull-down menu. As with OPEN LOOK and Motif menus, cascading menus in Windows are indicated by a right-facing arrow or similar symbol next to a command name on a pull-down menu, and provide access to a submenu of commands. Cascading menus provide a sneaky way to cram lots of commands on an otherwise unthreatening menu bar, but they can be abused. For example, users of a certain publishing program (which shall remain unnamed here) must wade through menus that cascade five, six, seven, or more levels deep!

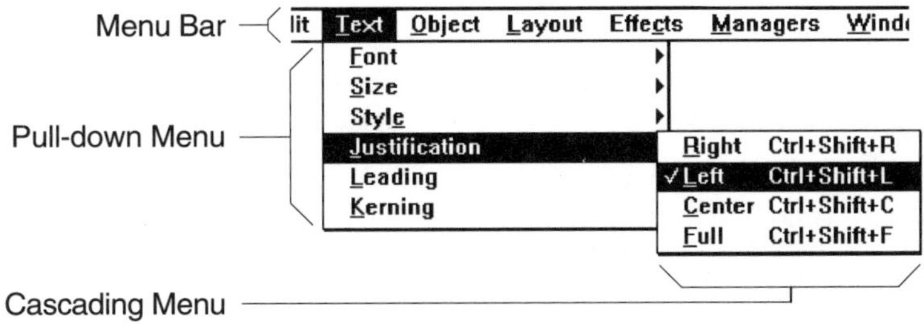

Figure 3-8   Cascading Menu

When it comes to pull-down menus, Windows applications running under Wabi use standard Microsoft Windows mouse conventions—that is, they do not inherit the mouse characteristics of the Solaris environment, although they work basically the same way in both environments. Specifically, you can click once with the left mouse button on a menu name to display a drop-down list of commands, then choose the command you want by clicking on it, again with the left mouse button.

There are a few subtle differences, however, in the way you use Windows menus and menus in OPEN LOOK or Motif-based applications:

- **Right mouse button support** – Unlike OPEN LOOK or Motif, Microsoft Windows-based applications are not nearly so enlightened in their support of the right mouse button. For example, the right mouse button has no effect on pull-down menus under Windows; only the left button is used. OPEN LOOK and Motif applications can be configured to use both right and left buttons.

  Also, most OPEN LOOK and Motif applications provide pop-up menus appropriate to the given context when you click with the right mouse button anywhere in a document or application window. Windows applications, for example, Microsoft Word 6.0 for Windows, have just gotten around to providing this kind of support, and most do not provide it at all.

- **Menu names as buttons** – In applications written for the OPEN LOOK windowing environment (but not those written for the Motif environment), menu names are displayed as buttons on menu bars. The idea here is that you can click on the menu name, like a button, to carry out the current default command for that menu. For example, in the Solaris Text Editor, clicking with the left mouse button on the File menu either saves the document (if it needs to be saved), or displays the File Open dialog box (if the document does not need to be saved). More important, you can configure your OPEN LOOK system so that clicking with the left mouse button performs *only* the default action—to display the drop-down menu on systems so configured, you must use the right button.

Dialog Boxes

Because they speak the language of a *user-friendly* kind of interface, Windows applications frequently want to engage in dialogs with you.... To aficionados of the UNIX command line, the Windows *dialog boxes* (a kind of pop-up window, illustrated in Figure 3-9) through which these exchanges take place can seem, at best, like chatty clerks at a retail store counter. Such users would rather go to an unadorned warehouse to purchase their books or VCRs, and would rather buy their paper products and pasta in bulk.

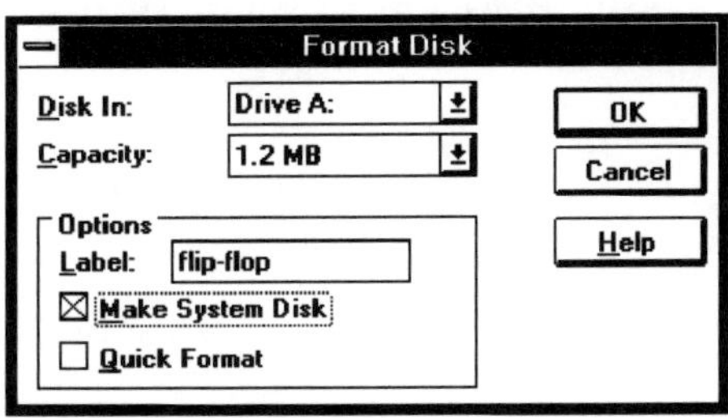

Figure 3-9   Simple Windows Dialog Box

By contrast, neophyte users are often intimidated by complex dialog boxes, which appear to bristle with controls and jargon, and fairly resemble the cockpit of a jet plane. Such users *don't* want to make too many choices; they just want to press a button or pick a menu command and have everything done for them automatically and perfectly.

How can a single interface component so neatly fail to meet the needs of these two types of users? Because the interface is designed for the users who fall in the middle—the rest of us—who want to make some choices, but don't want to (or can't) remember lots of command-line options.

Dialog boxes are compromises; controls are clustered within them, sometimes arbitrarily, into functional groups, with the designer's hope that you'll be able to find the controls you want for a given task in one location. For example, a paragraph format dialog box in a word processor might provide controls for line spacing, indentation, tabs, justification, and so forth. The design goal is to minimize the amount of "mousing around"—jumping from menu to menu to menu—required to accomplish a given task. In addition, dialog boxes can be designed to provide visual feedback that is not possible with a pull-down menu or command line.

With these points in mind, it is now possible to explain the different types of Windows dialog boxes, their purposes, and their various controls.

 The term *dialog box* is not used in the Solaris/OPEN LOOK environment. Instead, in OPEN LOOK, everything is either a window pane, pop-up window, or notice window; the various types of Windows dialog boxes encompass similar functions. The term dialog box is sometimes used, albeit inconsistently, in applications written for the Motif environment.

As far as the general user is concerned, there are four types of dialog boxes used in Windows. From a programmer's standpoint, you could categorize Windows dialog boxes into a larger number of groups, according to various classification schemes, but there is no reason to wade through all that here.

The four general types of dialog boxes in the Microsoft Windows environment are summarized in Table 3-4, and are explained in more detail in the paragraphs following the table.

Table 3-4   Windows Dialog Box Types

Type	How It Works	Where It Is Used
Application Modal	You must respond to and exit the dialog before doing anything else in the application, but you can switch to other applications.	The most common type of dialog in Windows. Displayed, for example, by the Windows File Manager Copy command.
System Modal	You must respond to and exit the dialog before doing anything else on your system; you can't switch to other applications.	Particularly nasty; usually displayed in response an egregious error on your part, or a program crash.
Application Modeless	You do not need to respond to the dialog before resuming work in your application; the dialog remains visible until you explicitly exit it.	The friendliest kind of dialog, but until recently, not used often in Windows. Dialogs with similar behavior are very common in Solaris and Motif.
Application Semimodal	You can perform a limited number of activities in your application, outside the dialog, while the dialog is displayed.	Provides an alternate means for entering dialog info. For example, a spell checker may let you correct a word *in situ* but allow no other editing.

Wabi 2: Opening Windows

- **Application modal dialog boxes** – These are the nice, run-of-the-mill dialog boxes you can show your mother (who has moved in with you and usurped your computer) or your children (who know more about your computer than you do). Unlike system modal dialogs, application modals allow you to switch away to other applications, and they can be dismissed without fear of retribution from the operating system.

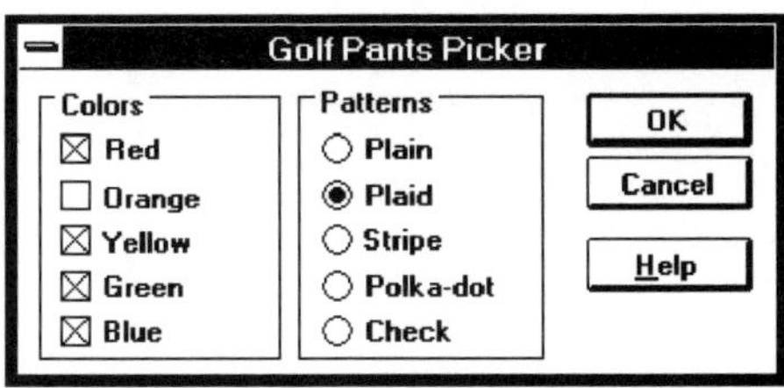

Figure 3-10 Pleasant Application Modal Dialog Box

Most of the dialog boxes in Windows applications nowadays are application modals, although some forward-thinking products are starting to use modeless dialogs more often, because they do not force the user's hand, and they are more suited for repetitive activities (see below).

Typically, application modals allow you to select from any number of options related to a given function. After making your selections, you enable or initiate them by pressing a dialog box button labeled OK (or Yes, or Do It!, or some other enabling phrase). If you change your mind, most application modals also provide a Cancel button to back out of the given process. Some especially friendly dialogs also provide a Help button, which leads to an on-line help system.

- **System modal dialog boxes** – This category of dialog box primarily comprises the annoying ones that pop up over whatever you are doing, and display messages like:

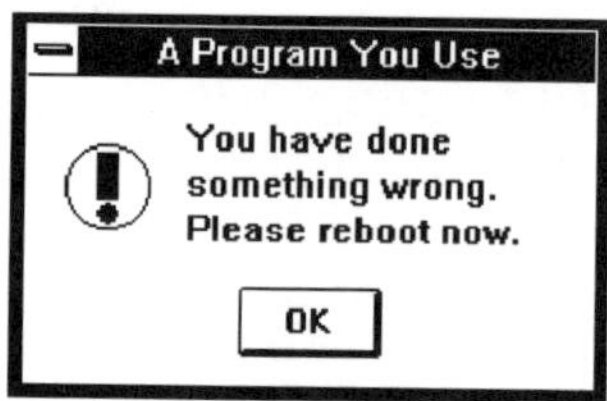

Figure 3-11 Annoying System Modal Dialog Box

"No!" You shout, "It's not okay!" By definition, system modal dialog boxes cannot be ignored—that is, you cannot switch to another application or do anything else until you satisfy the persnickety demands of the modal.

One of the nice things about Wabi is that it runs under UNIX, which is more stable than DOS. Under DOS/Windows, if an application crashes, it often brings down the whole system, forcing a warm reboot or hard reset. By contrast, under Wabi, if an application crashes, you can simply restart Wabi—you do not need to reboot your system.

- **Application modeless dialog boxes** – These are the most pleasant sort of dialog boxes. Easy-going, *sans souci*, they'll just hang around, waiting for you, while you're off gallivanting elsewhere in your application. You can use them or not, or ask them to leave—hey, no big deal. Unfortunately, such dialog boxes are still rare in the Windows environment, although they are quite common in the OPEN LOOK and Motif environments.

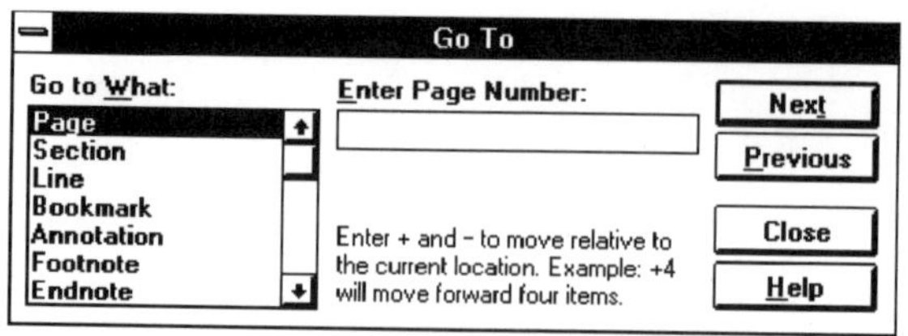

Figure 3-12 Come-What-May Application Modeless Dialog Box

Wabi 2: Opening Windows

In their most common manifestation, application modeless dialog boxes resemble applications modals, with similar sets of buttons; the major difference here is that you need to explicitly exit them to get them off your screen.

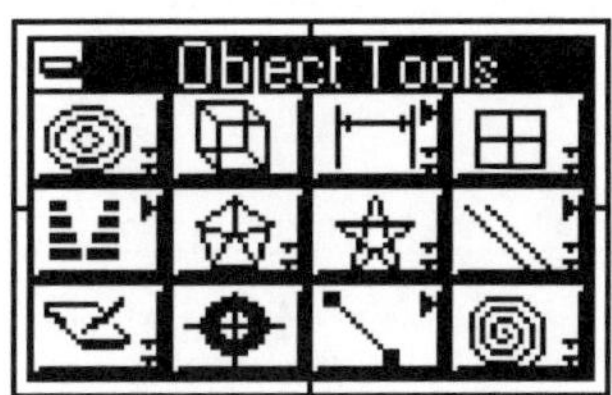

Figure 3-13 Application Modeless Dialog Disguised as a Tool Box

In addition, the *floating tool boxes* found in many Windows graphics applications, like CorelDRAW!™ (yes, the product name includes the exclamation mark) are actually application modeless dialog boxes, cleverly renamed to make you think you are using a tool from your familiar physical environment (please pass the application modeless hammer).

- **Application semimodal dialog boxes** – The rarest of dialog boxes, a hybrid of the modal and modeless, these dialogs tease you by letting you perform a limited number of functions outside the dialog before snatching back control. You sometimes see this kind of dialog, for example, in spelling or grammar checkers, which may allow you to edit a word in your document, but not allow any other actions in the application.

Dialog Box Controls

Windows dialog boxes present their choices to you through a wide variety of *controls*, some of which are more obvious than others. In many cases, these controls are designed based on familiar metaphors from the electromechanical world, like switches, dials, and sliders. Table 3-5, starting on the next page, summarizes the "standard" dialog box controls, as defined in *The Windows Interface: An Application Design Guide* (Microsoft Press, 1992). While some applications use nonstandard controls, the ones listed in Table 3-5 cover 90 percent or more of those you are likely to encounter.

Table 3-5   Common Windows Dialog Box Controls

What It Looks Like	What It's Called	How It Works
OK	Command Button	The most common control in dialog boxes. Click once with the mouse to activate the command with which it's associated. You can also use the Tab key to highlight the button, and then press Space or Enter.
◉ Enabled ○ Disabled	Option Button	Also called *radio button*. Represents a single choice in a list of mutually exclusive choices; that is, you can pick only one option from a group of related radio buttons. When the button is filled, the option is selected; when the button is empty, the option is unselected.
☒ Enabled ☐ Disabled	Check Box	Represents a choice that can be enabled or disabled, alone or in combination with other related check box options. When the check box has an X in it, the option is selected; when the check box is empty, the option is unselected.
☒ Enabled ☐ Disabled ▨ As Is	3-state Check Box	Similar to a check box, but provides a third setting, in which the box is filled with a gray pattern, which represents "as is" or "I don't care—ignore it or leave it unchanged."
Century Schoolbook Century-WP **Century725 BdCn BT** Century725 Cn BT Clarendon Cn BT CMBX10	Standard List Box	Similar in function to option buttons, in that you can only select one option at a time. List boxes are used when the list of options may vary, or when the list is very large, or when there's no space for a list of radio buttons. The currently selected option is highlighted in the list; use the scroll arrows or arrow keys to see other options. You can also press the first letter of the option in which you are interested to quickly jump to that option. Finally, in most dialogs, double-clicking on an option selects it and closes the dialog.

Wabi 2: Opening Windows

What It Looks Like	What It's Called	How It Works
Unix Closed Unix / DOS / Unix / VMS / MVS Dropped	Drop-down List Box	Similar to standard list boxes; the primary difference is that drop-down list boxes initially display only one option (the default or current selection). To display other options, click the down-arrow or press Alt+DownArrow.
Name:	Edit Box	Type or paste textual information into the edit box. Press End to jump to the end of the line; press Home to jump to the beginning. Double-click to select the entire line. Some edit boxes let you enter more than one line of text; to insert a carriage return in such edit boxes, press Ctrl+Enter or Shift+Enter.
8 8 / 9 / 10 / 11 / 12	Combo Box	Combination of a standard list box and an edit box. You can type an option setting in the edit box portion, or select an option from the list box portion. When initially displayed, the default or current selection is highlighted in both the edit portion and the list portion.
9600 Closed 9600 / 1200 / 2400 / 4800 / 9600 / 19200 Dropped	Drop-down Combo Box	Combination of a drop-down list box and an edit box. You can type an option setting in the edit box portion, or select an option from the list box portion. When initially displayed, the default or current selection is highlighted in the edit box portion, and the drop-down list is closed. To display other options, click the down-arrow, or press Alt+DownArrow.

What It Looks Like	What It's Called	How It Works
	Spin Box	Similar to an edit box in that you can enter an option setting by typing; differs from an edit box in that spin boxes can only accept a discrete set of values. You can use the up and down arrows to cycle through the list of acceptable values.
	Slider	Used to display and change option settings in a continuous, analog-style fashion. The illustration at left shows two common types of sliders, the lower of which resembles a basic scroll bar. Drag the slider with the mouse, or use the arrows at the end(s) of the slider to specify a value. The value you select is usually indicated by scale displayed beneath the slider. Some sliders also provide specific numeric or textual feedback, whereas others provide graphical feedback (for example, colors) in a small preview window.

Wabi 2: Opening Windows

This Thing Called DOS

When it's not running under Wabi in UNIX, Microsoft Windows runs under the DOS operating system. You must remember first and foremost: Windows is a *DOS program*; it is *not* an operating system.

Some people, of course, will argue that Microsoft Windows *is* an operating system—it's just not a complete operating system without DOS.... The important point for the purposes of this discussion is that Microsoft Windows was originally designed to run under DOS, and that makes it do weird things sometimes.

Although Wabi largely circumvents the hassles of DOS, understanding some of the implications of Windows' close association with DOS will help you understand why the Windows developers made some of their design decisions. Briefly, some things that may raise askew one or both of your eyebrows include:

- The memory-mapping games that Windows and DOS must play to actually use all of the physical memory that may be installed in a PC

- The absence, at the DOS operating system level, of file and resource sharing in a distributed network or multiuser fashion

- The lack of DOS support for true multithreaded, multitasking applications

- The restrictive file allocation and naming schemes used in DOS, compared to those used in UNIX

The remainder of this chapter explains each of these befuddling issues in more detail.

If you are not interested in why Microsoft Windows is occasionally a little bizarre, you can skip the next three sections of this chapter—Wabi obviates many of Windows' eccentricities. You should, however, read the last section in this chapter, "What's in a Name?," starting on page 73, for information about the different file naming schemes used in DOS and UNIX.

I... I Can't Remember

Everything Windows and Windows programs can do is defined by the restrictions of DOS and, hence, by the restrictions of the Intel 80386/ 80486/Pentium microprocessor architecture. Perhaps the most significant of these restrictions are the convolutions through which Windows and DOS must go to make physical memory available to applications.

Walking Backwards

The first IBM PCs, introduced in 1981, used an Intel 8088 processor. The 8088 was a 16-bit processor with an 8-bit data bus, and it could address a maximum of 1 megabyte (MB) of memory. Of this 1 MB, the IBM PC designers reserved 384 kilobytes (K) for use by system ROMs and hardware devices (like video adapters). This left only 640K of memory that could be accessed by application programs.

IBM chose the 8088 processor to retain backward compatibility with CP/M applications running on Z80-based computers, which represented the largest segment of the personal computer market at that time. Later, after IBM had blown the rest of the market out of the water, the PC switched to the 8086, essentially the same chip but slightly faster and with a 16-bit data bus. MS-DOS, the operating system chosen to run on the first IBM PCs, unfortunately inherited the 640K memory limitation endemic to the 8088/8086, and has been hobbled with it ever since—all in the name of backward compatibility.

To be sure, there have been significant advances in the architecture of Intel's line of microprocessors since the 8088, some of which have made the 640K barrier irrelevant for savvy applications. One of these advances was the introduction of *protected mode* operation (see below); the other advance was the addition of extra address lines to allow *x*86 processors to work with more than 1 MB of memory.

For example, the 80286, a 16-bit processor internally and externally, and blessed with an extra memory address line, could address up to 16 MB of memory. Next came the 80386, the first 32-bit processor in the *x*86 line, followed by the 80486, and the Pentium (nee 80586). These three 32-bit chips can address up to 4 gigabytes (GB) of memory—a truly impressive number.

Protect Me

Simply adding address lines was not enough to make such extra memory useful. More to the point, to access memory above 1 MB, *x*86 processors need to be set to a special operating state called *protected mode*. The 80286 was the first in the *x*86 series to employ protected mode functions, using 16-bit memory registers. The 80386 and later processors took protected mode a step further by working with 32-bit memory registers.

Protected mode operation allows the processor to access memory above 1 MB, and also provides some additional features, such as virtual memory, and support for the separation of tasks in a multitasking environment. In addition to the ability to run in 32-bit protected mode, 80386 and higher processors are also able to run in *virtual 8086* (*V8086*) mode. V8086 mode allows for the creation of multiple virtual 8086 machines; that is, multiple DOS applications can each think they are running on their own 8086 machine with its own 1 MB of memory.

Finally, to retain backward compatibility, *x*86 processors need be able to operate in a vanilla, non-protected mode, otherwise known as *real mode*. Thus, we arrive at the four modes used by 80386 and higher processors:

- **8086 real mode** – Where it all began; performs like an 8086 CPU, including the 640K memory restriction for applications.

- **16-bit protected mode** – All memory up to 16 MB can be accessed via 16-bit registers; first used in the 80286. *This is the processor mode used by Windows 3.x.*

- **32-bit protected mode** – All memory up to 4 GB can be accessed via 32-bit registers; used only by 80386 and higher processors. *This is the processor mode used by Solaris for x86.*

- **Virtual 8086 mode** – Creates the illusion of multiple, virtual 8086 machines running in real mode.

Why, you may ask, is it called protected mode? And who is being protected? Briefly, *protected mode* refers to a processor's ability to let multiple applications use the same physical memory while duping each application into believing that it has complete and exclusive access to that memory. *x*86 processors do this by creating a dynamic index of running applications and the segments of memory used by those applications; segments are mapped as needed in and out of an active state.

Extending and Expanding

As the Ginsu™ Knife guy says, "But wait! There's still more!" It's not enough to have protected mode, and it's not enough to have all this memory above 1 MB; you still need to provide a means by which applications can get at this memory. Enter the *Microsoft Extended Memory Specification* (*XMS*).

Under DOS, to access memory above 1 MB—referred to as *extended memory*—you must have some sort of XMS device driver. In the DOS world, the most ubiquitous of these drivers—the one included with Microsoft Windows—is called HIMEM.SYS.

Because Wabi runs under UNIX, Microsoft Windows under Wabi does *not need* to use HIMEM.SYS or any other DOS extended memory driver. Although HIMEM.SYS is present in your wabi/windows directory when you install Windows with the Wabi Windows installer, this is just a vestigial copy—*it is not used by Wabi*! Well then, you may ask, why is it there at all? Because some Windows applications need to check for its existence—not even whether it's running, mind you—before they will start.

In the context of the magical DOS world above 1 MB, you may have also heard of *expanded memory*. This is memory above 1 MB that is made to look as if exists in the conventional memory space below 1 MB. Again, a special expanded memory driver is needed to use expanded memory under DOS. The expanded memory driver included with DOS is called EMM386.EXE; other popular third-party drivers include Quarterdeck Software's QEMM®, and Qualitas' 386Max™.

As with extended memory drivers, expanded memory drivers are a moot point under Wabi—*expanded memory drivers are not needed!*

It's Not a Bug; It's an Enhancement

This brings us to *386 Enhanced Mode*, the most advanced operating mode used in Windows 3.*x*. 386 Enhanced Mode takes advantage of 16-bit protected mode in 80386 and higher processors, and provides three primary enhancements over the Windows fallback, *Standard Mode*:

- More memory protection and a greater capacity, compared to Standard Mode, for multitasking Windows applications. Note that this is not true *preemptive* multitasking, à la UNIX (see "Walking and Chewing Gum," later in this chapter).

- The ability to run multiple DOS applications (in virtual 8086 mode, for those of you that have been paying attention) in scalable windows alongside Windows applications. This benefit, however, is a nonissue in Wabi—DOS emulation under Wabi is provided by other programs, such as SunPC or Merge. Refer to Chapter 10, "Using DOS Applications," starting on page 248, for information about running DOS applications from Windows under Wabi.

- The ability to use *virtual memory*, in the form of a swap file, to provide more operating room for applications.

386 Enhanced Mode is the *only* Windows operating mode used under Wabi software; Standard Mode is not available from within Wabi. Also remember that DOS emulation is not provided directly by Wabi; opening a DOS shell from within Wabi launches the DOS emulation program of your choice.

I'm Okay, and It's All Mine

Compared to UNIX, DOS is a relatively simple single-user operating system—the operative term here is *single-user*. The implications of this, among other things, are that there are no inherent, operating system-based mechanisms for file sharing, file locking, and file protection. Nor are there built-in tools for network management; the concepts of user names, logins, and home directories are foreign. Nor are there such niceties as built-in store-and-forward mechanisms, to provide the groundwork for email and network-based file distribution.

Again, this is where Wabi combines the strengths of UNIX with the popular DOS/Windows-based applications. Wabi creates its files and directories on a UNIX system. When you install Windows and Windows applications, they are installed on a UNIX system. Any directory or disk partition that can be accessed through your UNIX system can be accessed through Windows under Wabi. Whether it is in UNIX, DOS, Macintosh, HPFS, or whatever format, if it can be mounted through Solaris, it can be accessed through Wabi.

Walking and Chewing Gum

Another implication of its single-user heritage is that DOS is inherently a single-tasking operating system—that is, it can do one thing at a time. The introduction of protected mode operations in Intel *x*86 processors made it possible to multitask applications, but to this day, DOS is still a single-user system. Windows, based in DOS but sneaking along with 16-bit protected mode operations, has pulled a rabbit out of a knit cap by providing some level of multitasking capabilities.

But do not be confused: Multitasking under Windows is not true *preemptive* multitasking as provided in UNIX. What this means is that processing does not take place according to need—a process cannot grab the CPU's attention when it might really need it—but instead must wait in queue with other running processes. Perhaps more importantly, when a process under Windows finally gets the attention of the CPU, it can hog it all and not give any other processes a chance.

For example, Windows applications are legendary for getting into some infinite loop, not letting go of the CPU or other resources, and taking down the whole system in a ball of digital flames. The beauty of Wabi (beauty is as beauty does) is that, because it runs as a process under UNIX, which is much better at multitasking, when an application crashes, it almost never takes the rest of the world with it.

 This point does require some clarification. All Windows applications running under Wabi run within a single Wabi process. That is, if you are running a Microsoft Excel spreadsheet, CorelDRAW!, and Microsoft Word for Window under Wabi, they are all running together in one Wabi process in UNIX. Consequently, if one of those applications crashes in such a way that would bring down a PC, it will also usually bring down Wabi. The difference is that it does not bring down the rest of your Solaris system.

What's in a Name?

DOS and UNIX use different schemes for naming files and directories. In particular, there are five differences, described in Table 3-6, that can cause some confusion when working with Windows applications under Wabi software.

Table 3-6   Some Confusing File Name Differences Between DOS and UNIX

Difference	Explanation
	File name length – DOS file names are limited to eight characters plus a three-character extension; for example, `FILENAME.DOC`. By comparison, UNIX file names can be up to 255 characters.
AaBbCc	**Uppercase/lowercase** – In DOS, it doesn't matter whether you enter a file name in uppercase or lowercase letters; DOS converts it all to uppercase. UNIX allows for mixed-case file names.
ÅßÉÑØÜ	**Special characters** – There are a number of characters that are not legal in DOS file and directory names, some of which are legal in UNIX. These characters are listed in Table 3-8 on page 76. Note in particular that DOS directory names are separated by backward slashes (\), but in UNIX they are separated by forward slashes (/).

Table 3-6   Some Confusing File Name Differences Between DOS and UNIX (Continued)

Difference	Explanation
	File attributes – DOS is not very clever when it comes to associating file attributes with a given file. For example, there is no inherent mechanism in DOS for determining with what application a given file is associated. Similarly, beyond a simple `.EXE`, `.COM`, or `.BAT` extension in the file name, DOS has no way of knowing whether a file is some sort of executable. Windows provides only a rudimentary way of associating files with applications based on the file's extension name; for example, files with a `.DOC` extension may be associated with Word for Windows. In Solaris, files are usually registered with the operating environment (in `/etc/magic` or the `~/.cetables` directory), so that the file name has little to do with the file's attributes—the operating environment knows what kind of file it is no matter what you call it.
	File securities – Because DOS is a single-user operating system, there are no mechanisms for true file security. In DOS, a file can be designated as hidden, read-only, system, or archive, but that's it—there are no privileges or securities based on file ownership, user groups, and so forth.

These differences can cause problems because Windows applications, even though they are running in UNIX under Wabi, can only work with DOS file names. For example, you cannot save a CorelDRAW! illustration with a twenty character file name, even though it would be legal in UNIX.

In general, Wabi automatically handles the differences between the two operating environments, mapping file names, attributes, and securities as needed, so you don't have to worry about it. Having said this, there are a few points you should remember:

- **Long file names** – Wabi automatically creates alias names for file names that are too long. The first five characters of the original name are preserved, followed by a tilde (~), followed by two variable characters. For example, a UNIX file named `reallylongfile` might be mapped to the DOS name `REALL~7G`. Note that this is only an *alias* name; the original UNIX name is retained outside of Wabi; that is, the file name displayed in Windows File Manager might be `REALL~7G`, but an `ls` command issued at the Solaris command prompt would list the file as `reallylongfile`.

Wabi 2: Opening Windows

The two variable characters used when truncating long file names may appear to be random, but they are, in fact, generated by deterministic methods—that is, they ain't random. The advantage to this is that the aliases assigned by Wabi to long file names remain consistent among your Wabi sessions. A file named REALL~7G remains REALL~7G from session to session. This makes it possible, for example, to maintain OLE links between Windows application files (see "DDE, OLE, and Packager" on page 298). If the variable portion of the aliases were generated randomly, such OLE links would break.

The variable portion of Wabi alias names can be any pair of alphanumeric characters (A–Z, 0–9). This makes for a total of 36^2, or 1296, possible combinations. What, you may ask, happens if you have more than 36^2 files with the same first five letters in the same directory? Well, first of all, if you have that many files named like that, you need to do something else with your time—*get a life!* Seriously though, that extremely rare case will cause problems for Wabi, the only solution to which is to rename some of the files in UNIX.

- **Uppercase and special characters** – The general rule when using Wabi is that any character that requires the use of the SHIFT key to enter it will be treated as a *special character.* File names containing any special characters—uppercase or the characters listed in Table 3-8—are mapped by Wabi with alias names, similar to the aliases created for long file names. With this method, uppercase characters are handled as unshifted, and special characters are replaced by tildes, followed by any legal characters. File names are always padded out to eight characters, using tildes if no other characters are available. Table 3-7 shows some examples of Wabi alias names.

Table 3-7   Examples of Wabi Alias Names

UNIX Name	Wabi Alias	UNIX Name	Wabi Alias
Clips	CLIPS~VP	c.lips.o	C~LIP~ID.O
Cl	CL~~~~62	clipcloP	CLIPC~LU
ClPo	CLPO~~F1	Clp.iooo	CLP~I~CX

Note that many Windows applications display file names in lowercase characters, while some others don't. The point is, DOS and Windows ignore the shift states of characters.

Table 3-8   Illegal Characters in DOS/Windows File Names

Character	How It's Used in DOS	Character	How It's Used in DOS
.	**Period** – Separator for three-letter file or directory name extensions.	;	**Semicolon** – Sometimes used as a command-line option separator.
,	**Comma** – Sometimes used as a command-line option separator.	:	**Colon** – Suffix indicating a drive or port name. For example, `D:`, `LPT1:`.
/	**Forward slash** – Command-line option separator. (In UNIX, used to separate directory paths.)	<	**Open angle bracket** – Redirects command output to a file or device. For example, `debug < win.com`.
\	**Backward slash** – Separates directory names in path statements. For example, `C:\DOS\OLD`.	>	**Close angle bracket** – Redirects command output to a file or device. For example, `dir > lpt1:`.
[	**Open square bracket** – An escape sequence prefix for some *very* arcane ANSI commands.	|	**Pipe/vertical bar** – Redirects command output to another command. For example, `type` *file* `| more`.
]	**Close square bracket** – A command delimiter in some programming languages.	+	**Plus sign** – Concatenates (combines) files when used, for example, with `copy`.
=	**Equal sign** – Assigns values to variables. For example, `PATH=C:\DOS`.	"	**Double quote** – Delimiter for literal strings in some programming languages.
?	**Question mark** – Single-character wildcard. For example, `LO?K.TXT` could be `LOOK.TXT` or `LOCK.TXT`.	*	**Asterisk** – Multiple-character wildcard. For example, `M*.DOC` could be `MOO.DOC` or `MEOW.DOC`.

Wabi 2: Opening Windows

- **File attributes and securities** – Wabi automatically maps relevant file attributes and securities between DOS and UNIX. Not surprisingly, though, some attributes and securities have no meaning, or slightly convoluted meanings, in one or the other operating system. For example:

  - The DOS `archive`, `system`, and `hidden` attributes have no meaning in UNIX.
  - The UNIX `execute` privilege has no meaning in DOS.
  - The DOS `read only` attribute is equivalent to no `write` privileges in UNIX.
  - In UNIX, directories are files; in DOS they are FAT table entries.
  - DOS has no concept of `user`, `group`, and `other` permission levels. Files created in Wabi inherit the `umask` values from the UNIX environment in which the Wabi process is running.

With these points in mind, Table 3-9 summarizes how Wabi maps various file attributes between DOS and UNIX.

Table 3-9   Attribute Mapping Between DOS and UNIX

DOS Attribute		UNIX Attribute
Read Only (ro)	⮕	Mapped to `no write`.
System (s)	⮕	Not mapped; not changed.
Archive (a)	⮕	Not mapped; not changed.
Hidden (h)	⮕	Sets `setuid` bit (s).
Normal access; not ro or h.	⬅	(rwx) Read-Write-Execute
Normal access; not ro or h.	⬅	(rw-) Read-Write
Mapped to ro; file can be executed.	⬅	(r-x) Read-Execute
Normal access; not ro or h.	⬅	(-wx) Write-Execute
Mapped to ro; file can be executed.	⬅	(r--) Read
File not displayed, doesn't exist.	⬅	(-w-) Write
Mapped to ro; file can be executed.	⬅	(--x) Execute
File not displayed, doesn't exist.	⬅	(---) No Privileges

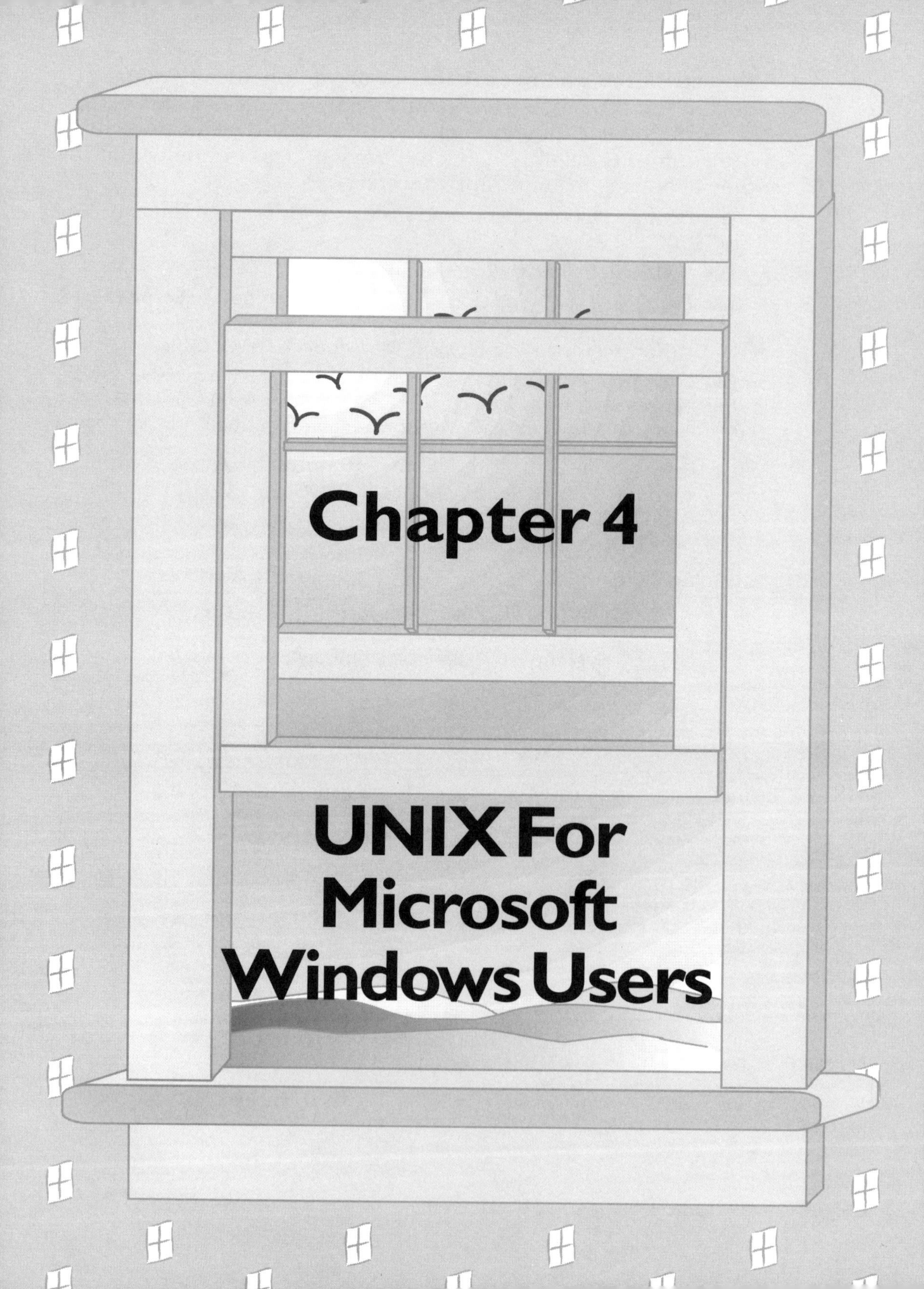
Chapter 4
UNIX For Microsoft Windows Users

U NIX gets a bad rap for being difficult to use, from the standpoint of the general user. This is unfair—after all, it's really not much more difficult than DOS....

User-friendly – adj. *Programmer hostile. Generally used by hackers in a critical tone, to describe systems that hold the user's hand so obsessively that they make it painful for the more experienced and knowledgable to get any work done.*

– Eric Raymond, *The New Hacker's Dictionary*, 1991

By implication, UNIX is a very powerful operating system, and *many* programmers (but not all: see the *Hacker's Dictionary* entry for "UNIX weenie") find UNIX to be a more technically satisfying operating system in which to program.

But truly, UNIX is not so difficult when you compare it to DOS. Most UNIX commands are no less mnemonic and no more arcane than their DOS counterparts, and in many ways the flexibility of UNIX makes things easier than DOS for the user, not more difficult. Many of the difficulties in UNIX are simply a consequence of the fact that UNIX does much, much more than DOS.

The *joy* of Wabi is that you don't need to worry much about the UNIX underpinnings—you can continue to live in your happy world of Windows "productivity applications" while still reaping the benefits of a robust multiuser operating environment that can also, by the way, run *many* powerful programs. The goal of this chapter, then, is to give you just enough information about UNIX to be dangerous (or tedious) at parties....

In This Chapter

About UNIX

UNIX is the most widely used multiuser, multitasking, general-purpose operating system in the world today. It can run on an extraordinarily wide variety of computer equipment—from PCs to microcomputers to mainframes—and is, in fact, the *lingua franca* of the world's largest computer network, the Internet.

The UNIX operating system was created in 1969 at Bell Laboratories by Ken Thompson. Rumor has it that Thomson invented UNIX so he could play games on his PDP-7 computer, which he salvaged after Bell Labs abandoned its MULTICS (the big brother of UNIX) project.

Dennis Ritchie (the C programming language deity) is generally considered to be the coauthor of UNIX. In the years 1972-74, UNIX was reimplemented almost entirely in C, which made it the first operating system that was truly portable—that is, it became relatively easy to port UNIX to different hardware platforms by recompiling its C source code. (The programmers in the audience may be cringing just now—*nothing* is that easy—but UNIX *is* a heck of a lot easier to port than most other operating systems.)

As UNIX evolved, it was embraced by the academic and scientific communities. Because of the generally experimental mind-set in those populations, and because of the wide availability of UNIX source code, UNIX was hacked and extended and tweaked and refined for different purposes, the product of which was a veritable tower of babbling operating systems. Eventually, by the mid 1980s, AT&T consolidated the various flavors of UNIX into a standard operating system. These efforts resulted first in System III, and finally in System V—the phylum from which the most popular strains of UNIX today are descended.

UNIX System V Release 4.0, released in 1989, and its ancillary System V Interface Definition (SVID), form the standard on which SunOS™, HP/UX®, IBM/AIX®, and SCO/UNIX are based. The bare-bones command-line interfaces of these systems have, in turn, been augmented by graphical, windowing environments (no, Microsoft did *not* invent such environments) like OPEN LOOK, OSF/Motif, and HP OpenVue™ (these particular environments are, in turn, implementations of the X Window System standard—see "About X Window" on page 100).

Basic UNIX Concepts

UNIX is founded on the concepts of multiple users, multiple tasks, timesharing, and interoperability. Before going any further, let's define these terms, because they are totally foreign to DOS.

- **Multiple users** – This one is easy: it means more than one user. The implications, however, are more complex. To support multiple users, an operating system must have some means of identifying those users, preventing them from getting in each other's way, and making it difficult for them to wreck each other's stuff. On the more optimistic side, it means providing tools with which multiple users can share data and programs, exchange messages, and generally apprise one another of each other's existence. Hence the concepts of logins, user names, privileges, protections, file locking, email, and so forth.

- **Multiple tasks** – Again, nominally simple: it means doing more than one thing at a time. Again, however, the implications are complex, and the details of their implementation are beyond the scope of this book. For the purposes of running Wabi, all you need to know is that, unlike Microsoft Windows, UNIX provides true *preemptive* multitasking. Program *threads* can operate independently of each other and other programs. This makes it possible, for example, for one program to update the display (using the video subsystem) while another program does a database lookup (using CPU and disk resources). By contrast, under Microsoft Windows, you would get the dreaded hourglass until one or the other activities was completed.

- **Timesharing** – The ability to allow authorized user access to programs, data, and resources (like printers, modems, and disks) on a system. Equally important is that users can gain such access *when they need it*; a user does not have to wait for other users to get off the system, within certain volume limits, before being allowed access.

- **Interoperability** – The sharing of programs, data, and resources among different machines in a relatively seamless way. UNIX's portability is also the basis for its interoperability.

At its highest level, UNIX can be divided into three primary components:

- **Kernel** – Provides core operating system functions
- **File system** – Hierarchical naming structure for files and directories
- **User shell** – The user interface through which you interact with the operating system

Of these three components, the file system and the user shell are of the greatest interest to Wabi users.

The UNIX File System

The basics of getting around in the UNIX file system are of interest to Wabi users because Wabi, Windows, and any Windows applications you install under Wabi will reside in UNIX.

Like DOS, UNIX provides a hierarchical file and directory structure, as illustrated in Figure 4-1. That is, *files* reside in *directories*, and directories reside in other directories. In Windows parlance, directories are also sometimes referred to as *folders*.

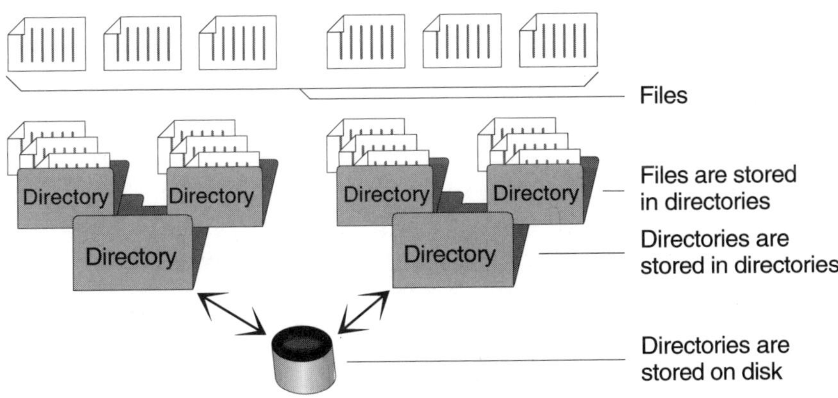

Figure 4-1   Hierarchical Relationship of Files and Directories

From a practical standpoint, there are several important differences between the DOS and UNIX file systems:

- In DOS, file names are limited to eight alphanumeric characters, plus a three character extension. For example, `FILENAME.DOC`. UNIX file names can be up to 255 characters.

- DOS file names are not case-sensitive—that is, forget about the SHIFT key. UNIX file names are case-sensitive; you can mix uppercase and lowercase characters.

- There are several characters you can't use in DOS file names, but which you can use in UNIX. (See Table 3-8 on page 76).

- Directory names in DOS are separated by backslashes (\); in UNIX, they are separated by forward slashes (/). For example, you could have a DOS directory named `\STUFF\LETTERS`. The same directory relationship in UNIX would be represented as `/STUFF/LETTERS`.

- The concepts of file security attributes, as provided in UNIX, are mostly not present in DOS.

These differences are explained in (excruciating) detail in Chapter 3, in the section "What's in a Name?" on page 73.

Wabi goes a long way towards smoothing out the differences between the two file systems, so you don't have to worry about them. For the most part, when running Windows applications under Wabi, you name and work with files and directories just as you would under DOS. There are two exceptions to this:

- **When you are installing Wabi** – Wabi installation requires at least some knowledge of how to get around in the UNIX file system. This requirement is minimal, however, and the installation instructions provided with Wabi software pretty much hold your hand through the process.

- **When you want to mount (connect to) a UNIX directory** – In Wabi, you mount—that is, connect to—UNIX directories so that they appear as disk drives to Windows applications. To do this, you need to understand how UNIX directories are named. Mounting directories is explained later in this chapter, and also in Chapter 5, "Using Wabi Software," and in Chapter 6, "Managing Drives."

The NFS File System

The Solaris operating environment is based on the *NFS®* distributed file system. In most cases, when using Wabi, you will be working with NFS-based files and directories. You may also, on occasion, find yourself connecting to other file systems, but NFS will probably be the most common system you will use with Wabi.

NFS is a UNIX-based distributed file system, developed by Sun Microsystems, that enables computers on a network to cooperatively access each other's files in a transparent, seamless manner. That is, from the user's standpoint, remote file systems (those that are on machines other than the user's) are indistinguishable from local file systems (those that are actually on the user's machine).

For example, instead of duplicating a set of directories on all machines on a given network, the NFS file system lets you have one common set of directories on a machine that is shared by all other systems. Each user sees that set of shared directories as local to his or her own workstation.

The file name and attribute mapping scheme used by Wabi (see "What's in a Name?" on page 73) is based on the NFS file system.

NFS Mount Points and Wabi Drives

A *mount point* is a location in an NFS directory structure at which you want to make a network connection from within Wabi. Such connections appear to Windows applications running in the Wabi environment as *virtual disk drives*—otherwise known, in Wabi parlance, as *Wabi drives*.

To Windows applications running under Wabi, Wabi drives appear to be regular PC disks—like a drive E: or F: You can treat Wabi drives pretty much the same way as regular PC disks; you can save, copy, move, rename, and delete files, and install and run applications.

For example, you could define an NFS directory named /home/yourstuff as a mount point, and then assign drive letter P: as the Wabi drive to represent that directory in Windows applications running in the Wabi environment. From Windows File Manager in Wabi, you could then click on the drive icon for P: to display the files in /home/yourstuff.

In the above example, /home/yourstuff is considered to be the root directory on the P: drive. Therefore, any subdirectories off that root are also accessible to you, provided that you have sufficient network *privileges*. For example:

Table 4-1   Sample Wabi Drive Assignments

NFS Directory Name	Wabi Drive Name
/home/yourstuff	P:\
/home/yourstuff/mail	P:\mail
/home/yourstuff/work	P:\work
/home/yourstuff/work/daysoff	P:\work\daysoff

This privileges thing is very important in the UNIX world—you may not (and probably don't) have access to all files and directories on your network. Access privileges are associated with your UNIX user account, which is described on the next page, in "Who Are You?"

Going Home

For general users, the most important, and most frequently accessed directory is your home directory. This is the directory in which you store your day-to-day data files, your email files, and many of your custom system configuration files, among other items. For example, your home directory may be named /home/president.

When viewing directory names, particularly in documentation or configuration files, you may occasionally encounter a tilde (~), and wonder what the heck it means. In UNIX, the tilde in directory paths represents your home directory. For example:

        /home/president/letters

is the same as:

        ~/letters

Who Are You?

To support the practical implications of multiple users, UNIX provides the concept of *user names*. A user name is a unique name used to identify a user to the operating system. Every user on a UNIX system must have a *user account*, the two primary identification components of which are a user name and a unique *password* associated with that name.

You enter your user name and password in response to *login* prompts when you first try to access a system. This login process is explained in more detail later in this chapter, in "Logging In" on page 96.

After identifying yourself to the system, UNIX is then able to automatically determine or configure various operating system components for you; for example, your home directory, your PATH environment variable, default configuration files, and so forth. Your user account also has associated with it a set of *privileges* (or *permissions*), which are the degrees to which you are allowed access to files, directories, and devices on your network or your machine. UNIX privileges are explained in more detail in the next section, "May I?"

UNIX users are also usually grouped into sets of users, collectively called *user groups*. Any single user can belong to one or more user groups, the specific list of which is part of user's account information. Like individual users, each user group has associated with it a set of privileges. This makes it possible to provide and manage collective access to, say, a set of document directories.

May I?

All access to files, directories, and devices (like printers) in UNIX is closely controlled by various permissions. Of particular interest to Wabi users are file and directory permissions, which you can control and sometimes need to modify. By contrast, device permissions are usually managed by your system administrator.

File and directory permissions are based on user and group accounts, and can therefore be divided into the following three user categories:

- **User** – You

- **Group** – Anyone in any of the user groups to which you belong

- **Other (or World)** – Everyone else

You can assign the following permissions to files and directories:

- **Read** (r) – The file can be viewed.

- **Write** (w) – The file can be modified.

- **Execute** (x) – The file can be run (only for programs or scripts). In the case of directories, the directory can be switched to; in UNIX you can only change to directories for which you have execute permission.

You can change the permissions on your own files and directories by using the UNIX chmod command. Alternatively, from within Wabi, you can use the Microsoft Windows File Manager to change some (but not all) permissions. The mapping of permissions between UNIX and Windows is described in detail in Table 3-9 on page 77.

Briefly, to use the chmod command, enter chmod, followed by a 3-digit value (4-digit values are another story) representing user, group, and world permissions respectively, followed by a file name. Figure 4-2 illustrates how to set chmod values.

Value	Permission		
7	r	w	x
6	r	w	
5	r		x
4	r		
3		w	x
2		w	
1			x
0	-	-	-

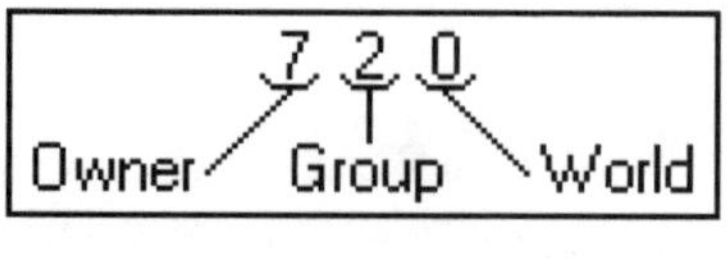

7 2 0

Owner   Group   World

The first digit represents permissions for owner; the second, for group; the third, for world (or other). For example:

```
chmod 720 myfile
```

sets permissions for myfile to 720, which means rwx for owner, w only for group, and no privileges for world.

Figure 4-2   Setting chmod Values

Wabi 2: Opening Windows

Table 4-2 lists some common `chmod` values.

Table 4-2   Common `chmod` Values

Value	Meaning
755	Owner: `rwx`; Group: `r-x`; World: `r-x`
700	Owner: `rwx`; Group, World: no access
777	Unrestricted access to all
666	`rw-` access to all

 Remember, in UNIX, directories are just another kind of file. You use `chmod` to change directory permissions the same way you change file permissions. Moreover, you cannot switch to a directory unless it has execute permissions!

umask and You Shall Receive

Your user account has associated with it default file and directory permissions. That is, every file or directory you create is assigned a default set of permissions. This default set of permissions is assigned (and can be changed) with the UNIX `umask` command.

The `umask` command is similar in many ways to `chmod`. The differences between the two, however, can be subtle and confusing:

- **Global versus local** – `chmod` is used to change permissions on an *as needed* basis; that is, you change permissions for specific files and directories. By contrast, `umask` is used to set *global* permissions—your `umask` setting is applied everywhere, to all files and directories you subsequently create. You use `chmod` to specifically override the `umask` setting on a file-by-file basis.

- **Positive versus negative** – `chmod` lets you specify what people *can* do to files; `umask` is the obverse of that concept—it specifies what you *can't* do to files. Think of `umask` as a filter (or a mask); the holes in the mask (values not set) are the permissions that are allowed to pass through.

Figure 4-3 illustrates how to set `umask` values. Compare these values to those shown for `chmod` in Figure 4-2 on page 88.

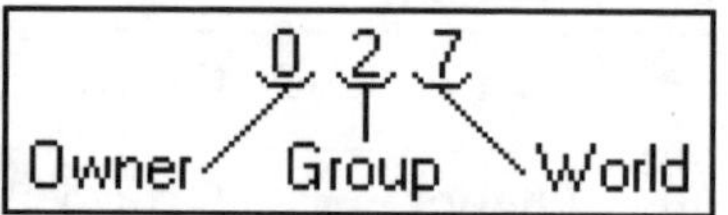

Value	Permission
0	r w x
1	r w
2	r x
3	r
4	w x
5	w
6	x
7	- - -

Figure 4-3 Setting `umask` *Values*

Table 4-2 lists some common `umask` values.

Table 4-3 Common `umask` *Values*

Value	Meaning
022	Anyone can read and execute a file; only the owner can write; for a directory, anyone can list the contents.
077	No access for anyone other than the owner.
000	Unrestricted access all.

Some Common DOS and UNIX Commands

Now that you've been sufficiently terrified by the concepts of `chmod` and `umask`, it is time to assuage your dismay by explaining some common DOS commands—with which you should already be comfortable—and their UNIX counterparts.

If you should ever find yourself stranded at a UNIX command prompt outside of Wabi, refer to Table 4-4, which lists DOS commands and their UNIX equivalents. Note that this is not an exhaustive list; just some of the basic commands are listed here.

Wabi 2: Opening Windows

DOS Command	UNIX Command	Comments
attrib	chmod or umask	Change the attributes of files or directories; note that many DOS attributes have no UNIX equivalents, and vice versa. Refer to Table 3-9 on page 77 for more information.
cd	cd or chdir	Change directories.
chkdsk	df -k fsck	Display disk statistics; fsck, for disk repair, is run automatically at bootup.
cls	clear	Clear the screen.
copy	cp	Copy files and directories.
del	rm	Delete files; also directories in UNIX.
dir	ls	Display the contents of a directory.
edit/edlin	textedit or vi	Edit text files; texedit is Solaris only.
find	grep	UNIX find finds files; grep finds strings.
format	format	Format diskettes and hard drives.
help	man	Get help on a specific command.
mkdir (md)	mkdir	Create new directories.
path	env or setenv	Display or set PATH environment variable.
print	lpr or lp	Print files.
rename (ren)	mv	Rename files; mv lets you rename directories or move to another directory.
rmdir (rd)	rmdir or rm -r	Remove directories.
type	more or cat	Display the contents of a file; more displays one screen at a time; cat displays continuously.
ver	uname -sr	Display operating system version number.

Getting Help

As described briefly in Table 4-4, you can display help text for most UNIX commands by using the `man` command. To use `man`, enter the `man` command followed by the command for which you want help. For example:

    man grep

displays help text for the `grep` command.

You can also use `man -k`, followed by a keyword, to display all commands associated with that keyword. For example:

    man -k copy

displays a list of all help topics that have anything to do with copying.

Climbing Into Your Shell

As mentioned at the beginning of this chapter, the second primary component of the UNIX operating system of interest to Wabi users, after the file system, is the *user shell*. The user shell is the face that UNIX puts on when people are around. In its raw, even *naked* state, UNIX is not all that good-looking. Similar to DOS, you get a bare, character-mode command line that doesn't say much—but will quickly do what you tell it to if you are specific, literal, and don't screw up.

When UNIX gets its clothes on, however, it can be a sartorial wonder, interface-wise. The range of interfaces for UNIX—graphical, textual, windowing and otherwise—is impressively (some would say confusingly) large and customizable. These interfaces can generally be divided into two categories:

- Character-mode command lines

- Graphical, mouse-driven windowing environments

In terms of character mode command-line interfaces, the most common are the C, Korn, and Bourne shells. Again, these are roughly similar in appearance to the common DOS command line, but are, in fact, far more powerful. For example, among other things, the C shell provides a *scripting* language with a syntax reminiscent of the C programming language. This lets you create scripts (analogous to DOS batch files) that can contain logical flow controls, nested functions, variables, and so forth—much more advanced than their DOS counterparts. Moreover, you can run one shell from within another shell of a different type; for example, you could start a Korn shell from within a C shell. When integrated with a multitasking windowing environment like OPEN LOOK, you can run different or multiple command shells simultaneously, each in its own window.

In terms of graphical interfaces, numerous environments are available. For example, OpenWindows—the graphical environment included in the Solaris package—is based on the OPEN LOOK windowing system. OPEN LOOK, in turn, is an implementation of the X Window System, which is a network-based, low-level windowing system developed at MIT in 1984 (see page 100). Similarly, Hewlett-Packard provides OpenVue, which is also derived from the X Window system.

Wabi software is an X Window application, and utilizes the X Toolkit (similar to the Microsoft Windows API). This makes Wabi software especially portable between various X-based UNIX environments (see "Wabi Operating Environments" on page 17). For example, the SunSoft version of Wabi software is compiled to run in the OpenWindows environment, using the OPEN LOOK window manager. The X Window System is explained in more detail later in this chapter, and in Chapter 2, "How Wabi Works."

Basic Networking Concepts

Like DOS, UNIX can run on standalone PCs, without being connected to any network. Unlike DOS, UNIX was designed for and shines in a networked environment. Being a multiuser operating system, UNIX provides many network utilities and resources; DOS, by contrast, is totally reliant on other programs and add-ons for its network support.

More often than not, when you use UNIX, you will be connected to a network of some sort. With this in mind, it may be useful here to explain a few basic networking concepts, as they apply to Wabi users.

What Is a Network?

In computing, a *network* refers to hardware devices, such as two or more computers, that are connected by communications hardware and software so they can share resources.

- Networking software running on each networked device handles the communications process between hardware devices, and provides the means through which the user or other application programs can work with the resources being networked.

- The software rules governing network communications are referred to as *protocols*; Solaris software (and hence Wabi software) is based on the widely available *Internet Protocol* (IP). This is often implemented in a protocol stack referred to as *Transfer Control Protocol/Internet Protocol* (TCP/IP). Wabi uses TCP/IP, but also supports the Windows Sockets (Winsock) networking interface, which allows some applications, such as Lotus Notes, to communicate through the network directly.

- The hardware connection between networked devices commonly consists of Ethernet® or TokenRing® cabling and interface *ports*, but may also include modems on telephone lines, serial cables, or wireless devices.

- Commonly shared resources on a network include printers, application programs, data, and data storage devices. For example, a person may be at a workstation that does not have a hard disk. That person can use the network facilities to store data files on a *remote* machine on the network.

Local Versus Remote

The term *local* refers to the computer at which you are physically located—that is, *your* computer—or any peripheral device, such as a printer, that is directly attached to your computer. Devices on the network, other than your local computer and directly attached peripherals, are said to be *remote* or *network* devices. Thus, a printer attached to a remote computer on the network is referred to as a *remote printer* or *network printer*; a printer attached directly to your computer is a *local printer*. A remote computer that provides data file storage and retrieval services for your local machine is called a *remote file server* or a *network file server*. Figure 4-4 illustrates the relationships between some basic network components.

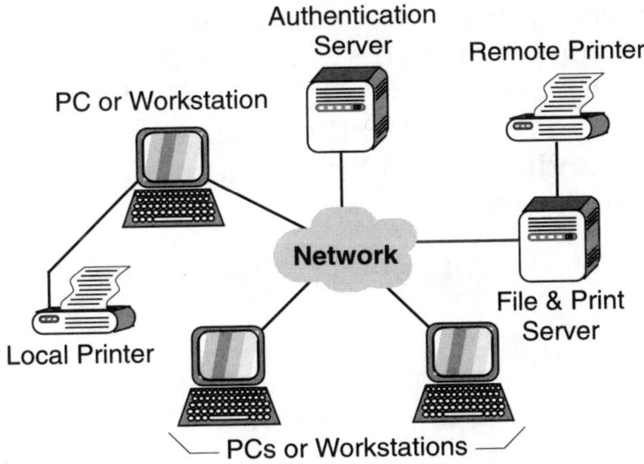

Figure 4-4   Basic Network Components

Servers and Clients

In networking, a *server* (also called a *host*) is any computer that performs services for other computers on the network. Computers that use any of these services are called *clients*. For example, a computer that provides data file storage and retrieval services is called a *file server*; a computer that accesses those files is a *client*.

Theoretically, any computer on a network can act as a server for other computers. Conversely, some computers may provide more than one kind of service. The specific design of any given network depends on the available hardware and software resources. For example, even though there may be a network-accessible printer directly attached to your computer, you may not want to have a lot of network traffic directed through your computer to access that printer.

Logging In

Logging in (also *logon* or *login*) refers to the process by which you identify yourself to a given computer or network system, usually by specifying your *user name* and *password* in response to a login *prompt* when you attempt to connect to a server. Whether your UNIX system is connected to a network or is a standalone machine, you must log in before doing anything else on the system.

For example, the first prompt you see after booting a Solaris-based workstation is:

```
login:
```

After entering your user name, you are next prompted to enter the password associated with your user name. In UNIX, you must have a specific user name—you can't just enter any name—and a unique password, usually assigned by a system administrator, before being allowed access to the system.

When you log in, the system usually runs a login script of some sort, which sets up your default environment, loads programs, sets configuration parameters, and so forth—similar in many ways to the `AUTOEXEC.BAT` and `CONFIG.SYS` files under DOS.

Authentication Servers

On most (but not all) NFS-based networks, the machine handling the login process is referred to as an *authentication* (or login) server. Authentication servers contain password databases and other user information files that describe the devices and files to which you are allowed access.

For example, an authentication server may contain a list of other servers to which you are allowed to connect. After you log in through an authentication server, the network becomes "aware" of your user name and the privileges associated with your user account; you can then connect to other authorized servers and devices, if any.

User names, passwords, and privileges are usually assigned by a system administrator, who is responsible for maintaining the operability and security of one or more machines on the network.

The root User

The `root` user is the user name of the *big cheese* on a UNIX-based computer—he or she has *complete* access to the machine, for better or worse, and can perform system-level maintenance or destruction. The `root` user is a *machine*-level, rather than network-level, concept; that is, every machine has one `root` user. More to the point, the `root` user on one computer is not the same `root` user on another computer or on the network as a whole.

When you log in as `root` on a given machine, and then enter the appropriate `root` user password, you gain access to every file on that machine. This is useful for system maintenance and configuration chores, but is not used for everyday work on your system. For example, installing or removing Wabi software requires that you log in as `root`. When you actually use Wabi software, however, you should log in using your regular user name (that is, not `root`).

nobody Is Somebody

In the world of computers, where counting starts with the number 0, rather than 1, it should not be surprising that in UNIX, nobody is somebody. That is, you can use the name nobody to log in to a network and, in most cases, be allowed a limited level of network access.

The user name nobody is the name to use when you do not or cannot log in to a network through an authentication server. Usually, however, you cannot get much work done when you are logged in as nobody—for example, you might not be able to view or edit your own files.

The specific privileges granted to nobody are assigned by your system administrator, and can vary widely from system to system.

Naming Network Drives

Each hardware device on a network must somehow identify itself to the network software before any type of network communications—such as logins, printing, or file transfers—can take place. Hardware devices are identified at the software level by at least two different kinds of labels:

- **Server (or host) name** – A unique alphanumeric name assigned to a network device, such as a workstation or file server. Analogous to user names, server names provide a convenient way to refer to hardware devices.

- **Internet address** – Commonly referred to as an *IP address*; a unique 32-bit, dot-separated, numeric address assigned to each hardware device on the Internet. An *internet* is a collection of networks connected in such a way that they can act as a single, virtual network; the *Internet* (with a capital "I") is the largest internet in the world.

For example, a file server on a network could be named bigfilemachine, and be assigned an IP address of 129.148.20.125. Server names and IP addresses are assigned by your network administrator.

Domain Name System

Internet addresses are cryptic and unwieldy, and not at all convenient to remember. As an alternative, the Internet provides a hierarchical naming system called the *Domain Name System* (DNS), which is not only easier to use than 12-digit numbers, but offers a number of system management features that are of interest to system administrators.

From the standpoint of the user, DNS provides a mechanism for resolving —or associating—mnemonic machine names (that is, names with letters in them) with their corresponding numeric Internet addresses.

DNS is based on the concept of Internet *domains*, which for our purposes here can be loosely defined as a naming scheme for subgroupings (or *subnetworks*) within a network. For example, a university might include the following domain-name definitions in the network environment:

```
profs.history.princeton.edu
grad.history.princeton.edu
admin.bursar.princeton.edu
housing.bursar.princeton.edu
```

In this example, `princeton` is a subnetwork (or subnet) in the `edu` domain; `history` and `bursar` are subnets in the `princeton` domain, `profs` and `grad` are subnets in the `history` domain, and `admin` and `housing` are subnets in the `bursar` domain. A file server named `bigfilemachine` in the `grad` domain would have the following fully qualified DNS name:

```
bigfilemachine.grad.history.princeton.edu
```

Device Names and Wabi

When mounting network drives through the Wabi Configuration Manager (see Chapter 6, "Managing Drives"), you may sometimes need to specify network mount points (directories) that are not local to your machine, or not even local to your network. In such cases, you would use DNS names for specifying the server to which you want to connect. For example, to connect to a directory named `/public/library` on the server `bigfiles.grad.history.princeton.edu`, you would use the name:

```
bigfilemachine.grad.history.princeton.edu:/public/library
```

About X Window

As mentioned earlier, Wabi is based on the X Window System. This makes it possible to compile Wabi to run on a wide variety of platforms, under a variety of X-compliant windowing systems.

The X Window System is a network-based graphical windowing system initially developed in 1984 at the Massachusetts Institute of Technology. It has been adopted as the low-level windowing standard by a consortium (the X Consortium) of industry leaders like Sun, IBM, Hewlett-Packard, DEC, and AT&T. X11R5 (X Version 11, Revision 5), the version on which most popular windowing systems (like OPEN LOOK) for UNIX are based, was released in 1991. The most recent version, Version 11, Revision 6 (X11R6) was released in May of 1994.

X Window (*X* for short) is based on a *client-server* model, in which application programs (*clients*) communicate with a display device indirectly via a display program (the *server*). Client programs do not need to run on the same machine as the server program, which makes the X Window system particularly suited for distributed computing environments.

X Window is a *low-level* windowing standard in that it is a set of specifications defining rudimentary mechanics for window controls and behavior. Most X-derived window managers add higher-level, platform-specific features—that is, the particular "look and feel" of dialog boxes, mouse actions, and menu behavior. For example, the Solaris OPEN LOOK window manager and HP's OpenVue are both based on the X Window standard, but each has its own unique feature and design elements, and the two environments look fairly different from each other.

X Window Terminology

From the standpoint of the Wabi user, what you see from within Wabi is Microsoft Windows—not UNIX, and not X Window. Because Wabi utilizes X Window resources, however, you should be aware of some potentially confusing terminology and interface quirks you may encounter.

Clients and Servers

Perhaps the most confusing terminology twist in the X Window system is the use of the term *client* and *server*. In X, the concepts are basically flip-flopped from what you might expect in a networking context, as described on page 96. Specifically, in X:

- An X *server* is a process that provides windowing services to an application, or client process. For example, the OPEN LOOK window manager running on your local computer is an X display server. In this model, the client and the server can run on the same machine or on separate machines.

  X servers handle user input from the keyboard and mouse, and send it to a client application, which is usually running remotely on a host on the network. The client, in turn, sends the server the contents of the application window and other program responses for display on the server screen.

- An X *client* application is a program that receives its input and/or displays its output on a local X terminal or workstation (the display server in this scenario). On "dumb" X terminals, most X client applications run on a remote client host—that is, the bulk of the processing performed by the program occurs remotely—with only input/output occurring locally on the display server. On more robust workstations, many client applications run locally on the display server. In the case of Wabi, it is usually run locally on your machine.

Confused yet? Not to worry—from your standpoint, Wabi runs locally on your machine, displays locally on your machine, and accepts mouse and keyboard input locally on your machine—the concept of Wabi X clients and servers is moot. If, however, you want to get tricky, and try out some of the X remote display capabilities with Wabi, refer to the instructions in Chapter 14, "Tips and Tricks," starting on page 288.

 For a nice description of the hows and whys of the X Window system, written for general users, read the *X Window System User's Guide* (Valerie Quercia and Tim O'Reilly; O'Reilly & Associates, Inc., 1990.).

Resources

X Window and the applications running under X Window get their configuration information about each other—details about the window manager being used, colormaps, fonts, and many other items—from X *resource* files. These resource files are similar to the `.INI` files used by Microsoft Windows and Windows applications.

For example, applications tell X Window how their dialog boxes should look and behave—such as what's in them, when they should be displayed or closed, their relationships to other dialog boxes—via a series of *hints* registered in one or more application resource files. Similarly, the `.Xdefaults` file sets workspace color, mouse input characteristics, and defines window borders and styles, among other things, which are used by the application.

Colormaps

In the X Window System, *colormaps* are tables of information that are loaded into memory, and which describe all the colors that a given display can handle. X-based applications can also provide their own colormaps, which can override the default colormap used by a given hardware device. Multiple colormaps can be loaded into memory, but only one colormap can be actively displayed at a time.

Similarly, Microsoft Window provides a color mapping scheme that is hardware dependent—you tell Windows what kind of display you are running, and it in turn gives to Windows applications only those colors it thinks the display hardware can handle.

Wabi must translate the Windows color mapping schemes to X colormaps. Where possible, Wabi uses the default X colormap; when necessary, it will swap in a custom *virtual colormap* as needed. This can sometimes cause excessive color flashing when switching between Windows applications running under Wabi and other non-Windows applications running on your Solaris desktop. You can mitigate this problem, however, by changing various settings in your `WIN.INI` file.

Information about these `WIN.INI` settings, as well as a more detailed explanation of colormaps and how Wabi uses them, are provided in Chapter 11, "Managing Colors," starting on page 264.

Font Servers

In the X Window System, a *font server* is a machine on the network containing font files used by local display servers. Display servers on the network download fonts as needed from the font host. Font files can be quite large; therefore, some networks may have a machine that is dedicated to the task of font serving.

In X Window, a *font server* is also a software process that manages the distribution and display of X fonts according to the X *font service protocol*. Wabi software includes its own font server, `wabifs`, which interacts with an X server via the font service protocol.

One of the most important new features of Microsoft Windows 3.1 was the addition of TrueType font technology. TrueType is a scalable outline font display and print technology, bundled with Microsoft Windows, which provides a WYSIPMWYG (What-You-See-Is-Pretty-Much-What-You-Get) way to view fonts on screen and print on your printer.

Wabi 2.0 used X font files, and shipped with several bitmapped and TrueType fonts. Wabi 2.1, however, bypasses the X font file resources and uses TrueType and Windows system fonts exclusively.

Refer to Chapter 12, "Fonts and Wabi," for more information about `wabifs` how Wabi works with fonts.

Don't Worry, Be Wabi

For people who are coming from the worrisome world of DOS, with its memory limitations, real mode and protected mode switching, IRQ conflicts, DMA channel selection, and so forth, there are many things about which you no longer need to concern yourself when using Wabi.

True, UNIX can be complicated in its own ways—enough to engender a classic nerd culture—but also true is that most people have a system administrator or three to take care of all that stuff(!).... This section describes those DOS sorts of things about which you no longer need worry when running your Windows applications under Wabi software.

AUTOEXEC.BAT and CONFIG.SYS

Wabi uses `AUTOEXEC.BAT` and `CONFIG.SYS` files primarily to fool Windows applications that modify these files during installation into thinking that they have done their deed and they can end the installation successfully.

The only things Wabi looks at in `AUTOEXEC.BAT` are the `PATH` statement and any other environment variables (like `SET VAR=`*value*) put there by an application—Wabi software simply ignores *everything* in `CONFIG.SYS`.

Extended and Expanded Memory

Windows under DOS goes a long way toward circumventing the problems associated with DOS extended, expanded, and conventional memory constrictions (as explained on page 70). The problem is getting out of DOS and into Windows in the first place.

Well, forget about it. In UNIX, there are no such things as extended, expanded, and conventional memory.

Memory Managers

Because extended, expanded, and conventional memory are moot points under Wabi, you don't need to even think about memory management programs like MEMMAKER, QEMM, EMM386.EXE, and the like.

SMARTDRV and Other Disk Caching Programs

Microsoft Windows relies on DOS for its input/output (I/O) services, such as access to disk read/write functions. Similarly, Windows under Wabi gets its I/O services from UNIX. Consequently, disk caching programs like SMARTDRV.EXE are unnecessary. Even better, Wabi does everything in true 32-bit mode.

Device Drivers

DOS device drivers, which are usually loaded under DOS via a CONFIG.SYS file, are not used under Wabi. As mentioned earlier in this section, all statements in CONFIG.SYS are ignored by Wabi. On the negative side, if your application requires such a driver, like a scanner driver, chances are it will not work under Wabi.

Wabi does not work at all with virtual device drivers. Programs that use virtual device drivers are not compatible with Wabi. See "Supported Applications" on page 6 for more information.

386 Enhanced Mode

Wabi software runs in Windows 386 Enhanced Mode. That's it. Forget about Standard Mode. Moreover, Solaris, which provides a true 32-bit processor environment (even on Intel platforms), does a lot of things better than Windows in 386 Enhanced Mode under DOS; for example, more robust multitasking and more DOS sessions (with an appropriate DOS emulator, like SunPC or Merge).

Wabi also has no use for the settings managed with the Windows 386 Enhanced Mode Control Panel tool—this set of Control Panel functions is not installed when you install Windows under Wabi with the Wabi Windows Install program.

What, you may ask, happens to all those nifty things like swap files and 32-bit disk access? The fate of these functions is described below.

Virtual Memory

The virtual memory setting in the 386 Enhanced Mode Control Panel tool lets you specify the type and size of a disk-based *swap file*. Such swap files are used by Windows to simulate physical RAM memory when none is really available.

UNIX provides similar swap file services for Wabi, but does it better than Windows under DOS. UNIX swap space is more flexible and performs better than Windows swap files.

32-Bit Disk Access

32-bit Disk Access is also a setting in the 386 Enhanced Mode Control Panel tool that is irrelevant under Wabi.

Solaris, on both Intel (*x*86) and RISC (SPARC) platforms provides true 32-bit disk access. Under DOS, Windows uses 32-bit disk access to avoid a couple of processor mode switches between real mode and protected mode when performing disk reads or writes. Under UNIX, such mode switching is unnecessary, because disk I/O functions are miles away from the world of DOS. Windows 32-bit disk access also does not work with all disk controllers—specifically any controller that works with disk sectors of 1024 bytes. UNIX controllers have no such problems.

Device Contention

Windows under DOS is not very clever when it comes to managing contention between serial ports. For example, if two applications are competing for the same port, Windows can sometimes freeze to the point of requiring a hard system reset—it all depends on how well behaved the Windows applications are.

Wabi, because it runs through UNIX, handles such contention more gracefully, and simply tells the offending applications to please stop talking so loudly and wait their turn. When the port becomes available, the UNIX operating system releases it to Wabi.

PIF Files

PIF files exist in the DOS/Windows environment so Windows can figure out how to futz with conventional memory and OEM-hardware-mapped, character mode displays in DOS applications. Because Wabi does not actually run DOS applications itself, but rather spawns a separate DOS emulation program like SunPC or Merge, Wabi does not have to do any such futzing, and PIF files are unnecessary. DOS applications run better under such emulation because they are running in DOS, rather than in DOS-in-Windows.

Chapter 5

Using Wabi
Software

O kay, we've explained what Wabi software is and how it works. We've described UNIX, DOS, and Microsoft Windows. Now what? It's time to actually *use* the software. *It's time to get to work!*

I like work; it fascinates me. I can sit and look at it for hours. I love to keep it by me; the idea of getting rid of it nearly breaks my heart.

– Jerome K. Jerome, *Three Men in a Boat*, 1889

Culture, as I understand it, is essentially a product of leisure. The art of culture is therefore the art of loafing.

– Lin Yutang, *The Importance of Living*, 1937

In This Chapter

Installing Wabi Software

The specific installation instructions you should follow to install Wabi software depend on the particular Wabi package you are using. For example, the instructions for SunSoft Wabi 2.1 differ from those for SunSoft Wabi 2.0, which differ from those for HP Wabi 2.0, and so forth. Therefore, you should refer to the installation instructions included with your Wabi package.

Having said this, there are several common steps involved with installing any version of Wabi software.

➤ *Common steps for installing Wabi software*

   1. **Verify that your system meets the system requirements for installing and running Wabi software.**
   2. **Remove your old version of Wabi software and Wabi patches, if any.**
   3. **Install the new version of Wabi software and any required operating system patches.**
   4. **Start Wabi software for the first time.**
   5. **Install Microsoft Windows under Wabi.**

Again, the instructions for performing the first three steps will vary, depending on the particular Wabi package you are installing. Refer to the installation instructions included with your Wabi package for more information.

The fourth step, starting Wabi software for the first time, causes several files and directories to be created automatically on your system. This happens no matter which Wabi package you use, This process is described in the next section in this chapter.

The final step, installing Microsoft Windows under Wabi, is required for all versions of Wabi software. This process is also described later in this chapter, in "Installing Microsoft Windows" on page 114.

Starting Wabi for the First Time

After you install your Wabi package, the next phase of Wabi software installation happens automatically when you start Wabi for the first time. When you do, the Wabi program creates or updates your personal Wabi user directory, including several subdirectories. By default, this directory is named $HOME/wabi. If you are upgrading from a previous Wabi release, your existing $HOME/wabi directory and its contents are preserved.

During this process, the Wabi program checks for adequate space in your Wabi user directory for all required subdirectories and files. If there is not enough space, the Wabi program warns you and stops the installation. If this occurs, remove items as necessary from your home directory (or the directory in which your Wabi user directory is located) to free up space.

About Your Personal Wabi Directory

The Wabi startup script creates your personal wabi directory as a subdirectory of your home directory. Within that directory, it creates a windows subdirectory. These two directories are analogous to the C:\ and C:\WINDOWS directories on a DOS-based PC configured to use Microsoft Windows.

After your personal wabi directory is created, the Wabi Windows Install Program prompts you to install Microsoft Windows software. You must do this before you can use the Wabi program. Installing Microsoft Windows software under Wabi is described later in this chapter, in "Installing Microsoft Windows" on page 114.

You *must* install Microsoft Windows under Wabi, using the Wabi Windows Install program, as described in this chapter. *Do not* use the Microsoft Windows SETUP.EXE program.

To Create Your Wabi Directory in Another Location

You can tell Wabi to create your personal `wabi` directory in a location other than your home directory by setting the `WABIDIR` environment variable before you start the Wabi program. You can do this by using the commands below, where *pathname* is the directory path in which you want to place your personal `wabi` directory.

> ### To set *WABIDIR* in the C shell

```
setenv WABIDIR pathname
```

> ### To set *WABIDIR* in the Bourne or Korn shell

```
WABIDIR=pathname; export WABIDIR
```

Include this statement in your `.cshrc` or `.profile` file in order to use this directory each time you start Wabi. If you do not, the next time you start Wabi, another `wabi` directory will be created in your home directory.

If You Are Upgrading From a Previous Wabi Release

The first time you start the Wabi program after the new release is installed, your `wabi` user directory is updated. All Windows applications you have installed remain, and all changes you have made to your Wabi configuration, such as drive mappings, will be unchanged. See the Wabi Release Notes in the Wabi Tools group for more upgrade information.

Whether or not Microsoft Windows is currently installed on your system, however, the Wabi Windows Install program starts automatically, and prompts you to install Microsoft Windows software.

- If Windows is not already installed on your system, you must install it before you can use Wabi 2.0 or 2.1 software.

- If Windows was installed on your system under your old version of Wabi software, you must reinstall it so Wabi has access to some additional Windows files that were not previously needed.

Instructions for installing Microsoft Windows under Wabi software are provided in the next section of this chapter.

➤ To start the Wabi program for the first time after installation

1. **If you are still in a superuser session from the installation, return to normal user status by entering the `exit` command.**

2. **At a UNIX command prompt enter:**

   ```
   /opt/SUNWwabi/bin/wabi &
   ```

   The directory path indicated in this command is for the SunSoft (Solaris) version of Wabi 2.1; the directory path you should enter may vary, depending on your version of Wabi software.

   The Wabi program creates or updates your personal Wabi directory under your home directory (or the directory to which the `WABIDIR` environment variable points).

   When this process is completed, the Wabi Windows Install program starts so you can install Microsoft Windows. If you are upgrading from a previous Wabi release, you must reinstall Microsoft Windows. The Wabi 2.1 version of the Wabi Microsoft Windows Install program installs some files that were not installed in Wabi 2.0 and Wabi 1.*x*.

3. **Continue with the instructions in the next section, "Installing Microsoft Windows."**

Installing Microsoft Windows

The final procedure in the Wabi software installation process is to install or reinstall Microsoft Windows into your personal `wabi/windows` directory with the Wabi Windows Install program. The Wabi Windows Install program starts automatically the first time you start the Wabi program. You must install Microsoft Windows before you can use Wabi.

 You *must* use the Wabi Windows Install program to install Microsoft Windows under Wabi software. *Do not* use the Microsoft Windows `SETUP.EXE` program. Also note that Microsoft Windows software is not included with Wabi—you must supply your own licensed copy.

If you are using Wabi 2.1 software, you can install Microsoft Windows 3.1 or 3.11, or Microsoft Windows for Workgroups 3.11. However, bear in mind that the Wabi program does not support all of the network features in Windows for Workgroups. Read "Microsoft Windows for Workgroups 3.11" on page 302 for details about supported and unsupported features.

 If you are using Wabi 2.0 software, you can only install Microsoft 3.1 or 3.11—Wabi 2.0 software does not support Windows for Workgroups. Windows for Workgroups is supported under Wabi 2.1 software only.

The Wabi Microsoft Windows Install program lets you install Windows from diskettes, CD-ROM, or a network drive. You cannot use the Wabi Windows Install program to install Microsoft Windows onto a network server, although you can perform such an installation with a DOS-based computer or a DOS emulation program. See the section "Installing Windows on a Network Server" on page 118 for more information.

The following two sections describe how to install Microsoft Windows from diskette (similar instructions apply to CD-ROMs), and from Wabi's drive `R:`, respectively. Following that is the section on installing to a network server.

Installing Windows From Diskette

Installing Windows from diskette is the method that is most similar to the procedure by which you would install Windows on a DOS-based PC.

➢ *To complete Wabi software installation by installing Microsoft Windows from diskette*

These instructions assume that you have followed the Wabi installation instructions as described in this chapter. This means that Wabi has been installed, and you have just started Wabi for the first time. The Wabi Windows Install program then starts automatically, and displays its opening dialog box (Figure 5-1).

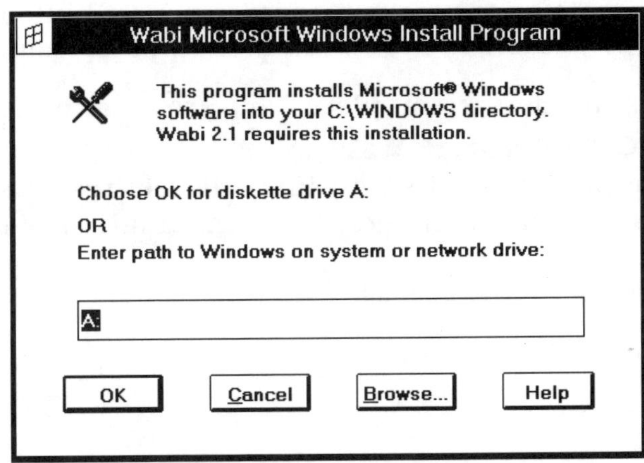

Figure 5-1   Initial Wabi Windows Install Program Dialog Box

1. **Specify the letter of the drive in which the first Windows installation diskette is inserted.**

   Wabi supports the connection of two diskette drives: drive A: and drive B:. The default connection is diskette drive A:.

   If you are using drive A: to install Windows software, choose OK to accept the default designation. If you are using drive B:, change the designation from A: to B:.

   You are prompted insert Windows installation disk 1 into the diskette drive.

2. **Insert the first Windows installation diskette into the specified diskette drive, and then choose OK.**
   The files on disk 1 are installed in your `C:\WINDOWS` directory, which is mapped to your `wabi/windows` directory.

The destination directory, `C:\WINDOWS`, cannot be changed. The Wabi Windows Install Program does not support installation of Microsoft Windows to another location. However, you can change the location of your personal `wabi` directory by setting the `WABIDIR` variable, as explained on page 112.

A progress meter in the dialog box increments as files are installed. When disk 1 installation is complete, you are prompted to insert disk 2.

3. **Insert Windows installation disks as prompted.**
   Repeat this procedure for the remaining disks.

If your diskette drive does not provide an eject button, you can eject diskettes by clicking in the Wabi window and pressing Meta+E.

When installation is complete, you are prompted to restart Wabi.

4. **Choose OK to restart Wabi.**
   The Wabi program exits and immediately restarts, displaying Windows Program Manager. Wabi installation is now complete.

Installing Windows From Wabi Drive R:

If your Microsoft Windows software is copied on a hard drive or network directory accessible to your operating system, you can install it into the Wabi program by using Wabi drive R:, which is assigned to your / (root) directory.

To install the Microsoft Windows software from drive R:, you enter R: and the path the Wabi program can use to locate the Windows files. You can also use the Browse button to navigate through the directories accessible to your system and locate the Microsoft Windows files.

For example, if the Microsoft Windows 3.1 diskettes are copied into /usr/apps/install/win31.dsk, you would enter the following in the entry field of the Wabi Microsoft Windows Install Program's initial dialog box, shown in Figure 5-1:

```
R:\usr\apps\install\win31.dsk
```

You can use either a DOS path or a UNIX path. The back slash (\) is used in DOS path names. The forward slash (/) is used in UNIX path names. The Wabi program accepts both types of path names, provided you use one type of slash within a path.

You must have read permission to access the directory containing the Windows files. If you cannot access this directory because of a permission problem, change the permissions by using the chmod command or see your system administrator.

After you've entered the drive letter and path and chosen OK, the Wabi program installs the Windows files in your $HOME/wabi/windows directory. A progress meter in the dialog box increments as files are installed.

As installation nears completion, the Wabi Tools group and Microsoft Windows Main, Accessories, Games, and Startup groups open. When installation is complete, you are prompted to restart Wabi.

When you choose OK, the Wabi program exits and immediately restarts, displaying Windows Program Manager.

Installing Windows on a Network Server

The Wabi Windows Install program can only be used to install Microsoft Windows files into a Wabi user environment. If you want to install Microsoft Windows onto a network server so that users can install Windows from the server, you can use the procedure for placing Windows files on a network server that is described in your Microsoft Windows documentation. The documented procedure requires a DOS emulator or DOS computer on your network so you can run the DOS command `setup /a`. Using DOS emulators in conjunction with Wabi software is described in Chapter 10, "Using DOS Applications."

If you do not have a DOS computer or DOS emulator on your network, refer to your UNIX documentation for information about accessing DOS file systems. Once you are able to access the DOS diskettes from your operating system, you can use UNIX commands to copy the diskettes to a network server and set read permission on the files.

Once you have installed Microsoft Windows to a network server, Wabi users can use the Wabi Microsoft Windows Install program to install Windows files into their Wabi environments, as described in "Installing Windows From Wabi Drive R:" on page 117.

The Wabi Windows Install program does not allow you to set up your system to access a shared copy of Microsoft Windows. Each user must have his or her own copy of Windows in `$HOME/wabi/windows`, and must have a Microsoft Windows software license.

What Wabi Installation Does

Wabi installation creates several directories on your system, and installs numerous program and configuration files. These files and directories can be divided into two general areas:

- **The Wabi system directory** – This area is created when you install the Wabi software from the distribution media. The directories within this directory contain UNIX executable and binary files, many of which are copied into other directories. The default location of the Wabi system directory depends on your operating system. It could be `/usr/wabi`, `/usr/lpp/Wabi`, `/opt/SUNWwabi/wabi`, or some other directory. Refer to the installation instructions you received with your Wabi package.

- **The `$HOME/wabi` user directory** – This area is created within your home directory the first time you start the Wabi program. (However, if you set the `WABIDIR` variable, your `wabi` user directory may be located elsewhere.) The directory is expanded and modified as you install applications. The directories within this directory contain resource, program, and initialization files. Symbolic links in this directory point to other locations.

In addition to these directories, the Wabi program uses initialization (`.ini`) files to provide application compatibility and to control program configuration. Initialization files are located in the `$HOME/wabi/windows` directory. By changing settings in these files, you can change various Wabi configuration items. Initialization files are discussed later in this chapter, in "Initialization Files" on page 122.

Wabi System Directories and Files

A system of directories and files is created during the first phase of installation. These directories and files contain UNIX binary programs and other executable files. Table 5-1 lists the directories created during the installation process on all operating systems. Do not alter these directories or files within them in any way unless you are following a procedure documented in this book or in the *Wabi User's Guide*.

Table 5-1   Wabi System Directories and Files

Directory Name	Directory Contents
bin	The Wabi program's UNIX executable files and scripts, such as `wabi` (the Wabi startup script), `wabiprog` (the main Wabi executable), and `wabifs` (the Wabi font server).
drvr	Files related to the Wabi kernel driver, which provides file locking in the Solaris environment. The `clearlocks` program is located in this directory.
icons	Icon image files used in the Solaris environment.
lib	Internal Wabi scripts and image files, and the `locale` subdirectory, which contains language-specific Wabi files.
man	Text pages displayed when you enter the `man wabi` command.
printers	Drivers, initialization files, and help files for HP LaserJet III and Epson printers.
wbin	Wabi utility programs, executable files, libraries, and initialization files.

Your Wabi system directory may contain additional directories specific to your operating system.

$HOME/wabi Directories and Files

The first time you start Wabi, it creates a system of directories and files within a `wabi` subdirectory in your home directory. Table 5-2 lists the directories and files created the first time you start the Wabi program.

Table 5-2 $HOME/wabi Directories and Files

File or Directory	Function
autoexec.bat	File required to complete the installation of application programs that look for and modify it automatically. This file may contain PATH statements, which Wabi uses to locate installed applications, and SET statements for setting environment variables used by applications. PATH and SET commands are the *only* commands that Wabi uses in this file. If you add other commands, Wabi ignores them.
config.sys	File required to complete the installation of application programs that look for and modify it automatically. The Wabi program ignores all statements in this file.
fc	In Wabi 2.0 and earlier, this directory contained font information for your display. This information is not needed in Wabi 2.1, so if you have this directory you can delete it.
tmp	Directory for storing temporary files; required by some application programs. The directory contains no Wabi files, and may contain nothing at all, but you should not delete it.
wabihome	Symbolic link to the Wabi system directory.
windows	Directory containing Microsoft Windows files and Wabi program resource and initialization files. This directory also contains links to various executables in the Wabi system directory. Initialization (.ini) files installed by applications may also be stored in this directory
windows/system	Directory containing font files and dynamic link libraries (.dll) installed with Windows, and utilities and files related to installed printer drivers. Some files are links to files in the Wabi system directory. This directory may also contain font files and dynamic link libraries installed by applications.

Initialization Files

Initialization (`.ini`) files are contained within the $HOME/wabi/windows directory. These files are used to control certain configuration items for the Wabi program and Microsoft Windows programs. Some of these files are updated automatically by the applications you install. When you install applications, the installation programs may add `.ini` files for the applications to this directory. Table 5-3 lists initialization files and the functions each provides.

Table 5-3   Initialization Files

File Name	Function of File
win.ini	Provides compatibility with Windows applications (many applications modify it automatically during installation). This file also stores the window color settings you make from Control Panel. You should not edit this file unless instructed to do so.
system.ini	Provides compatibility with Windows applications.
wabi.ini	Used to store Wabi-specific settings made through Configuration Manager. This file also stores default system settings for various operating system platforms. In general, you should not edit this file directly; make all changes through Wabi Configuration Manager.
progman.ini	Used by Windows Program Manager to maintain lists of groups and their contents and other miscellaneous settings. Do not edit this file directly.
control.ini	Used by Windows Control Panel to store Wabi environment settings. Do not edit this file directly.

What Wabi Looks Like

As mentioned in Chapter 1, in "The Thing That Isn't There," Wabi doesn't have much of an interface of its own. What you see is basically Microsoft Windows, with just a few minor cosmetic differences (for example, see Figure 3-5 and Figure 3-6 on page 56).

As with Microsoft Windows on a DOS-based PC, the default *program shell* used by Wabi 2.1—that is, the interface through which you launch and manage Windows applications—is the Microsoft Windows Program Manager. Program Manager (see Figure 5-2) provides tools for working with *program items* (in the form of icons representing applications or documents), and *program groups* (sets of program items). Complete information about using the Microsoft Windows Program Manager is provided in the *Microsoft Windows User's Guide*, which is included with your Microsoft Windows software package. You can also press F1 at any time in Program Manager to read Windows on-line help.

You can use a different program shell, if you wish, by specifying the name of the shell you want to use in the SHELL= statement in your Windows SYSTEM.INI file. For example, you could use Windows File Manager. Refer to your Windows documentation for instructions.

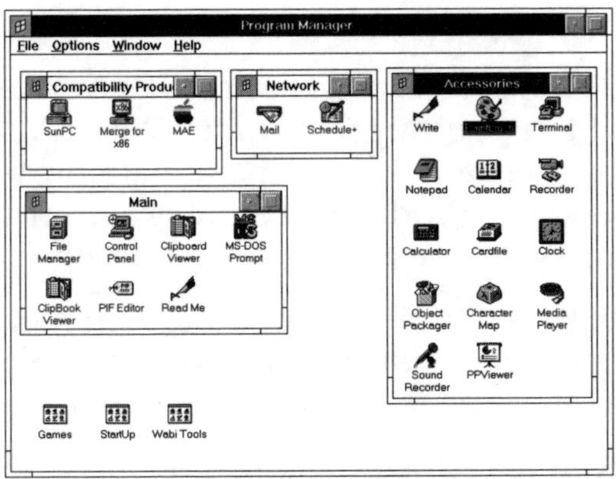

Figure 5-2   Default Windows Program Manager (WFWG 3.11) Under Wabi

Wabi does add or modify three things in Program Manager:

- A Wabi Tools program group is added.

- The Windows Main program group is modified.

- Wabi Configuration Manager is added to Windows Control Panel.

These changes are explained below.

Wabi Tools Program Group

When you install Microsoft Windows with the Wabi Windows Install program, as described in "Installing Microsoft Windows" on page 114, a Wabi Tools program group is added to your Windows Program Manager desktop.

The Wabi Tools program group, shown in Figure 5-3, contains three program items:

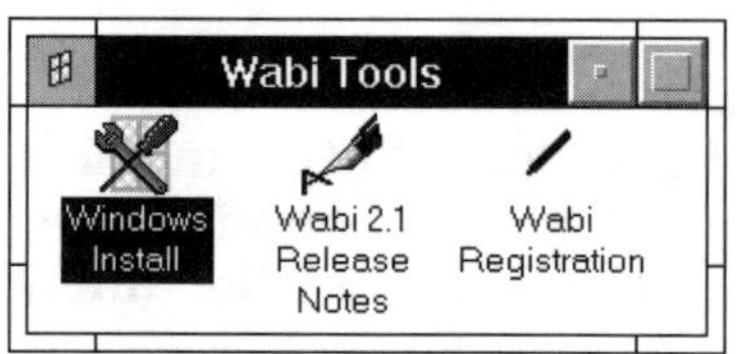

Figure 5-3   Wabi Tools Program Group

- **Wabi Windows Install** – Installs your Microsoft Windows package (which you supply) under Wabi. Microsoft Windows *must* be installed for the complete version Wabi to run; for this reason, the Wabi Windows Install program runs automatically the first time you start Wabi after installing the Wabi package.

  If you want to reinstall or upgrade your Windows software at another time, you *must* use the Wabi Windows Install program, rather than the SETUP.EXE program included with Windows.

- **Wabi 2.1 Release Notes** – Late-breaking news about Wabi 2.1 software; provided in Windows Write format.

- **(Solaris only) Wabi Registration Tool** – Automatically registers your Wabi package with SunSoft, Inc.

Windows Main Program Group

The Wabi Windows Install program does not install every Windows component; some of the these components are unnecessary under Wabi, while others don't work. In particular, you may notice that two programs are missing from the Main program group:

- **Print Manager** – Windows Print Manager is unnecessary (and doesn't work) under Wabi, because print spooling functions are handled by the (more robust) UNIX print spooler.

- **Windows setup** – The `SETUP.EXE` program included with Microsoft Windows *does not work* under Wabi. Consequently, the Wabi Windows Install program does not install `SETUP.EXE` on your disk, and the Windows Setup program item is excluded from your Main program group.

Wabi Configuration Manager Added to Windows Control Panel

Wabi Configuration Manager is a tool that lets you configure various Wabi options. It is added to the standard Microsoft Windows Control Panel as an extra *applet* (that is, a little application).

In Wabi 2.1, Configuration Manager provides tools for working with COM (serial) and LPT (parallel) ports, UNIX directory mount points (that is, Wabi drives), diskette drives, and DOS emulators. Wabi 2.0 also provided controls for mouse, sound, colors, and international settings; these settings are redundant with standard Control Panel tools, and so were omitted from Wabi 2.1. See Table 1-3 on page 13 for explanations of how Wabi Configuration Manager differs between Wabi 2.0 and 2.1.

General instructions for using Wabi Configuration Manager are provided later in this chapter.

Using Windows Control Panel

Most of the configuration settings used by Wabi software are also used under "regular" Windows, and you control these settings the same way in both environments. For example, you use the same tool, the Microsoft Windows Control Panel, to modify desktop colors, install printer drivers, configure COM ports, and so forth.

Some of Control Panel's settings, however, are irrelevant under Wabi, because certain Wabi functions are controlled by your native X Window operating environment, and not by DOS or Microsoft Windows. For example, mouse tracking speed is controlled by X Window, as are screen savers, desktop background patterns, and some COM port settings. If you change such settings with the standard Windows Control Panel tools, Wabi simply ignores them.

You use the Windows Control Panel under Wabi software the same way you use it in Microsoft Windows under DOS. The program item for Control Panel is located by default in the Microsoft Windows Main program group; double-click this program item (or select it and press Enter) to open Control Panel (Figure 5-4). If you need help using Control Panel, refer to the Control Panel on-line help (press F1 from within the Control Panel window) or refer to your *Microsoft Windows User's Guide*.

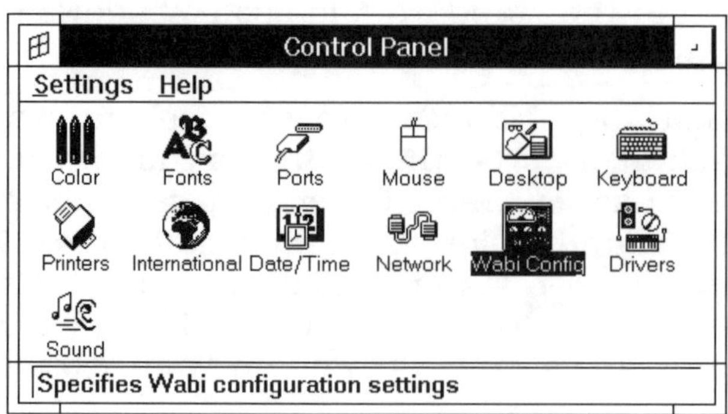

Figure 5-4   Microsoft Windows Control Panel

As mentioned earlier in this chapter, the Wabi Windows Install program installs the Wabi Configuration Manager in the Windows Control Panel. The Wabi Configuration Manger provides tools for setting options with which the standard Window Control Panel cannot work. Table 5-4 describes the purposes and limitations under Wabi of the various Microsoft Windows Control Panel settings.

Table 5-4   Microsoft Windows Control Panel Settings and Limitations

Color	The Color tool lets you change the colors used in Wabi windows. These color selections affect only your Wabi windows, and not any of your other X windows. Similarly, colors set with your X Window desktop tools do not affect Wabi windows.
Fonts	The Fonts tool lets you add or remove fonts used in your Wabi environment. You can also set TrueType options, as in the Microsoft Windows environment, though not all applications use the settings.
Ports	The Ports tool lets you change COM (serial) port settings such as baud rate, data bits, parity, stop bits, and flow control. However, many applications use their own settings for these port attributes, so the settings you select here may not be used. The Control Panel Ports tool also includes settings for Base I/O Port Address and Interrupt Request Line (IRQ), which Wabi ignores. In the Wabi environment, these port attributes are controlled by the UNIX device driver for the port. If you want to use a serial port with an application in the Wabi environment, it must be connected to the appropriate device driver for your operating system. The Wabi program is set up to work with the default drivers on all supported operating systems, so you probably will not have to change the connection unless you use a nonstandard driver.
Mouse	The Double Click Speed and Swap Left/Right Buttons settings work in the Mouse dialog box. Mouse Trails is ignored, and Mouse Tracking Speed is controlled through your X Window desktop. The X Window setting for mouse button order/swapping may also affect your Wabi environment, but the Wabi setting will not affect your X desktop. Double-click speed is independent in each environment.

Desktop	Many of the settings under the **Desktop** tool should not or cannot be used under Wabi. For example, the options for decorating the desktop background (**Pattern, Wallpaper**) do not work because the X Window desktop controls the background, or root, window. Use X Window tools for colors, patterns, and bitmaps in the root window. The **Screen Saver** option may not work on some platforms, and should *not* be used even if it does work. Your X desktop has its own screen saver mechanism, which works more efficiently and covers the whole display. Microsoft Windows screen savers use significant CPU time and do not cover the whole display. If you are using Wabi on a system you share with other users, the Microsoft Windows screen saver's heavy CPU usage will slow everyone down.
Keyboard	The **Keyboard Repeat** settings have no effect under Wabi. You can enable and disable keyboard repeat in your X Window desktop, and some X desktops may also be able to set the repeat delay rate.
Printers	The **Printers** tool lets you install printer drivers, set your default printer, set up printers, and connect them to ports. The Print Manager and options related to it (Transmission Retry, Device Not Selected) are not used by the Wabi program. You control your UNIX printers with UNIX printer management utilities only.
International	The **International** tool works the same under Wabi and Microsoft Windows. The only difference for the Wabi environment is that the **Keyboard Layout** option has no effect. You must use the WABI_KEYB environment variable to specify a keyboard language, as explained later in this chapter, in "WABI_KEYB" on page 147.
Date/Time	Wabi uses your computer's system clock to determine the time. You cannot change the date and time with the **Date/Time** tool.
Network	The **Network** tool has no function in the Wabi environment. All network services under Wabi are provided by UNIX.

386 Enhanced	The **386 Enhanced** tool does not appear in the Control Panel in your Wabi environment because there is no need for the 386 Enhanced settings in a UNIX operating system.
Drivers	The **Drivers** tool lets you install and remove multimedia drivers, just as in the Microsoft Windows environment. However, your platform may or may not support the use of multimedia. Multimedia features are supported under Wabi 2.1 software in the Solaris environment, if you have the necessary hardware. Multimedia features are not supported under Wabi 2.0 software. See "Using Multimedia Features" on page 235 for more information.
Sound	If your Wabi platform supports playing and recording waveform files, you can use the Sound tool to assign sounds to system events. If your Wabi platform does not support waveform playback and recording, you can only use the tool to enable and disable system sounds. See "Using Multimedia Features" on page 235 to determine if you have the correct hardware for sound in the Wabi environment.

Using Wabi Configuration Manager

The Wabi Configuration Manager lets you connect Wabi devices to UNIX counterparts. Once connected through Wabi, you can use familiar (that is, if you're a DOS user) DOS-type device names for printers, COM ports, drives, and diskettes from within your Windows applications.

Wabi Configuration Manager also lets you configure the commands used to launch a DOS emulator, if you have installed one on your system. This lets you start DOS sessions from the MS-DOS Prompt program item in the Main program group in Program Manager.

Connections you make in Configuration Manager apply to all Wabi windows and sessions. Common connections you might make or change include those between a Wabi virtual disk drive (`E:`, `F:`, and so on—see page 85) and a file system, a Wabi diskette drive (`A:` or `B:`) and a diskette device in your operating system, and a Wabi LPT port and a printer.

Some Configuration Manager connections require you to supply UNIX device names. In most cases, however, Wabi recognizes your operating system and supplies the appropriate default settings, which are defined in your `~/wabi/windows/wabi.ini` file. Infrequently, you may need to enter a unique or unusual setting in a Configuration Manager dialog box.

You open the Wabi Configuration Manager by double-clicking the Wabi Config icon (Figure 5-5) in the Microsoft Windows Control Panel. Alternatively, you can select the icon and press **Enter**.

Figure 5-5   Wabi Configuration Manager Icon

The Configuration Manager window contains several icons representing Wabi program tools, as shown in Figure 5-6.

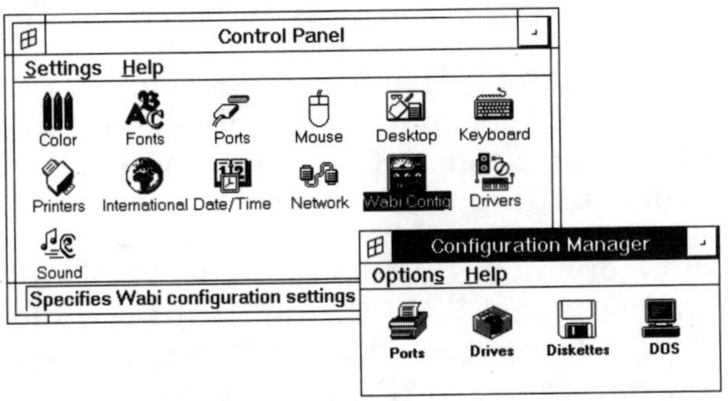

Figure 5-6   Control Panel and Wabi Configuration Manager

Configuration Manager comprises four tools. Each tool is represented by an icon and by a menu item on the Configuration Manager Options menu. Opening an icon for a tool or choosing a tool name from the Options menu produces the same result; that is, a dialog box associated with the tool is displayed.

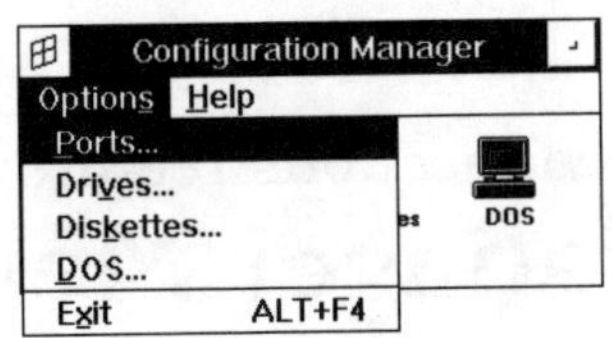

Figure 5-7   Wabi Configuration Manager Options Menu

Table 5-5 lists the tools provided by the Wabi Configuration Manager, and tells you where you can find instructions for using each tool.

Table 5-5   Wabi Configuration Manager Tools

Icon	Tool
Ports	Connect COM ports and LPT ports to UNIX devices. Refer to Chapter 8, "Managing COM Ports," for information about working with COM and LPT ports under Wabi. Refer to Chapter 7, "Managing Printers," for information about printing under Wabi.
Drives	Specify NFS directory mount points to use as Wabi virtual drives. Refer to "NFS Mount Points and Wabi Drives" on page 85 for information about Wabi virtual drives. See Chapter 6, "Managing Drives," for instructions on connecting to UNIX directories.
Diskettes	Assign Wabi diskette drives A: and B: to UNIX diskette device drivers. Refer to Chapter 6, "Managing Drives," for more information.
DOS	Specify the UNIX command used to start your DOS emulator. Wabi does not provide DOS emulation; you must provide your own emulator. See Chapter 10, "Using DOS Applications" for more information.

Configuration Manager Menus

Wabi Configuration Manager provides two drop-down command menus:

- **Options** – The primary menu; provides access to the four Configuration Manager tools. Choosing a tool from the Options menu is the same as double-clicking the icon for that tool in the Configuration Manager window. This menu also provides an Exit command, which lets you exit the Configuration Manager.

- **Help** – Provides several ways to access the Configuration Manager on-line help system. You can view a table of contents for the system, search for a specific topic, or get instructions for using the help system. The help system is in standard Microsoft Windows 3.1 on-line help format.

Configuration Manager Dialog Boxes

Each of the four tools in Wabi Configuration Manager has its own dialog box or set of dialog boxes. These dialog boxes use standard Microsoft Windows controls to perform various functions—that is, they look like Microsoft Windows dialogs, rather than X Window dialogs. Detailed information about Microsoft Windows dialog boxes in general is provided in Chapter 3, "Microsoft Windows For UNIX Users," in the sections titled "Dialog Boxes" and "Dialog Box Controls," starting on page 59.

Specific instructions for working with each of the tools in Wabi Configuration Manager are provided in various chapters. Each tool is explained in the larger context of a set of tasks and concepts to which it relates. For example, the DOS emulator tool is described in relation to running DOS applications under Wabi. Refer to Table 5-5 for the chapters and sections to which you should turn for tool-specific information.

Wabi Command-Line Options

Wabi provides several options you can use with the `wabi` command to start the Wabi program. These options are summarized in Table 5-6. The rightmost column in the table lists the page number on which you can find a detailed explanation for each given command.

Table 5-6   Wabi 2.1 Command-Line Options

Option	Example	Purpose	Page
<none>	`wabi`	Starts Wabi normally.	*111*
-display *display_name*	`wabi -display myscreen`	Displays Wabi on a remote system.	*135*
-fs +fs	`wabi -fs` `wabi +fs`	Start Wabi without (–) or with (+) Wabi font server.	*136*
-LF	`wabi -LF`	Displays Wabi with large fonts on a small screen.	*137*
-p	`wabi -p`	Starts a separate Wabi process; must be used with the -s option.	*138*
-SF	`wabi -SF`	Displays Wabi with small fonts on a large screen.	*137*
-s *filename*	`wabi -s notepad.exe`	Starts an application directly, without using your program shell.	*140*

In all cases, the command-line options are *case-sensitive*—those shown in uppercase must be entered uppercase, and vice versa. Also note that the commands in this section pertain specifically to Wabi 2.1 from SunSoft, Inc. Other versions and other manufacturer's products may support different command-line options.

Displaying Wabi On a Remote System

`-display`

You can direct the Wabi display to a remote system or X terminal. That is, you can run Wabi on one machine, but have its display and keyboard input on another. This can be useful if want to view and use Wabi on a system that cannot run it locally, or if you want to run Wabi on a central computer and display it on X terminals.

You can display Wabi on an available remote system by using the `-display` command-line option when starting the Wabi program. To direct the display to a remote system every time the Wabi program is started, you can set the `DISPLAY` environment variable in your UNIX environment. If you do set the UNIX `DISPLAY` variable, be aware that the displays of all other X applications you subsequently start may also be sent to this system, depending on where the variable is set. See your UNIX documentation for information about setting the `DISPLAY` variable.

Wabi software accesses local resources, like diskette drives, on the system on which it is running. You cannot access the diskette drive of a remote system on which the Wabi program is being displayed.

➤ *To display Wabi output on a remote system*

1. **Set the remote system to allow access to its display.**
   Enter the following command at the UNIX command line on the remote system:

   ```
   xhost +remote_host
   ```

2. **Start Wabi on your system with the** `-display` **option followed by the remote host name and** `:0`
   For example, to display Wabi output on a remote system named `myscreen`, enter:

   ```
   wabi -display myscreen:0
   ```

   Screen output is sent to the remote system with the specified host name.

To send the Wabi display to a remote system every time Wabi is started, you can set the `DISPLAY` environment variable in your UNIX shell. For example, to always display Wabi output on a remote system named `myscreen`, enter one of the following commands:

- If you use the C shell:

  ```
  setenv DISPLAY myscreen:0
  ```

- If you use the Bourne or Korn shell:

  ```
  DISPLAY=myscreen:0;export DISPLAY
  ```

If you do set this variable, be aware that all other X Window applications you start subsequently from the same UNIX command shell will be displayed on the remote system.

Starting Wabi Without the Font Server

```
-fs
+fs
```

By default, Wabi automatically starts the Wabi font server, `wabifs`, if there is an available X server—either local or remote—running the X11R5 font service protocol. `wabifs` speeds up the display of fonts in the Wabi environment by passing TrueType and bitmap font information to the X server, which in turn rasterizes the fonts for display. If an X server is not available, `wabifs` does not start, and all font handling is done within `wabiprog`. (See "X Font Services" on page 31 for more information.)

In general, you should let the Wabi program determine whether or not there is an available X server with which `wabifs` can interact; if such a server is available, `wabifs` starts automatically and life is good. However, for occasional troubleshooting purposes, you can manually disable the font server if you find that Wabi performs slowly or erratically, fontwise. To do this, start Wabi with the `-fs` option.

Although it is highly unlikely, it is possible that the Wabi program could falsely identify your X server as one that does not support the X font service protocol. If, however, you know that your X server *does* support the font service protocol, you can use the `+fs` switch to force Wabi to use it. From a practical standpoint, however, you will probably never use the `+fs` option.

Wabi 2: Opening Windows

For example:

- **-fs** – Forces Wabi to not use the font server
- **+fs** – Forces Wabi to use the font server; if you are wrong and a font server is not available, Wabi refuses to start

➤ *To force Wabi to NOT USE the font server*

➡ **Start Wabi with the** -fs **option.**
For example:

```
wabi -fs
```

➤ *To force Wabi to USE the font server*

➡ **Start Wabi with the +fs option.**
For example:

```
wabi +fs
```

Displaying Wabi With Smaller or Larger System Fonts

`-SF`
`-LF`

The Wabi program adjusts the size of the system fonts it uses in dialog boxes, icon labels, and menus according to the size of the display screen you use. On a large display screen (one with more than 640 horizontal pixels), the Wabi program uses a system font approximately 20 pixels high. On a small display screen (one with 640 or fewer horizontal pixels), it uses a system font approximately 16 pixels high. You can use the -LF and -SF command-line switches to override the default and have Wabi use larger or smaller system fonts.

- **-SF** – Forces Wabi to use small fonts on a large screen; this option has no effect on small screens
- **-LF** – Forces Wabi to use large fonts on a small screen; this option has no effect on large screens

➤ **To display Wabi with small fonts on a large screen**

➥ **Start Wabi with the** `-SF` **option.**
For example:

```
wabi -SF
```

➤ **To display Wabi with large fonts on a small screen**

➥ **Start Wabi with the** `-LF` **option.**
For example:

```
wabi -LF
```

In both procedures, note that `-SF` and `-LF` are case-sensitive—they must be entered in uppercase letters.

Starting Multiple Wabi Processes

`-p`

Normally, every Windows application you run under Wabi is executed within a single Wabi process. For example, if you run Microsoft Word for Windows and CorelDRAW!, both would be executed within one instance of Wabi. In this example, the UNIX `ps` command (which shows you what processes, or programs, are running on your system) would show a single `wabiprog` process. If Wabi is running, and you start another instance of Wabi, the two processes are combined, so there is still only a single Wabi process running.

This is not all that different from what Microsoft Windows does on a DOS-based PC; start Windows once, and all your Windows applications run within it. Unlike Wabi, however, you simply can't start a second instance of Windows under DOS. With Wabi, you can choose to:

- Start additional instances of Wabi, which will all be combined with the first.

    or

- Start additional instances of Wabi, but have each run as its own separate process.

The first choice is the default—if you don't do anything to override it, only one Wabi process will run on your system at a time, and all your Windows applications will run within that process. The second choice, running multiple Wabi processes, can be desirable if you want an application to be as "bullet-proof" as possible. That is, by running one or more of your Windows applications in their own process (which, from a practical standpoint, means their own memory space), the crash of one Windows application running in one process will usually have no effect on another application running in another process.

This is markedly different from Windows under DOS, where the crash of one application often takes down your entire system. By running your Windows applications in separate Wabi processes, the crash of one application will (in most cases) have no effect on any other applications.

To start separate Wabi processes, enter the `wabi` command with the `-p` option. This option *must* be used in combination with the `-s` switch, which is described in the next section.

 You must use the `-p` switch in combination with the `-s` switch. If you do not do this, Wabi will attempt to start two instances of Program Manager, which can cause unpredictable results if Program Manager attempts to access the same files at the same time.

There is one major advantage and one minor disadvantage (depending on your point of view) to running Windows applications in separate Wabi processes:

- Windows applications run in their own memory space, which makes it nearly impossible for a crash in one Windows application to affect other Windows applications or Wabi.

- OLE, DDE, and Windows Clipboard functions are not supported when Wabi is run this way. Cut-and-paste is supported, but only through X Window mechanisms. For example, you could copy text from a Windows application to a Solaris application, like `textedit`, and then copy it from `textedit` to another Windows application. In this scenario, cutting and pasting of graphics objects is not supported. (See "Cut, Copy, and Paste" on page 290 for more information about using cut-and-paste features in Windows applications running under Wabi software.)

➤ **To run Windows applications in separate Wabi processes**

1. **Start the first Wabi process normally.**
   For example:

   ```
   wabi
   ```

2. **Start the next Wabi process with the `-p` and `-s` switches.**
   For example:

   ```
   wabi -p -s g:\word6\winword
   ```

   This example starts Microsoft Word for Windows (located in this example on drive `G:` in the `\word6` directory), in a new Wabi process, bypassing Windows Program Manager.

3. **Start other Wabi processes, as needed, using the `-p` and `-s` switches.**
   If you omit the `-p` switch, this Wabi process is joined with the first Wabi process, started in Step 1.

Starting Windows Applications Directly

`-s`

Normally, you start Wabi, which starts Program Manager, and from there you start your Windows applications. However, you can, if you wish, bypass Program Manager entirely, and launch a Windows application directly from the UNIX command line. To do this, start Wabi with the `-s` option, followed by the name (and directory path, if necessary) of the Windows application you want to run. `-s` is often used with the `-p` option.

➤ **To start a Windows application directly from the UNIX command line**

➡ **Enter the `wabi` command with the `-s` option, followed by the name of the application you want to run.**
   For example:

   ```
   wabi -s directory\application
   ```

   Replace *directory* with the directory in which the application you want to run is located, if it is not already in your environment `PATH`. Replace *application* with the name of the application.

See Chapter 9, in the section titled "Running Windows Applications" on page 220, for more about using the `-s` option.

Wabi 2: Opening Windows

Exiting Wabi

Exiting Wabi is the same as exiting Microsoft Windows under DOS. Specifically, to exit Windows or Wabi, choose the Exit command from the Program Manager File menu, or double-click the Control-menu box in the upper-left corner of the Program Manager window.

If you prefer, you can also press Ctrl+Esc to display the Windows Task Manager, select "Program Manager" from the displayed list of tasks, and then choose End Task.

➤ *To exit the Wabi program*

1. **Save any open files.**
   If you try to exit before saving, individual applications prompt you as needed to save your work.

2. **Choose Exit from the Program Manager File menu.**
   Alternately, press Alt+F4, or double-click the Control-menu box in the upper left corner of the Program Manager window.

   The Exit Windows confirmation message is displayed.

3. **Choose OK.**
   Program Manager closes and the Wabi program terminates.

   If you change your mind, choose Cancel to keep Program Manager open and remain in the current Wabi session.

Getting Help

The SunSoft version of Wabi 2.1 software provides context-sensitive Windows on-line help, complete on-line documentation in Solaris AnswerBook format, and general reference information in a text-based UNIX manual (man) page.

Windows On-Line Help

Wabi 2.1 software includes context-sensitive on-line help for Wabi Configuration Manager. You can view this on-line help through the Configuration Manager's Help menu, or by choosing the Help button or pressing FI in any of Configuration Manager's dialog boxes and most error messages.

Also be sure to look at the status bar at the bottom of each Configuration Manager dialog box. This status bar displays information about the dialog box item currently under the mouse pointer. As you move the pointer around in a dialog box, the status bar message changes.

Most Windows applications, including Program Manager itself, also provide on-line help. Pressing FI anywhere in these applications generally displays application-specific help. Pressing FI again displays help about using the Windows on-line help system.

AnswerBook Documentation

The SunSoft *Wabi User's Guide* is provided on-line in Solaris AnswerBook format. You may or may not have installed this AnswerBook package, with the `pkgadd` command, when you installed the Wabi program package.

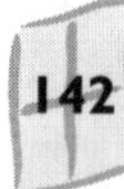

Wabi man Page

A man page of information is available for all versions of the Wabi program. This man page describes command-line options, provides examples of various startup modes, and describes Wabi environment variables. To display the Wabi man page, enter the command `man wabi` at any UNIX command prompt.

➤ *To view the Wabi man page*

⇒ **Enter the following command at a UNIX command line:**

```
man wabi
```

The initial screen of Wabi man page information is displayed. Press the spacebar to view additional screens.

If the `man` command indicates there is no Wabi man page, you may have to add it to your man pages `MANPATH` environment variable, as explained below.

To be able to display the Wabi man page, you must have the Wabi man page directory included in your man pages `MANPATH` environment variable. The Wabi installation procedure may have taken care of this for you already; it varies depending on your native operating system. Some operating systems set a `MANPATH` environment variable in your `.login`, `.cshrc`, or `.profile` file. If you cannot view the Wabi man page, you may have to modify your `MANPATH` environment variable.

➤ *To add the Wabi man page to your MANPATH setting*

1. **Open a UNIX command window.**
2. **Determine where the** `MANPATH` **environment variable is set.**
   Examine your `.login` and `.cshrc` (if you use the C shell) or `.profile` (if you use the Bourne or Korn shell) to locate this variable.

3. **Set your** MANPATH **variable to include the Wabi man page directory.**

If MANPATH does not exist in `.login`, `.cshrc`, or `.profile`, use a text editor to enter the following line in the appropriate file:

a. **If you use the C shell, add the following line to either your** `.login` **or** `.cshrc` **file:**

```
setenv MANPATH parentdirectory/man
```

b. **If you use the Bourne or Korn shell, add the following line to your** `.profile` **file:**

```
MANPATH=parentdirectory/man;export MANPATH
```

parentdirectory is the directory where the Wabi system software is located; for example, `/usr/wabi`.

c. **If** MANPATH **is set in one of these files already, use a text editor to update your** MANPATH **variable by adding the following at the end of the** `setenv MANPATH` **or** `MANPATH=` **statement:**

parentdirectory`/man`

For example, if the Wabi system software is located in `/usr/wabi`, your MANPATH directory is `/usr/wabi/man`.

Be sure to separate the Wabi entry from existing MANPATH entries with a colon. Save and quit the `.login`, `.cshrc`, or `.profile` file once you've added this statement.

4. **Update your operating system to recognize the new** MANPATH **entry.**

Enter one of the following commands, depending on the file in which your MANPATH statement is located:

```
source .login
```

or

```
source .cshrc
```

or

```
. .profile
```


Wabi 2: Opening Windows

Wabi International Settings

Because the Wabi environment consists of programs, libraries, and files from both the UNIX world and the Microsoft Windows world, it is affected on several levels by the international settings of both those environments. In UNIX, you can set environment variables. In Microsoft Windows, you can install localized Windows versions and change International options in Windows Control Panel.

UNIX Environment Variables

On the UNIX side, the Wabi program can be localized through three environment variables: `LANG`, `WABI_KEYB`, and `WABI_CODEPAGE`. The `LANG` variable affects your entire X Window desktop, while the `WABI_KEYB` and `WABI_CODEPAGE` variables affect only the Wabi program.

LANG

If your version of the UNIX operating system contains international language libraries, you can use the UNIX environment variable `LANG` to enable the Wabi program to use a particular language, or locale, as it is called in the UNIX world. International versions of the Wabi program use the locale settings to determine which language to use to display Wabi error and status messages, Wabi on-line help, and Wabi graphical user interface components, such as the Configuration Manager menus.

Table 5-7 lists valid locale values for the `LANG` environment variable.

Table 5-7   Locales for `LANG` *and* `WABI_KEYB` *Environment Variables*

Language – Country	Locale	Equivalent DOS Variable
English – United States	en_US or C	KEYB_us
English – United Kingdom	en_UK	KEYB_uk
Danish – Denmark	da	KEYB_dk
Dutch – Netherlands	nl	KEYB_nl
Finnish – Finland	fi	KEYB_su
French – Belgium	fr_BE	KEYB_be
French – Canada	fr_CA	KEYB_cf
French – France	fr	KEYB_fr
French – Switzerland	fr_CH	KEYB_sf
Spanish - Latin America	es_LA	KEYB_la
Spanish – Spain	es	KEYB_sp
German – Germany	de	KEYB_gr
German – Switzerland	de_CH	KEYB_sg
Italian – Italy	it	KEYB_it
Norwegian – Norway	no	KEYB_no
Portuguese – Portugal	pt	KEYB_po
Swedish – Sweden	sv	KEYB_sv

Wabi 2: Opening Windows

➤ *To set the LANG environment variable*

1. **Enter one of the following commands before starting your X Window desktop:**
   For example, before starting OpenWindows, enter:
   - In the C shell:
     ```
     setenv LANG locale
     ```
   - In the Bourne or Korn shell:
     ```
     LANG=locale;export LANG
     ```

   For example, to specify French as the locale/keyboard type, enter one of the following commands:
   - In the C shell:
     ```
     setenv LANG fr
     ```
   - In the Bourne or Korn shell:
     ```
     LANG=fr;export LANG
     ```

   Refer to Table 5-7 for a list of valid locale values.

2. **Start your X Window desktop.**

WABI_KEYB

The LANG environment variable also sets the keyboard to the locale you specify. The Wabi program supports the WABI_KEYB variable to let you specify a keyboard that is different from that specified by the LANG variable. The WABI_KEYB variable overrides the keyboard specified by the LANG variable, but only for the Wabi environment and applications running within it.

The LANG and WABI_KEYB variables use a two-letter or four-letter abbreviation to identify the locale. Table 5-7 lists the locale abbreviations.

1. **Enter one of the following commands before starting Wabi:**
   - In the C shell:

     ```
     setenv WABI_KEYB locale
     ```
   - In the Bourne or Korn shell:

     ```
     WABI_KEYB=locale;export WABI_KEYB
     ```

   For example, to specify French as the keyboard locale, enter one of the following commands:
   - In the C shell:

     ```
     setenv WABI_KEYB fr
     ```
   - In the Bourne or Korn shell:

     ```
     WABI_KEYB=fr;export WABI_KEYB
     ```

   Alternatively, to set the environment variable statements required to establish French international settings with an English-language (U.S.) keyboard, use the following commands:
   - In the C shell:

     ```
     setenv LANG fr
     setenv WABI_KEYB C
     ```
   - In the Bourne or Korn shell:

     ```
     LANG=fr;export LANG
     WABI_KEYB=C;export WABI_KEYB
     ```

   Refer to Table 5-7 on page 146 for a list of valid locale values.
2. **Start the Wabi program.**

WABI_CODEPAGE

The WABI_CODEPAGE variable lets you specify which code page Wabi should use for OEM character translation. Microsoft Windows uses the code page set in DOS. Since DOS is not used in the Wabi environment, the Wabi program uses code page 437 by default. If you want to use a different code page, specify the code page with this environment variable.

Table 5-8 lists valid values for the WABI_CODEPAGE environment variable.

Table 5-8   WABI_CODEPAGE Environment Variable Settings

Code Page	Country	Code Page	Country
437	United States	861	Iceland
850	Western Europe	863	Canada
860	Portugal	865	Denmark

➤ **To set the *WABI_CODEPAGE* environment variable**

   1. Enter one of the following commands before starting Wabi:
   - In the C shell:

     ```
     setenv WABI_CODEPAGE nnn
     ```
   - In the Bourne or Korn shell:

     ```
     WABI_CODEPAGE=nnn;export WABI_CODEPAGE
     ```

   For example, to specify the 850 code page, enter one of the
   following commands:
   - In the C shell:

     ```
     setenv WABI_CODEPAGE 850
     ```
   - In the Bourne or Korn shell:

     ```
     WABI_CODEPAGE=850;export WABI_CODEPAGE
     ```

   Refer to Table 5-8 for a list of valid WABI_CODEPAGE values.

   2. Start the Wabi program.

International Versions of Microsoft Windows

Most of the text you see when you run Wabi is provided by Microsoft
Windows; the amount of user interface text provided by Wabi software is
relatively small by comparison. You can install one of several different
language versions of Microsoft Windows into your Wabi environment; this
determines the language in which most of the user interface is displayed.

Before you install a localized version of Microsoft Windows, you must first set the LANG variable in your UNIX environment to the language of the Windows version you want to install. Do this before starting Wabi. In international versions of Wabi software, the Wabi Windows Install program uses the LANG setting of the system on which it is running to determine the language to display the user interface.

International Settings in Control Panel

Applications running under Wabi use the international options set in your WIN.INI file. You can customize these international settings by using the Microsoft Windows Control Panel International dialog box (Figure 5-8).

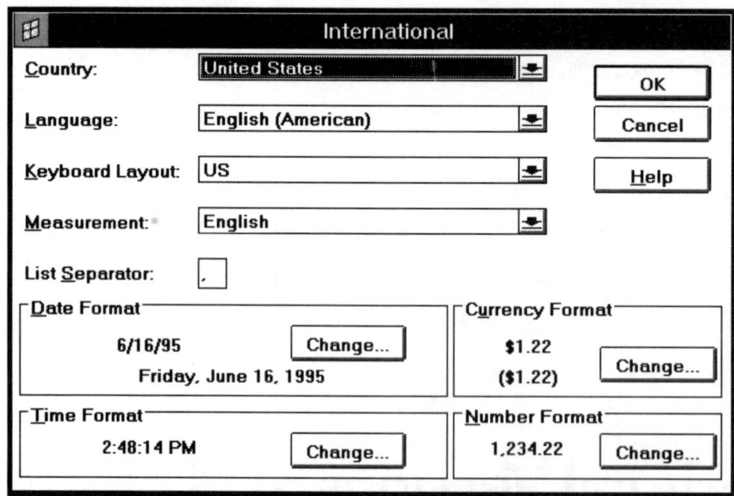

Figure 5-8   Control Panel International Dialog Box

Some applications have their own menus or commands for setting certain international formats. Settings selected within a given application take precedence over the Control Panel settings. Also, the International options set in the International dialog box are used by Windows applications, and not by the Wabi program itself.

The International dialog box works as it does in the Microsoft Windows environment, except for the Keyboard Layout setting, which Wabi ignores in favor of the `WABI_KEYB` variable. Briefly, the International settings are:

- **Country** — Sets the default Date, Time, Currency, and Number formats to the values normally used in the selected country

- **Language** — Used by applications to determine how to sort characters

- **Keyboard Layout** — Microsoft Windows uses this setting to determine how to interpret your keystrokes on keyboards designed for various languages; in the Wabi environment, the `WABI_KEYB` variable performs this function, so this setting has no effect

- **Measurement** — Specifies English or metric measurement

- **List Separator** — Specifies the character used between list items

- **Date/Time/Currency/Number** — Specifies the formats to use for dates, times, currency, and general numbers

➤ *To change International settings*

1. **Open the Microsoft Windows Control Panel.**
   The Windows Control Panel program item is located by default in Program Manager's Main program group.
2. **Open the International icon.**
   The International dialog box displayed.
3. **Change the settings you want.**
   Press F1 to get help about any of the settings in this dialog box.
4. **Choose OK to accept your settings and exit the dialog.**
   Choose Cancel to ignore your changes and exit the dialog.

International Compose Key Sequences

The Wabi program supports Compose key sequences. If your keyboard provides a Compose key, you can use it to produce special characters. See your keyboard documentation for details about using the Compose key.

Chapter 6

Managing
Drives

Wabi software lets you work with local, CD-ROM, and network disk drives as if they were all local fixed drives on your computer. This is useful for a number of reasons: the ability to share files and (licensed) applications in a workgroup setting, the ability to move from machine to machine but still have access to your files, and increased capacity and flexibility for storing your programs and data. This latter point is more important than it might appear at first glance; applications written for today's graphical windowing environments are notorious for being disk and memory hogs, and Microsoft Windows applications are no exception.

640K ought to be enough for anybody.

– William H. Gates III, 1982

All progress has resulted from people who took unpopular positions.

– Adlai Stevenson, 1954

In This Chapter

Topic	Page
Disk Drives Under Wabi	*154*
Diskette Drives	*155*
Wabi Drives	*162*
Wabi Network Drives	*174*
CD-ROM Drives	*176*

Disk Drives Under Wabi

Wabi uses two general kinds of drives:

- **Diskette drives** – Drives A: and B: are diskette drives. These drives connect (map) to diskette devices defined in your UNIX operating system. Diskette drive A: is set up for you by Wabi and assigned automatically as the default diskette drive. (You can change this assignment.) If your computer has a second diskette drive, use diskette drive B: to represent this drive.

- **Wabi drives** – Drives C: through Z: represent Wabi drives, which are functionally similar to the local disk drives, CD-ROM drives, and network drives used on DOS-based systems. A Wabi drive can be assigned to a directory on a drive physically located within your computer, or to a virtual disk drive—that is, a directory that is physically located on a remote system and accessed, or mounted, over the network by your operating system. (See "NFS Mount Points and Wabi Drives" on page 85 for more information about virtual disk drives under Wabi.)

  Wabi does not know if a drive's assigned directory is local or on a network, because it accesses the drive through a directory path. The physical location of the directory is transparent to you and to the Wabi program.

Diskette Drives

To use a diskette drive under Wabi, you must connect it to a UNIX operating system diskette device. A device is a UNIX operating system file, similar to a DOS device driver, that allows you to access a physical device, such as a diskette drive. Once you make this connection, Wabi uses it for all subsequent sessions, or until you change the connection. Most likely, the Wabi program's default connection will work for your operating system, and you can use the diskette drive without changing the diskette connection to the device.

Diskette Connections Dialog Box

The Diskette Connections dialog box (Figure 6-1) lets you work with Wabi diskette drive connection settings. You open this dialog box from within Wabi Configuration Manager by clicking the Diskettes icon, or by choosing Diskettes from the Configuration Manager Options menu. As the Diskette Connections dialog box opens, the Wabi program scans your operating system device directories for diskette devices.

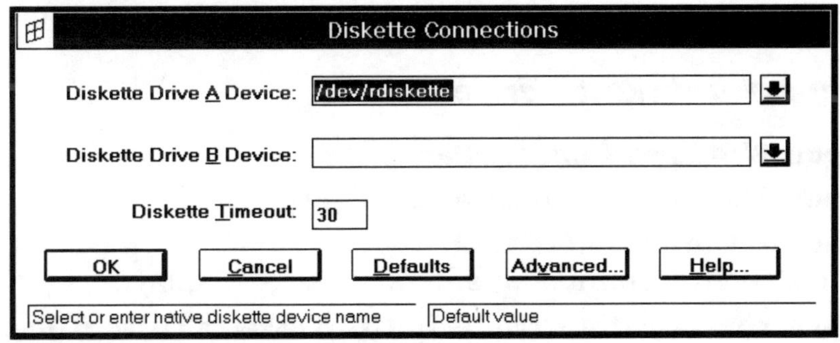

Figure 6-1   Diskette Connections Dialog Box

As diskette device file names are scanned, they are validated. If a device name is valid, the Wabi program adds it to the list of available diskette drives that appear in the drop-down list associated with diskette drive A: and diskette drive B:. Note that the Wabi program uses *raw* UNIX device files. (See your UNIX operating system documentation for information about raw devices.)

In the Diskette Connections dialog box, you select diskette device assignments for drives A: and B:, if applicable, and specify a Diskette Timeout period (see below).

Wabi provides a default assignment for drive A:, which you can change. No default assignment is provided for drive B:. The field to the right of each Diskette Drive name displays the current assignment. If you click the down-arrow to the right of a field, a list of additional diskette device names is displayed. You select a device name by clicking it.

- **Diskette Timeout** – You can specify a timeout period (in seconds) for the diskette device. Wabi releases control of the diskette drive if the device has not been used after this period of time, allowing other programs to use the diskette drive while Wabi is running. Wabi regains control the next time you access the diskette through an application running under Wabi.

- **Unlisted diskette device** – You can connect a Wabi diskette drive to an unlisted diskette device by typing the device path and name directly in the text box associated with diskette drive A: or B:. This can be useful if you want to connect to a device that you know exists, but does not appear in the list.

➤ *To connect a diskette drive*

1. **Open Windows Control Panel.**
2. **Open Wabi Configuration Manager.**
3. **Choose the Diskettes tool.**
   The Diskette Connections dialog box is displayed.
4. **Open the Diskette Drive A list or Diskette Drive B list.**
   A list of prevalidated diskette device names is displayed.
5. **Select a diskette device name in the list.**

6. **Choose OK to accept your selection and close the Diskette Connections dialog.**

   Alternatively, choose Cancel to close the dialog box without making changes.

   When you choose OK, the diskette device you've chosen is connected to the selected diskette drive letter.

➤ *To change the diskette drive timeout period*

1. **Open Windows Control Panel.**
2. **Open Wabi Configuration Manager.**
3. **Choose the Diskettes tool.**

   The Diskette Connections dialog box is displayed.

4. **Enter the desired timeout period (in seconds) in the Diskette Timeout field.**

   This period is the number of seconds the diskette must be idle before Wabi releases control of the drive.

5. **Choose OK to save your setting and close the Diskette Connections dialog.**

   Alternatively, choose Cancel to close the dialog box without saving your changes.

➤ *To manually enter a diskette device name*

1. **Open Windows Control Panel.**
2. **Open Wabi Configuration Manager.**
3. **Choose the Diskettes tool.**

   The Diskette Connections dialog box is displayed.

4. **Open the Diskette Drive A list or Diskette Drive B list.**

   A list of prevalidated diskette device names is displayed.

5. **Enter the path and name of the desired diskette device file.**

6. **Choose OK to save your setting and close the Diskette Connections dialog.**

   Alternatively, choose Cancel to close the dialog box without saving your changes.

   When you choose OK, Wabi validates your entry. If the entry is valid, the diskette device you entered is connected to the diskette drive. An error message is displayed if the entry you typed is not a valid device name.

Advanced Diskette Drive Options

Wabi software is configured to detect default diskette device locations and naming patterns used by most UNIX operating systems. In some cases, however, these defaults may not match the locations or patterns used in your particular system. For example, if you relocate diskette devices to a directory not normally used to store them, the Wabi program will not know where to look for these device files. When this is the case, you must tell Wabi where the diskette device files are located.

You use the Advanced Diskette Drive Options dialog box (Figure 6-2) to provide Wabi with the information it needs to find and use diskette devices that are named or located in a nonstandard manner. You access the Advanced Diskette Drive Options dialog box by choosing the **Advanced** button in the Diskette Connections dialog box.

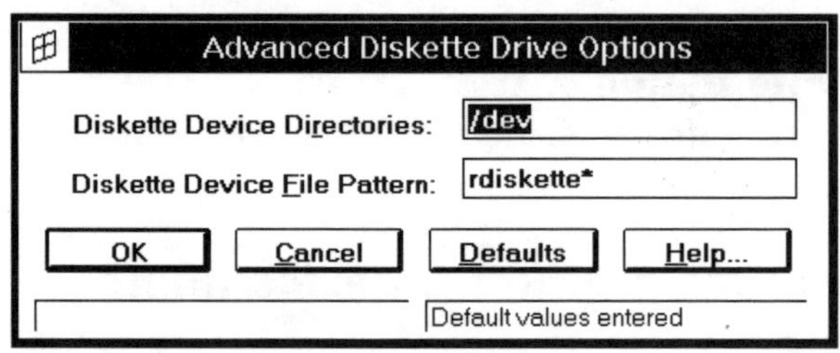

Figure 6-2   Advanced Diskette Drive Options Dialog Box

You can enter two items in this dialog box:

- **Diskette Device Directories** – Specify the names of directories that Wabi searches for operating system diskette devices. You can specify more than one directory, with directory entries separated by commas with no surrounding spaces.

- **Diskette Device File Pattern** – Specify the device file-naming pattern (convention) used in your UNIX operating system. You can specify more than one pattern, with pattern entries separated by commas with no surrounding spaces.

Wildcard characters are allowed in file pattern entries. An asterisk (*) can replace a group of characters, and a question mark (?) can replace a single character. You can indicate a range of possible values for a single character by using brackets. For example, you can use [0-9] to match a value from 0 through 9. If you enter the pattern rfd[0-9]*, Wabi finds file names such as rfd0, rfd1floppy, rfd3c, and rfd9xyz. Remember that Wabi uses raw diskette devices.

➤ *To access an alternate diskette devices directory*

1. **Open Windows Control Panel.**
2. **Open Wabi Configuration Manager.**
3. **Choose the Diskettes tool.**
   The Diskette Connections dialog box is displayed.
4. **Choose Advanced.**
   The Advanced Diskette Drive Options dialog box is displayed.
5. **Select the Diskette Device Directories field.**
   The field becomes active.
6. **Type the directory or directories in which diskette devices are located.**
   Separate multiple entries with commas; do not use spaces.
7. **Choose OK to save your setting and close the Diskette Connections dialog.**
   Alternatively, choose Cancel to close the dialog box without saving your changes.

   When you choose OK, Wabi validates your entry. If the entry is valid and the directories exist, each time you connect a diskette drive to a diskette device, Wabi searches for device files in the directories you specified.

➤ *To reset the diskette device directories to the default*

1. **Choose Defaults in the Advanced Diskette Drive Options dialog box.**
   The default diskette devices directories are restored.
2. **Choose OK to save your settings and exit the dialog.**

➤ *To access an alternate diskette device file pattern*

1. **Open Windows Control Panel.**
2. **Open Wabi Configuration Manager.**
3. **Choose the Diskettes tool.**
   The Diskette Connections dialog box is displayed.
4. **Choose Advanced.**
   The Advanced Diskette Drive Options dialog box is displayed.
5. **Select the Diskette Device File Pattern field.**
   The field becomes active.
6. **Type one or more file patterns.**
   Separate multiple patterns with commas; do not use spaces.
7. **Choose OK to save your setting and close the Diskette Connections dialog.**
   Alternatively, choose Cancel to close the dialog box without saving your changes.

   When you choose OK, the Wabi program validates your entry. If the entry is valid, each time you connect a diskette drive to a diskette device the Wabi program searches for diskette device files using the naming patterns you entered.

➤ *To reset the diskette device file pattern to the default*

1. **Choose Defaults in the Advanced Diskette Drive Options dialog box.**
   The default diskette device file pattern is restored.
2. **Choose OK to save your settings and exit the dialog.**

Diskettes and DOS

You cannot format DOS diskettes within the Wabi environment. Before you can use a diskette with Wabi, it must already be formatted for DOS. (All Microsoft Windows applications write to disk in DOS format.)

Some operating systems provide a command for formatting DOS diskettes. (In the Solaris environment, you can use `fdformat -t dos`.) Refer to your operating system documentation for information about formatting DOS diskettes. If your operating system is not able to format DOS diskettes, you can use preformatted diskettes, or you can format diskettes yourself on a PC running DOS.

You have several options for formatting DOS diskettes under UNIX:

- DOS diskettes can be formatted from a Solaris command prompt with the `fdformat` command. See the man page for instructions.
- If you have a DOS emulator installed on your system (see Chapter 10), you can start a DOS session and use the DOS `format` command.
- Note that you cannot use the Disk Format command in Microsoft Windows File Manager to format diskettes.

➤ *To format a DOS diskette*

1. **Open a UNIX operating system command window.**
2. **Place a diskette in the diskette drive.**
3. **Enter your operating system's diskette format command.**
   Refer to your operating system user's guide for more information. In the Solaris environment, the command is `fdformat -t dos`.

Wabi Drives

Wabi drives correspond to fixed, CD-ROM, and network drives on a PC, and are represented under Wabi by the letters C: through Z:. These drives serve as a gateway to the mounted file systems and directories of your operating system. By assigning drives to network-based directories—thereby creating Wabi (*virtual*) drives (see page 85)—you can access those directories as if they were local drives attached to your PC. Moreover, it does not matter whether those drives are formatted for UNIX or DOS; Wabi automatically maps file and directory formats and attributes so your Windows applications can access them. This process is explained in detail in Chapter 3, in the section titled "What's in a Name?" on page 73.

Remember, some UNIX file attributes don't map directly to DOS attributes, and vice versa (see Table 3-9 on page 77). For example, while a UNIX `no write` attribute can be mapped to the DOS `read-only` attribute, there is no UNIX equivalent to the DOS `archive` attribute. Also note that Wabi cannot lock files on DOS drives (for example, directories located in PCFS partitions). See the "File Locking and File Sharing" section later in this chapter for more information.

Wabi cannot tell if a drive is local or on a network, because Wabi accesses the drive through a directory path. The physical location of the directory is transparent to you and to the Wabi program. However, when you connect a drive to a directory, you can tell the Wabi program to represent the drive to applications as a network drive, whether the drive is local to your system or not. This feature is important to some Windows applications running under Wabi.

Drive Connections Dialog Box

You create and change drive assignments in the Drive Connections dialog box, shown in Figure 6-3. When you assign a drive to a directory, the Wabi program retains your drive assignment for all subsequent Wabi sessions, or until you change the assignment.

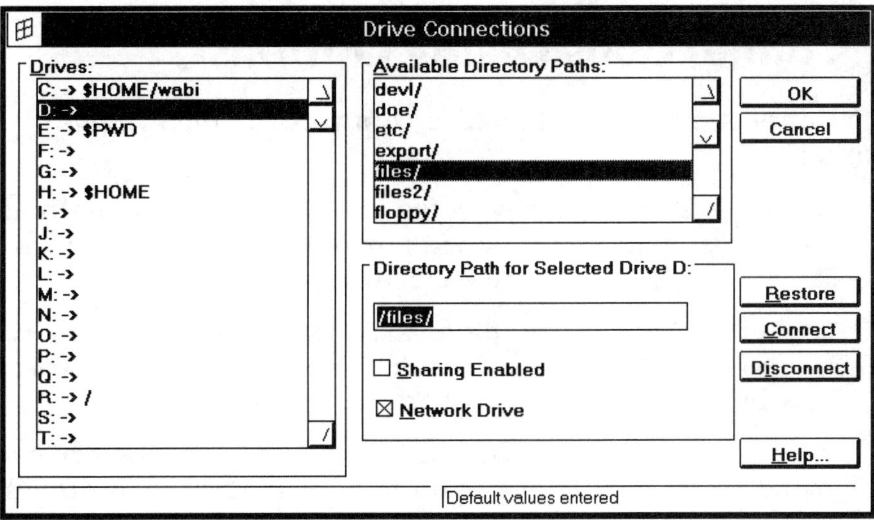

Figure 6-3   Drive Connections Dialog Box

Drive Connections Dialog Information

The Drive Connections dialog box provides three types of connection information:

- **Drives** – Presents a list of Wabi drives and their assignments. Drive letters that are not connected to a file system appear with no assignment.

- **Available Directory Paths** – Displays a list of mounted file systems and directories contained within the current directory. The highest-level directory available for viewing is the root (/) directory. When you click on a subdirectory within the root directory, the directories within the subdirectory are displayed. Double-click on a directory to see the directories within it and to add it to the drive path. By double-clicking on subsequent directories, you construct a path that you can assign to a drive. (../ takes you up a level in the directory hierarchy.)

- **Directory Path for Selected Drive *x*:** – Displays a scrolling text-entry field that indicates the path assignment of the selected drive. You can edit the path displayed in this field, or enter a new path.

Drive Connections Dialog Options

The Drive Connections dialog box also contains the following buttons and check boxes:

- **Restore** – Returns the selected drive's path to the path assigned when you opened the dialog box. Restore is not the same as Cancel—it resets only the selected drive.

- **Connect** – Assigns the path appearing in the Directory Path for Selected Drive list to the drive letter selected in the Drives list. This button is activated when a path is selected.

- **Disconnect** – Removes the path assignment of the drive selected in the Drives list. This button is activated when a drive letter with an assigned path is selected.

- **Sharing Enabled** – Enables or disables file sharing on the selected drive. An **x** in this check box indicates that file sharing is enabled. Note that file sharing in this context refers to an automatic locking mechanism that prevents simultaneous access to a given file by more than one user. This file-sharing mechanism, which is activated every time a file is opened, can exact a noticeable performance penalty with some applications. Specifically, Wabi needs to perform several extra operations each time an application opens a file, so if your application opens many files, you will probably see a degradation in performance. For this reason, file sharing is disabled by default under Wabi, and should generally be used only if you really need it. Note that file sharing works only on the Solaris version of Wabi software. See "File Locking and File Sharing" on page 169 for details.

- **Network Drive** – Checking this box makes the drive appear to an application as a network drive, whether the assigned directory is local or on the network. An **x** indicates that the selected drive is viewed as a network drive. By default, all drives except C: are viewed as network drives. See "Wabi Network Drives" on page 174 for more information.

Default Wabi Drive Assignments

When you first open the Drive Connections dialog box, notice that several drives are already assigned. Some of these assignments are permanent and you cannot change them. Table 6-1 lists the default assignments that you cannot change, and Table 6-2 lists the default assignments you can change.

Table 6-1   Default Wabi Drive Assignments You Cannot Change

Drive	Description
`C:  → $HOME/wabi`	The directory in which your Wabi user files are installed.
`R:  → /`	The root directory. Drive `R:` serves as a gateway to network file systems and to all directories on your system.
`W: → $WABIHOME`	The directory used to store Wabi program files.

If you select the `C:`, `R:`, or `W:` drive, the Available Directory Paths list is blank, and the Restore, Connect, and Disconnect buttons are disabled.

Table 6-2   Default Wabi Drive Assignments You Can Change

Drive	Description
`E:  → $PWD`	The directory that was current when Wabi was started.
`H:  → $HOME`	Your home directory.

New Drive Assignments

Making a new drive connection is a simple process; specifically, you do the following:

- Select a drive letter.
- Specify a drive path.
- Connect them.

Selecting a drive letter is easy: you click on any unassigned letter in the Drives list. This activates the Available Directory Paths list, which displays a scrolling list of root-level directories. Single-clicking a directory in this list places the directory in the assigned drive path. Double-clicking a directory in this list places the directory in the path and also opens the directory. The subdirectories available within the first directory are now displayed in the Available Directory Paths list. By sequentially navigating remaining directories, you can construct a path to the desired file system.

When you reach the destination directory, choose the Connect button. Wabi assigns the drive letter you selected to the path you constructed. To save assignments you make, choose OK.

You need adequate file permissions to access the files and directories you assign to Wabi drives. If you attempt to access a file or directory for which you do not have adequate permissions, you will see an error message indicating that a permission problem exists. Ask your system administrator about accessing files or directories for which you do not currently have permission.

➤ *To assign a Wabi drive*

1. **Open Windows Control Panel.**
2. **Open Wabi Configuration Manager.**
3. **Choose the Drives tool.**
   The Drive Connections dialog box is displayed.
4. **Select an unassigned drive letter from the Drives list.**
   The letter is highlighted.
5. **Select the directory to which you want to connect.**
   Navigate through the directories and files in the Available Directory Paths list until you reach the file system you want.

   Click a directory name to place it in the path. Double-click a directory name to place it in the path and view the directory's contents. The selected path is displayed in the Directory Path for Selected Drive list.
6. **Choose Connect.**
   The selected directory is assigned to the drive. The connection is displayed in the Drives list.

7. Choose OK to save your selection and exit the dialog.
Alternatively, choose Cancel to close the dialog box without saving
your changes.

Editing the Directory Path

In certain situations, you may want to edit a drive path assignment or
enter a drive path directly, rather than define one by sequentially clicking
on directories in the Available Directory Paths list. This might be the case if
you know the path, or if you want to include a variable such as $HOME in
the path.

The Directory Path for Selected Drive list allows you to enter a path directly.
To activate this list, select an assigned or unassigned drive letter. If you
select an assigned drive letter, the path assigned to the drive appears in
the list. If you select an unassigned drive letter, the list is activated but is
blank. Once the I-beam cursor appears in the list, you can edit an
existing path or type a new path.

➤ *To edit or enter a drive path directly*

1. **Open Windows Control Panel.**
2. **Open Wabi Configuration Manager.**
3. **Choose the Drives tool.**
   The Drive Connections dialog box is displayed.
4. **Select a letter representing the drive assignment you want
   to edit or enter.**
   The drive assignment is highlighted, and the path is displayed in
   the Directory Path for Selected Drive list.

   If you select one of the permanent drives, `C:`, `R:`, or `W:`, no path
   is displayed in the Directory Path for Selected Drive list because you
   cannot change this path.
5. **Select the Directory Path for Selected Drive list.**
   The text entry area becomes active.
6. **Edit or enter a directory path.**
   Alternatively, choose the Restore button to return the path to
   what it was when you entered the dialog box.

7. **Choose Connect.**
   The path displayed in the Directory Path for Selected Drive panel
   is assigned to the selected drive. The connection is displayed in
   the Drives panel.

8. **Choose OK to save your selection and exit the dialog.**
   Alternatively, choose Cancel to close the dialog box without saving
   your changes.

Disconnecting Drives

You can remove the connection for an individual Wabi drive, except for
drives `C:`, `R:`, and `W:`, by selecting a drive letter and choosing the
Disconnect button in the Drive Connections dialog box.

➤ *To disconnect a Wabi drive*

1. **Make sure the drive is not being used by any running
   applications.**

2. **Open Windows Control Panel.**

3. **Open Wabi Configuration Manager.**

4. **Choose the Drives tool.**
   The Drive Connections dialog box is displayed.

5. **Select the drive letter of the drive you want to disconnect.**
   The Disconnect button is activated.

   If you select one of the permanent drives, `C:`, `R:`, or `W:`, the
   Disconnect button is not activated because you cannot disconnect
   these drives.

6. **Choose Disconnect.**
   The path assignment is cleared for the selected drive.

7. **Choose OK to save your changes and exit the dialog.**
   Alternatively, choose Cancel to close the dialog box without saving
   your changes.

File Locking and File Sharing

Wabi supports both file locking and file sharing. These two concepts sound similar, but there are subtle differences between them.

- **File locking** – Prevents multiple users from accessing or modifying a file or, more typically, a *portion* of a file (like a database record) at the same time. File locking is supported on all Wabi platforms, but not on some UNIX partitions—for example, PCFS (DOS) partitions. File locking is enabled under Wabi by default.

- **File sharing** – Controls access to files *as a whole*. Sharing manages a set of access rights—what you can do to a file—and a set of deny modes—what you can't do to a file. File sharing is supported under Wabi software on Solaris platforms only, and is disabled by default.

These two features are explained in more detail below, and are summarized in Table 6-3 on page 171.

File Locking

Not all applications use file locking; for those that do, the sequence of events is basically as follows: When you open a file, or more commonly, when you access a portion of a file—for example, a database record—the application you are using automatically requests from the operating system a *file lock*. This file lock prevents other people from modifying the same portion of the file on which you are working; depending on how the lock is requested, someone else may still be able to work on a different portion of the same file. When you close the portion of the file on which you are working, the file lock is automatically cleared so other users can subsequently modify that portion of the file. The important thing here is that this all happens automatically; you need not dirty your hands to enable the locking feature under Wabi.

Without going into the gory technical details, it is sufficient to say that
Wabi software translates DOS-style lock requests made by your Windows
application into UNIX-style lock requests that are then made to the UNIX
lock daemon. In the Solaris environment, this lock daemon is called
`lockd`. Wabi software can translate lock requests on all platforms with
which Wabi is compatible.

There is, unfortunately, a catch in this automated rosy picture....
Not all UNIX file systems support lock requests. For example, lock
requests for files on a PCFS (DOS) partition will fail, which means that
you will not be able to access your file or database record.

In the context of using Wabi software, the workaround is to disable file
locking by setting the `WABI_NOLOCK` environment variable in the
command shell from which you start Wabi. For example, in the C
shell, enter the following command before starting the Wabi program:

```
setenv WABI_NOLOCK
```

Use this variable with caution, however, because it disables file
locking *throughout* Wabi, not just on DOS partitions. This opens the
door for you and your co-workers to handily trash files with
simultaneous writes.

Only set the `WABI_NOLOCK` environment variable if you are
encountering errors when trying to access files on DOS partitions.
Remember, many Windows applications don't make lock requests,
which means that you will never encounter errors, even when
accessing DOS partition files.

File Sharing

File sharing controls access and modification to files as a whole. Compare
this to file locking, which is usually used on only portions of a file. Under
DOS, file sharing is implemented by a terminate-and-stay-resident (TSR)
program named `SHARE.EXE`.

There is no direct equivalent to `SHARE.EXE` in the UNIX world; similar to
file locking support, Wabi software translates `SHARE.EXE` functions into a
combination of UNIX functions related to a UNIX lock manager. For a
variety of reasons, however, file sharing translation under Wabi software
is a far more cumbersome (that is, computationally intensive) process
than file lock translation. Because of this, file sharing is disabled by
default under Wabi. Also note that file sharing is supported under Wabi
only on the Solaris platform.

Wabi software does not actually use SHARE.EXE; calls from Windows applications to SHARE.EXE are intercepted and translated directly by Wabi. However, some Windows applications, for example, Microsoft Word for Windows 6.0, require the presence of the SHARE.EXE file in order to run. To satisfy such applications, when you install Windows with the Wabi Windows install program (see page 114), a file named SHARE.EXE is created in your Windows directory. Careful readers will note that this SHARE.EXE file is 0 bytes; it is a dummy placeholder put there solely to fool persnickety applications. Also note that a popular SHARE.EXE replacement, VSHARE.386, is a virtual device driver, and is therefore not supported under Wabi software.

 Solaris 2.5 software includes a new implementation of NFS, called NFS3, with which Wabi file sharing is not compatible. You should therefore not enable file sharing on drives mounted under the Solaris 2.5 operating environment using NFS3. NFS3 support is planned for future releases of Wabi software.

 If you really, really must, you can enable file sharing under Solaris 2.5 by forcing the operating system to not use NFS3 on selected drives. To do this, edit your /etc/vfstab file to include the statement vers=2 in the mount options field for the NFS file system from which you want to connect a Wabi drive using file sharing. This is not guaranteed to work, however, and it's certainly not for the faint-of-heart, so we're not going to say any more about it....

The Synopsis

Table 6-3 summarizes various aspects of file locking and file sharing features under Wabi.

Table 6-3   File Locking and File Sharing Under Wabi

Feature	File Locking	File Sharing
Description	Restrict access to file regions	Control access to entire files
Platforms	All Wabi platforms	Solaris platform only
Default	Enabled	Disabled
Restrictions	Not supported on all UNIX partitions (for example, PCFS)	Not compatible with NFS3 in Solaris 2.5

Using File Locking and File Sharing

As mentioned earlier, to use file locking features under Wabi, you do not need to do anything. If your Windows application uses file locking, it will be invoked automatically by the application. You can disable file locking by setting the `WABI_NOLOCK` environment variable—but be careful! (See the warning on page 170.)

By contrast, you enable file sharing on a drive-by-drive basis, using the Wabi Configuration Manager Drive Connections dialog box (page 162). Remember, though, because of the performance penalty sharing induces, you should only enable file sharing for drives on which you really need it.

When you enable file sharing on a given drive, every file opened on that drive comes under the jurisdiction of the file-sharing mechanism. This means that for every open file, the Wabi program creates a share lock, which takes time. Share locks are cleared when you close a file or exit the Wabi program.

Unlike file locks, share locks are not automatically removed when Wabi terminates unexpectedly. If this happens, you may have to clear share locks manually. On the Solaris platform (the only platform on which Wabi supports file sharing), the Wabi package includes a UNIX program that clears all locks. This program, named `clearlocks`, should be used with care.

The `clearlocks` program removes all file, record, and share locks between two machines, regardless of who created or who "owns" the locks. To run `clearlocks` on the machine on which the Wabi program terminated unexpectedly, enter the command `clearlocks` followed by the host name of the system on which the shared files are located.

➤ *To manually clear all file and share locks on a Wabi drive*

1. **Become** root **on your system.**
   You will need to enter your root password. If you do not know this password, ask your system administrator for assistance.

2. **Enter the following command:**

   ```
   /opt/SUNWwabi/drvr/clearlocks  hostname
   ```

   where *hostname* is the name of the NFS server on which you want to clear all file and share locks. Note that this server may different than the machine on which you are running Wabi.

3. **Exit your root session.**
   Use the exit command. You are returned to your normal user prompt.

➤ *To enable file sharing on a Wabi drive*

1. **Choose the Drives tool in Wabi Configuration Manager.**
   The Drive Connections dialog box is displayed.

2. **Select the drive letter of the drive on which you want to enable sharing.**
   The drive path is displayed in the Directory Path list.

3. **Select the Sharing Enabled check box.**

4. **Choose OK to save your selection and exit the dialog.**
   Sharing is enabled for the selected drive.

Wabi Network Drives

In the Wabi environment, the directory to which a drive letter is connected may reside on a local disk or on a remote disk on the network. To Wabi, and to UNIX programs in general, it does not matter where a directory path leads; the underlying operating system and network software keep track of file systems.

However, it does matter to some Microsoft Windows applications whether a given drive letter is a local drive, or is located somewhere else on the network. These applications may check to see if a particular drive letter is local or networked, and may behave differently in each case. For example, when you install an application onto a drive, the installation program may try to determine if the drive is networked. If it finds that the drive is networked, the installation program may present you with a number of installation options specific to servers, such as the location of shared program files and user directories. Also, some applications may not use file locking if they detect that the drive is local.

Wabi lets you control how the Wabi drives appear to applications. The Drive Connections dialog includes a **Network Drive** option that, when enabled, specifies that the selected drive is seen by applications as a network drive. When this option is not enabled, the drive appears to be a local hard drive to a Windows application running under Wabi.

Whether a drive is actually on a local UNIX file system or a remote file system doesn't matter to Wabi. You can make your Wabi drives appear to be local or networked regardless of where they are really located. Remember, though, that some Windows applications do not allow themselves to be run from networked drives. See the documentation included with your application to determine whether it can be used from a network drive.

By default, Wabi makes each drive appear as a network drive. In most cases you should leave the **Network Drive** option enabled so applications that can use file locking will detect a network environment and lock files as you open them. However, if you install or use an application that requires a local drive, you can disable the **Network Drive** option.

➤ **To set network drive status on a Wabi drive**

1. **Open Windows Control Panel.**
2. **Open Wabi Configuration Manager.**
3. **Choose the Drives tool.**
   The Drive Connections dialog box is displayed.
4. **Select the drive that you want to use as a network drive.**
   The drive is displayed in the Directory Path for Selected Drive list.
5. **Select the Network Drive check box to enable it.**
6. **Choose OK to save your selection and exit the dialog.**
   The drive now appears to applications as a network drive, whether it is connected to a local directory or a remote directory.

➤ **To set local drive status on a Wabi drive**

1. **Open Windows Control Panel.**
2. **Open Wabi Configuration Manager.**
3. **Choose the Drives tool.**
   The Drive Connections dialog box is displayed.
4. **Select the drive that you want to use as a local drive.**
   The drive is displayed in the Directory Path for Selected Drive list.
5. **Deselect the Network Drive check box to disable it.**
6. **Choose OK to save your selection and exit the dialog.**
   The drive now appears to applications as a local drive, whether it is connected to a local directory or a remote directory.

CD-ROM Drives

Wabi lets you access a CD-ROM device, provided the CD-ROM uses a media format the native operating system recognizes. For example, since the Solaris operating system can read only CD-ROMs that use the ISO, Rock Ridge and High Sierra File System (HSFS) formats, the Wabi program has this same limitation.

Connecting to a CD-ROM drive with Wabi is much like connecting any other Wabi drive. You mount the device on a mount directory in the native UNIX operating system, then assign a drive letter to the mount directory in the Drive Connections dialog in Wabi Configuration Manager.

You cannot use a CD-ROM drive to play music CDs or video laser disks under Wabi, but you may be able to play Microsoft Windows waveform files (`.WAV`) on some platforms. Wabi 2.1 on Solaris platforms supports the playing of `.WAV` and `.AVI` files, as described in "Using Multimedia Features" on page 235.

If you install an application that uses Microsoft CD-ROM extensions, and you have purchased the rights to use that application on your local system (not on a network), you may not be able to run your CD-ROM application.

This limitation is due to a protection mechanism that Microsoft Corporation has incorporated in much of its CD-ROM-based application software. This mechanism ensures that a CD-ROM application purchased for use on a local system is not capable of running on a network. Because the Wabi program accesses a local CD-ROM drive through a path in your operating system, it appears to a CD-ROM application running under the Wabi program that the application is being used on a network, not on a local CD-ROM drive.

Unfortunately, this limitation cannot be overcome by disabling the Network Drive option in the Drive Connections dialog box.

➤ *To access a CD-ROM drive through Wabi*

The specific commands required may vary, depending on your operating system. Some operating systems automatically make a compatible CD-ROM available when you insert the CD-ROM into the drive—for example, Solaris Volume Manager (vold) does this. If your operating system does this, begin with Step 7.

1. **Open an operating system command window.**
2. **Change to the root (/) directory.**
3. **Become superuser (su).**
4. **Create a directory named cdrom.**
5. **Mount the CD-ROM.**
   Make sure you can read the CD-ROM from the operating system before proceeding. For example, try to do an ls command on the /cdrom directory.
6. **Exit from superuser status.**
7. **Start Wabi, if it is not already running.**
8. **Open the Drives tool in Wabi Configuration Manager.**
9. **Select an unassigned drive letter in the Drive Connections dialog box.**
10. **Depending on whether you are using volume manager, enter one of the following in the** Directory Path for Selected Drive **list:**

    a. **If you are using volume manager, enter:**

    `/cdrom/volname`

    where *volname* is the volume label of your CD-ROM. Volume manager automatically creates this directory for you.

    b. **If you are not using volume manager, enter:**

    `/cdrom`

    If you mounted the CD-ROM in a directory other than /cdrom, use that name instead.

11. **Choose Connect.**
    The drive letter is assigned to the CD-ROM directory.
12. **Enable the Network Drive option, if desired.**
    See "Wabi Network Drives" on page 174 for more information.
13. **Choose OK to save the drive connection and exit the dialog.**
    Access the CD-ROM through the drive letter you assigned. For example, if you connected F: to /cdrom, you can run the setup program on the CD-ROM with the command F:\setup.

Chapter 7
Managing
Printers

You've worked, you've slaved; you now have a 300-page report, or a 17,000-cell spreadsheet, or a 150-slide presentation. You've got to show it to someone, you've got to get feedback, you've got to *print it....*

> *...a thick old-fashioned heavy book with a clasp is the finest thing in the world to throw at a noisy cat.*
>
> – Mark Twain, ca. 1890, (Replying to a lady, regarding the usefulness of books as gifts)

In This Chapter

About Printing Under Wabi

Wabi print functions bridge the gap between an application's printing method and the printing mechanism of your UNIX operating system. This all happens transparently under Wabi—once you establish Wabi printer settings and connections, you can simply issue print commands from within your Windows applications, just as you would under "regular" Microsoft Windows.

Under Wabi, when you issue a print command from within a Windows application, the application passes your print request to a Wabi or Windows printer driver. Up to this point, the print process is the same as printing in the Microsoft Windows environment. However, instead of sending the print request to a DOS LPT port, the Wabi program redirects the request to the native UNIX print spooling mechanism on your system, along with the name of a UNIX printer and a UNIX print command.

Your UNIX printing system processes print jobs from all applications you run on your desktop, whether they are running under Wabi or another UNIX application. UNIX printing is performed in the background, so you never have to stop your work while a print request is carried out.

You manage printers, print queues, and print jobs with the same UNIX printer management utilities and commands you normally use to manage printing on your UNIX system.

You do not need (and cannot use) a separate tool such as the Windows Print Manager to manage printing under Wabi. This is not a disadvantage, however, because UNIX-based print spoolers generally perform better and faster than Windows Print Manager.

Supported Printer Models

Wabi can use the following printer types:

- Text-only
- PostScript
- HP LaserJet™ III series
- Epson® FX, LX, and MX series

Wabi supplies and installs Wabi printer drivers for the HP LaserJet III and Epson printers. The Wabi program also installs two of the printer drivers supplied with Microsoft Windows: Generic/Text Only and PostScript Printer (using the Apple® LaserWriter® IINTX description).

Wabi can also use the additional PostScript printer descriptions supplied with Microsoft Windows; you can install these through the Windows Control Panel Printers tool, just as you would in Microsoft Windows under DOS.

For HP LaserJet III and Epson printers, you can use only the Wabi-supplied drivers. The drivers supplied with Microsoft Windows for these printers are not supported under Wabi 2.0 and 2.1. This is scheduled to change in Wabi 2.2, however.

Before Printing From Wabi

Before you can print from Windows applications running under Wabi, you must have access to a UNIX printer. You (or your system administrator) must configure your operating system environment to recognize the printer. If you can print on a printer by using a print command (such as `lp` or `lpr`) under UNIX, you will be able to access the printer under Wabi.

Configuring UNIX Printers

Normally, you do not need to do anything special to your UNIX printer configuration in order to print from Wabi. However, if you use one printer most often, you should designate it as your UNIX default printer. That way, the Wabi program will automatically send all its print jobs to that printer unless you specify a different printer.

If you want to print to an HP LaserJet III printer on an HP-UX print server, the printer definition on the server should be set up for a "dumb device" to prevent filtering by the print server.

Refer to your operating system documentation for more information about installing and accessing UNIX printers.

Default Wabi Printer Configuration

Wabi configures itself automatically to print in many UNIX environments without any additional action on your part. By default, Wabi assigns the PostScript Printer driver to port LPT1, and connects LPT1 to your UNIX default printer. These settings work for printing to PostScript printers in most situations. However, you can also use the Microsoft Windows Control Panel and Wabi Configuration Manager to change the default printing setup if you like. Note that on the Solaris platform, the Apple LaserWriter II NTX description for the PostScript driver is used by default.

Changing Print Settings

If the default Wabi print configuration is not appropriate for your needs, you can change the print settings in Microsoft Windows Control Panel and Wabi Configuration Manager.

Windows Control Panel Printers Dialog

You use the Windows Control Panel Printer dialog box (Figure 7-1) for selecting all print settings except those pertaining to the connection between Wabi LPT ports and UNIX printers.

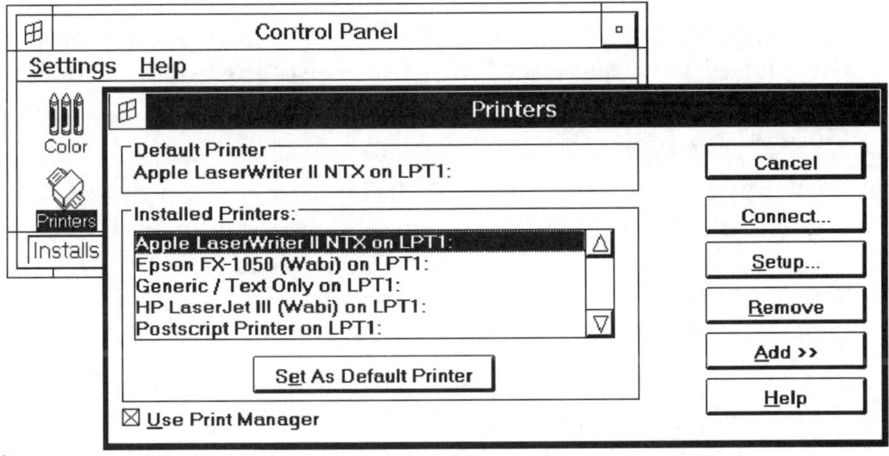

Figure 7-1   Windows Control Panel Printers Dialog Box

In the Wabi environment, you use the Control Panel Printers dialog to:

- Install a different printer description for a PostScript, HP LaserJet III, or Epson printer

- Change the printer setup of an installed printer

- Specify a new Wabi default printer

- Set up to print to a file

- Assign a directly connected serial printer to a COM port

- Assign a printer to a different LPT port

You perform these tasks in the Wabi environment the same way you would in the Microsoft Windows environment. The Printers dialog box and related dialog boxes work as they do in Microsoft Windows, with the following exceptions:

- Microsoft Windows Print Manager, whether enabled or disabled in the dialog box, does not run in the Wabi environment.

- Although you may be able to add an unsupported driver from the List of Printers, the Wabi program will not be able to use it. You can use only those drivers described in "Supported Printer Models" on page 181.

- Several items in the Connect dialog box, which opens when you choose the Connect button, are not applicable in the Wabi environment. The settings are: Device Not Selected, Transmission Retry, and Fast Printing Direct to Port. In Microsoft Windows under DOS, these settings affect Print Manager and DOS interrupts.

- The Network button located in the Connect dialog box opens the Port Selection dialog box in Wabi Configuration Manager, which you can use to connect a Wabi LPT port to UNIX printer.

Printer Output Connections Dialog

Use the Wabi Configuration Manager Ports tool to access the Printer Output Connections dialog box. This dialog box lets you connect an LPT port to a printer defined in your UNIX environment, and specify the UNIX print command to use for printing to that printer.

When you open the Ports tool, the Port Selection dialog box is displayed. Selecting the LPT port to which you want to connect, and then choosing the Connect button, displays the Printer Output Connection dialog box (Figure 7-2).

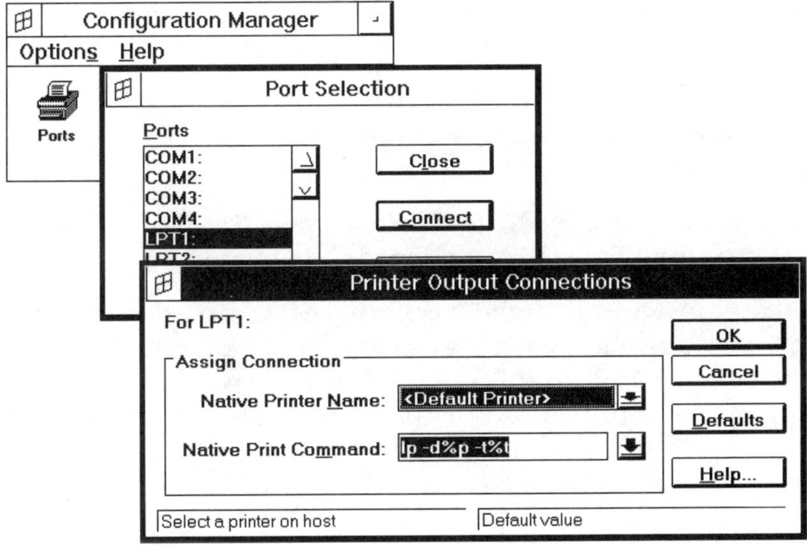

Figure 7-2   Wabi Printer Output Connections Dialog Box

Your UNIX operating system recognizes and addresses printers by their names; the implication here is that every printer you can use must have a name. In addition, your operating system uses a specific command to initiate a print job. When you connect a printer to a Wabi LPT port, you indicate the name of the printer you want to assign to the port and the command required to start a print job.

As illustrated in Figure 7-2, the Printer Output Connections dialog box contains a pair of functions in the Assign Connection group. The settings you specify in this group apply to the LPT port whose name appears in the upper-left corner of the dialog box.

The Assign Connection group contains two fields with drop-down lists:

- **Native Printer Name** – Displays a list containing the names of all the printers your system is configured to recognize and which you can access. The first name, `<DefaultPrinter>`, is a variable that specifies your current system default printer, which is the printer used when you print without specifying a printer name. When you assign a port to `<DefaultPrinter>`, print jobs sent to that port go to the current system default printer. If you change the default printer on your system, the Wabi program immediately uses the new default printer for `<DefaultPrinter>`.

- **Native Print Command** – Displays a list of operating system print commands.

To connect a printer to a Wabi LPT port, open the Native Printer Name list and select the name of the printer you want to use.

In most cases, you will not have to modify the Native Print Command entry. The default entry supplied with Wabi is usually correct. However, you can select the entry field and type in a command if you want. You can change the native print command to any command that you know works in your operating system to get the output you want from the printer. See your operating system documentation for information about commands used for printing.

After you select a printer by name and choose OK in the Printer Output Connections dialog box, the printer name and command are assigned to the selected LPT port.

The Defaults button in the Printer Output Connections dialog box restores the Wabi program default printer connection. This connection assigns the default printer specified in the Printer Settings dialog box to Wabi port LPT1. The default also specifies a generic print command.

Wabi 2: Opening Windows

The default print command includes two placeholders for parameters used with arguments to the print command:

- **%p** – Wabi replaces %p with a printer name. If the printer name is <DefaultPrinter>, Wabi omits the argument using %p when a print command is issued to the operating system. This makes the operating system use its default printer.

- **%t** – Wabi replaces %t with the print job title. Some operating systems require a print job title statement.

Using Other PostScript Printers

If you find that the printer output is not exactly what you want when you use the PostScript Printer driver, you should install the PostScript printer that matches your PostScript printer model. This lets Windows applications tailor themselves, according to your printer's capabilities, for paper size, multiple paper trays, envelopes, and so on. It also gives the application access to all the fonts on the printer. If your PostScript printer is a SPARCprinter, you should install the Apple LaserWriter II NTX printer driver.

In Microsoft Windows and in the Wabi program, all PostScript printers listed in the Control Panel use the same driver file, pscript.drv. However, each listed printer has its own printer description, which provides detailed information about the printer's capabilities. When you select and install a particular model of PostScript printer, you are installing the printer description, not the driver.

Using Epson and HP LaserJet III Printers

If you want to print to an HP LaserJet III or Epson printer, you must use the HP LaserJet III (Wabi) or Epson FX-1050 (Wabi) printer drivers. Wabi installs these drivers in your Wabi environment and assigns them to LPT1 the first time you start the Wabi program.

You must use the printers that include (Wabi) in the name in the List of Printers. The Wabi printer descriptions for Epson and HP LaserJet III printers are at the top of the List of Printers in the Control Panel Printers dialog, as shown in Figure 7-3. Other drivers in the list use the Microsoft Windows version of the drivers, which are not supported in the Wabi program.

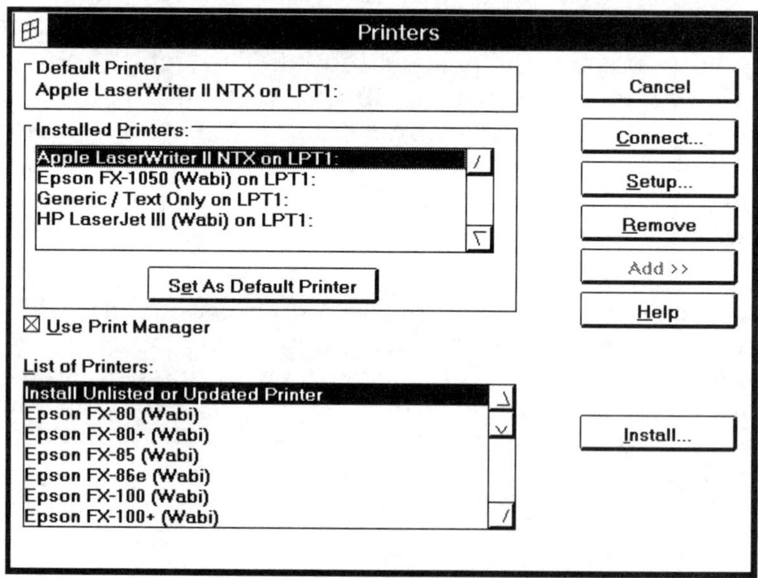

Figure 7-3   Printers Dialog Showing Wabi Printer Descriptions

Epson Models

The Epson printer driver provided with Wabi software supports many Epson printer models. If your Epson printer is not an FX-1050, you can install a printer description that matches your particular printer model. Table 7-1 lists the Epson printer models supported by the Wabi Epson printer driver:

Table 7-1   Epson Printer Models Supported by Wabi Printer Driver

FX-80	FX-80+	FX-85	FX-86e
FX-100	FX-100+	FX-185	FX-286
FX-286e	FX-800	FX-850	FX-1000
FX-1050	FX	LX	MX

If you have an Epson PostScript printer, you should use the appropriate PostScript driver, not the Epson FX-1050 driver.

HP LaserJet Models

The HP LaserJet III printer driver provided with Wabi also supports the LaserJet IIID and LaserJet IIIP models. If you have these models, you can install a printer description that matches them. The HP LaserJet III driver can also be used with LaserJet IV printers, although the driver may not be able to use all the LaserJet IV's capabilities. The driver cannot be used with LaserJet II printers. Note that the `HP LaserJet III (Wabi)` driver does not support font downloading with the HP Font Installer.

Epson or LaserJet III System Default Printer

Wabi is configured by default to print to PostScript printers. If you want your system default to be an HP LaserJet III or Epson printer, use Windows Control Panel to change the default printer setting to `HP LaserJet III (Wabi)` or `Epson FX-1050 (Wabi)`.

➤ *To install printer drivers for PostScript, Epson, or HP LaserJet III printers*

1. **Open Windows Control Panel.**
2. **Open the Printers tool.**
   The Printers dialog box is displayed.
3. **Choose the Add button.**
   The dialog box expands to include the List of Printers and an Install button.
4. **Select a printer driver appearing in the List of Printers.**
   You must choose either a PostScript printer model, or an HP LaserJet or Epson model that includes `(Wabi)` in the name. The Wabi HP LaserJet and Epson drivers are at the top of the list of printers, and are not listed alphabetically with the Windows printer drivers.
5. **Choose Install.**
   If you choose a Wabi HP LaserJet III or Wabi Epson driver, the printer is displayed in the list of Installed Printers immediately, and you can close the dialog box.

   If you choose a PostScript driver, such as TI® microLaser™ PS17, the Install Driver dialog tells you to insert the diskette containing a file needed for the printer.
6. **Insert the requested diskette and choose OK.**
   If your Microsoft Windows files are on a network drive, use the Browse button to locate the requested file, and choose OK.

   When installation is complete, the printer is displayed in the list of Installed Printers.
7. **Choose Close to exit the dialog.**

Using Text-Only Printers

You can print to text-only printers (such as dot-matrix printers) by using
the Generic/Text Only driver supplied with Microsoft Windows. You can
also use this driver to print plain text (not graphics) to most printers. If
your printer is not supported in the Wabi environment, you can assign
the Generic/Text Only driver to it and print draft-quality documents
without graphics.

Note that if your application lets you save a document as an ASCII text
file, you probably can print a text file without the generic printer driver.
PostScript printers can print text-only documents if they are configured
in the operating system to accept simple text input.

Changing the Wabi Default Printer

You set your Wabi default printer the same way you set your Microsoft
Windows default printer; that is, by using the Windows Control Panel.
The Set as Default Printer button in the Printers dialog box sets the selected
printer as the default printer.

Your Wabi default printer should connect to the UNIX printer you use
most frequently. For example, if most of your printing is done on an
Apple LaserWriter II NTX printer named speedy, attach the Apple
LaserWriter II NTX printer driver to a port such as LPT1, and then set
this printer as your default. Then use Wabi Configuration Manager to
connect Apple LaserWriter II NTX on LPT1 to the speedy printer. When
you print within an application, the application sends the job to LPT1,
and the Wabi program redirects the print job to speedy.

➢ *To define the Wabi default printer*

    1. Open Windows Control Panel.

    2. Open the Printers tool.
       The Printers dialog box is displayed.

    3. Select a driver/port combination in the Installed Printers list.

4. **Choose the Set As Default Printer button.**
The selected driver/port combination is assigned as the default, and is displayed in the Default Printer field.

5. **Choose Close to save your selection and exit the dialog.**
Alternatively, choose Cancel to close the dialog box without saving your changes.

Connecting to a UNIX Default Printer

You may find it convenient to use the same default printer for both your UNIX and Wabi print jobs. The Wabi program is set up this way initially. If you have changed your print setup, do the following to assign both defaults to the same physical printer:

- Use your operating system's printer management methods (UNIX commands or utilities) to assign a system default printer.

- Use Wabi Configuration Manager to connect LPT1 to <DefaultPrinter>.

- Use Windows Control Panel to connect a printer to LPT1 and set the printer as your Wabi default printer.

➢ *To connect a Wabi printer port to a UNIX printer*

1. **Open Windows Control Panel.**
2. **Open Wabi Configuration Manager.**
3. **Choose the Ports tool.**
The Port Selection dialog box is displayed.
4. **Select the LPT port to which you want to connect.**
The selected port is highlighted.
5. **Choose the Connect button.**
The Printer Output Connections dialog box is displayed.

6. **In the Assign Connection group, open the Native Printer Name list and select a printer name.**
   The selected name is highlighted.

   Select `<DefaultPrinter>` if you want to connect to your operating system's default printer.

   You must designate a default printer at the operating system level before you can use `<DefaultPrinter>`.

7. **In the Assign Connection group, open the Native Print Command list and select a printer command.**
   The command is highlighted.

   Alternatively, type in a different print command in the field. If you make no selection, the default print command is used.

8. **Choose OK.**
   The printer name and command you selected are assigned to the Wabi printer and port. The Printer Output Connections dialog box closes.

9. **Choose Close in the Port Selection dialog box.**
   The Port Selection dialog box closes.

➤ *To restore printer name and command defaults*

1. **Open Windows Control Panel.**
2. **Open Wabi Configuration Manager.**
3. **Choose the Ports tool.**
   The Port Selection dialog box is displayed.
4. **Select the LPT port you want to reset to the default values.**
5. **Choose the Connect button.**
   The Printer Output Connections dialog box is displayed.
6. **Choose the Defaults button.**
   Default Native Printer Name and Native Print Command entries replace existing settings.
7. **Choose OK to save your settings.**
   Alternatively, choose Cancel to exit the dialog box without saving your changes.

Printing to a File

You can set up a Wabi printer so that all print requests that are sent to the printer go to a file on disk instead of being printed. To do this, you can connect the Wabi printer to the FILE "port" instead of an LPT port. Use Windows Control Panel to do this.

You will be prompted for a file name whenever you print to this printer from a Windows application.

Some applications allow you to print a single print job to a file using a Print Setup option within the application's menus. If your application has this option and you only occasionally print to a file, it may not be necessary to set up a printer in this way.

Printing Directly to a Serial Printer

Within the UNIX environment, you can configure a serial printer so that you can send print requests through the UNIX print system. You can print from the Wabi environment to a serial printer configured in the UNIX print system, just as with any other printer configured in the operating system—that is, through a Wabi LPT port connected to the UNIX printer.

However, if you have connected a serial printer to a serial port on your UNIX system, you can also print directly to the printer through Wabi. To do this, first use Wabi Configuration Manager to make sure a Wabi COM port is connected to the serial device that controls the UNIX serial port. Then use the Control Panel to connect an appropriate printer driver to the COM port. See "COM Port Configuration" on page 200 for the steps required to connect a COM port to a UNIX serial device.

The printer's documentation should tell you what to use for COM port settings such as baud rate, flow control, stop bits, and suchlike. You should configure the port through the Windows Control Panel Ports dialog boxes.

Printing directly to a serial port generally is not recommended because it bypasses the UNIX print spooling system. This means you cannot use your usual print control commands or utilities to cancel or pause the print request. Also, printing directly to a printer is no faster than printing through the operating system's print system, and you must wait for the print job to finish before continuing to work in your applications.

Chapter 8
Managing COM Ports

Sometimes you need to go beyond your local- or wide-area network to access data or services. This is the primary use for COM ports— otherwise known as serial ports.

Banality is a symptom of non-communication. Men hide behind their clichés.

– Eugène Ionesco, *Notes and Counter-Notes, pt. 4,; "Further Notes, 1960,"* 1962

In This Chapter

About COM Ports Under Wabi

COM, or *serial*, ports provide a means by which you can connect to data sources or devices that are not on your local- or wide-area network. For example, you could use standard telephone services, via a modem connected to a serial port, to "dial in" to an information service like CompuServe®. Some printers, called serial printers, also use COM ports (rather than LPT ports) to connect to your computer.

 LPT ports are commonly used for connecting to printers, although some printers can also use a serial connection. Chapter 7, "Managing Printers" explains how to work with printers connected to either an LPT or COM port.

COM ports handle data across a single wire, one bit at a time. Compare this to LPT (parallel) ports, which handle data eight bits at a time. The advantage to COM ports over LPT ports (at least until recently) is that they can handle such communications in both directions—coming and going—and with an extremely wide variety of devices. This is where things get sticky, however.

To manage bidirectional communications, a COM port must be configured so that it can recognize when it's supposed to be talking and when it's supposed to be listening. Moreover, the COM ports on both ends of a communication link must agree upon the data format with which they are talking. Hence, there are several communications parameters, listed in Table 8-1, that must be identical for both COM ports in a given data communications link. You will encounter these terms often in the context of serial communications, so it is useful to review them here.

Table 8-1   Common Serial Data Communications Parameters

Parameter	Purpose
Baud rate	The speed at which data is transferred; roughly equivalent (I hear the engineers squirming) to bits per second. Named after the French engineer, Jean Maurice Emile Baudot.
Data bits	The number of sequential bits in a data stream that represent actual data, rather than data delimiters; provides a standard for dividing a stream of data bits into discrete chunks.
Stop bits	Related to data bits; the number of delimiter bits inserted between chunks of data bits in a data stream.
Parity	Specifies how the binary value of bits in a data stream are interpreted. That is, if a data stream is represented as a series of on/off electrical pulses, parity specifies whether the "on" pulse represents a binary 0 or 1.
Flow control	The pacing of data transfer; ensures that the receiving device can absorb the data sent before more is sent.

Under UNIX, COM ports are associated with serial device files, similar to LPT device files (described in Chapter 7). These device files provide the means by which the operating system can communicate with serial devices, like modems and printers, attached to the COM ports.

Wabi supports up to four COM ports—COM1, COM2, COM3, and COM4—although your computer probably has fewer than four ports available. Microsoft Windows under DOS theoretically supports four COM ports also, but does not do it particularly well. The problem is that under DOS, COM1 and COM3 share one Interrupt Request Line (IRQ), while COM2 and COM4 share another. Without going into all the details, two devices cannot use the same IRQ at the same time; Microsoft Windows tends to choke when it encounters such conflicts. This is much less of a problem under Wabi, because UNIX does not work with IRQs in the same way.

COM Port Configuration

Before you can use a COM port, you must be able to access the serial device files located in your UNIX operating system. Your operating system documentation contains instructions for accessing such device files. Once you have access to a serial device in your UNIX system, you can configure a Wabi COM port to access the device.

When a COM port is being used by another UNIX program, the port is not available to Wabi until that other program releases it. This could occur, for example, if your mouse connects through COM1, or if you are connected to a remote system with the UNIX `tip` command.

Configuring a COM port is a two-part process:

- Specify COM port settings through Windows Control Panel.

- Connect the COM port to an operating system serial device file through Wabi Configuration Manager.

COM Port Settings in Control Panel

You'll find the default Wabi COM port settings, listed in Table 8-2, appropriate for most serial communications situations. When using a COM port, try the default settings first. If these settings do not work, change them as necessary to establish and maintain communication.

Table 8-2   Default Wabi COM Port Settings

Parameter	Setting
Baud Rate	9600
Data Bits	8
Stop Bits	1
Parity	None
Flow Control	Xon/Xoff

 Many applications automatically adjust COM port settings by determining the settings required, overriding the current COM port settings.

You can change COM port settings with the Windows Control Panel Fonts tool, using the Settings for COM*x* dialog box, shown in Figure 8-1. You access this dialog box by opening the Control Panel Ports tool and selecting a COM port in the Ports dialog box.

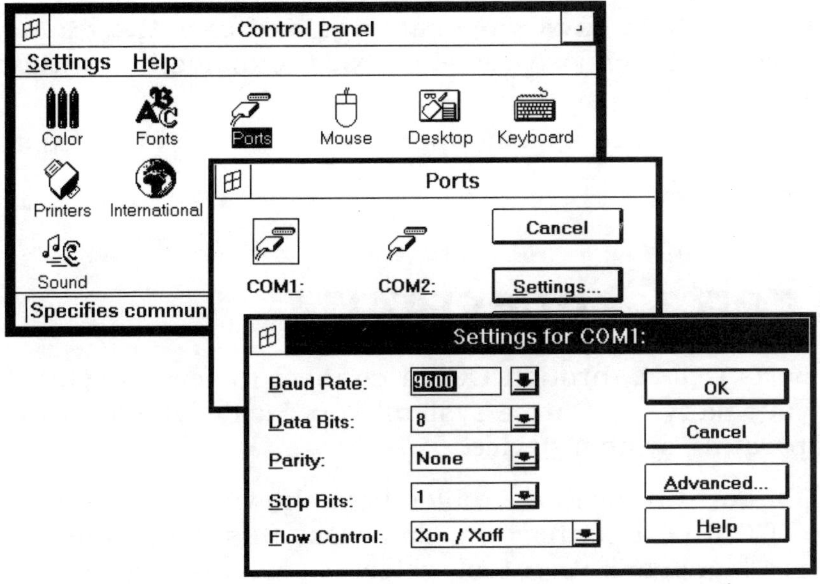

Figure 8-1   Windows Control Panel Port Settings Dialog Box

You change COM port settings under Wabi the same way you do in Microsoft Windows. The Settings for COMx dialog box works under Wabi as it does in Microsoft Windows, with the following exceptions:

- Hardware Flow Control is not supported. You should select either None or Xon/Xoff flow control.

- The Advanced Settings dialog, which you open by choosing the Advanced button, has no meaning in the Wabi environment; Base I/O Port Address and Interrupt Request Line (IRQ) are dependent on the operating system.

1. **Open Windows Control Panel.**
2. **Open the Ports tool.**
3. **Select a COM port and choose** Settings.
   The Settings for COM*x*: dialog box is displayed.
4. **Select settings for Baud Rate, Data Bits, Parity, Stop Bits, and Flow Control, as desired.**
   The settings you select must be the same as those for the device with which you want to communicate.
5. **Choose OK to save your settings and exit the dialog.**
   Alternatively, choose Cancel to exit the dialog box without changing settings.

   The settings you specify apply to the selected COM port.

COM Port Connections

The COM ports COM1 through COM4 connect to serial device drivers located in your native operating system. You decide which port to connect to which operating system device.

Use the COM Port Connections dialog box, shown in Figure 8-2, to make or change a COM port connection. To access this dialog box, open Configuration Manager's Ports tool, select a port, and choose Connect.

Wabi supplies a default COM Device Driver name for each COM port. You can change this default by selecting another name from the COM Device Driver list. This list displays the available device drivers for the port selected in the Port Selection dialog box. Open the COM Device Driver list to view the device driver names. You change a COM port's connection by selecting a different device driver name from the list.

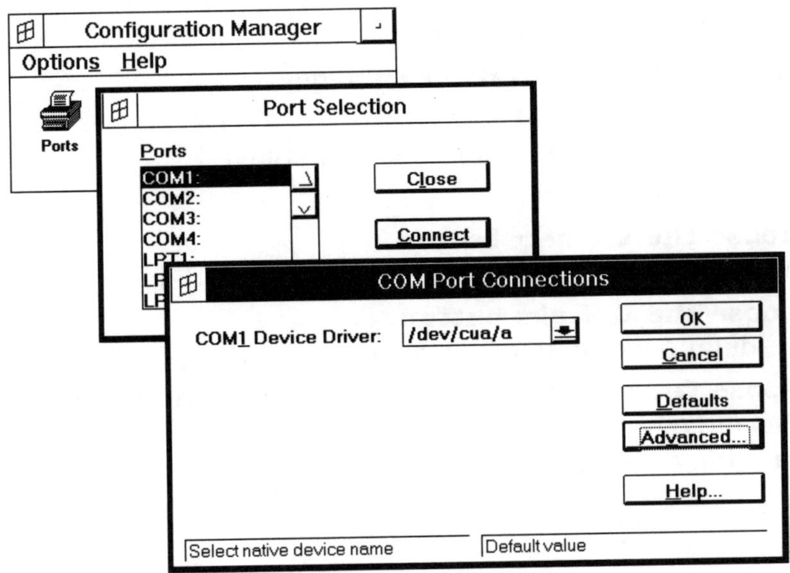

Figure 8-2   Wabi COM Ports Connection Dialog Box

➢ *To connect a COM port to a serial device file*

1. **Open Windows Control Panel.**
2. **Open Wabi Configuration Manager.**
3. **Open the Ports tool.**
   The Port Selection dialog box is displayed.
4. **Select a COM port.**
5. **Choose the Connect button.**
   The COM Port Connections dialog box is displayed.
6. **Open the Device Driver list.**
   A list of available serial devices for the selected port is displayed.
7. **Select a device name.**
8. **Choose OK to save your settings and exit the dialog.**
   Alternatively, choose Cancel to exit the dialog box without changing settings.

   The selected device is connected to the port.

➤ *To reset a COM port connection to the default*

1. **Open Windows Control Panel.**
2. **Open Wabi Configuration Manager.**
3. **Open the Ports tool.**
   The Port Selection dialog box is displayed.
4. **Select a COM port.**
5. **Choose the Connect button.**
   The COM Port Connections dialog box is displayed.
6. **Choose the Defaults button.**
   The default connection is restored for the port.
7. **Choose OK to save your settings and exit the dialog.**
   Alternatively, choose Cancel to exit the dialog box without changing settings.

Advanced COM Port Settings

Wabi searches for serial device directories and files based on default locations and file-naming patterns. In most cases, these defaults match the directories and naming patterns used by your operating system. In some cases, they may not.

For example, if you rename a serial device file using a nonstandard naming convention, the Wabi program will not be aware of the file. If you relocate a serial device to a directory not normally used to store it, the Wabi program will not know where to look for the device file.

When these situations occur, you must tell Wabi which directories to search and the naming patterns to look for when searching for serial device drivers. Think of these entries as "search templates" that are used whenever a device driver is called for.

You use the Advanced COM Port Options dialog box, shown in Figure 8-3, to provide Wabi with the information it needs to find and use serial devices named or located in a nonstandard manner. You access this dialog box by choosing the Advanced button in the COM Port Connections dialog box.

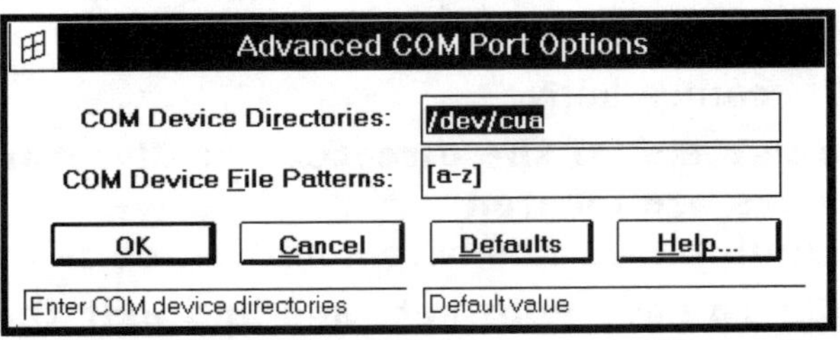

Figure 8-3   Wabi Advanced COM Port Options Dialog Box

You specify two settings in this dialog box:

- **COM Device Directories** – The list of UNIX directories in which Wabi searches for serial device drivers. You can include more than one directory in the list, with directory names separated by commas with no surrounding spaces.

- **COM Device File Patterns** – The device driver file-naming pattern. You can include more than one pattern in the list, with patterns separated by commas with no surrounding spaces.

  Wildcard characters are allowed in file pattern entries. An asterisk (*) can replace a group of characters, and a question mark (?) can replace a single character. You can indicate a range of possible values for a single character by using brackets. For example, you can use `[0-9]` to match a value from 0 through 9, or `[b-g]` to match a value from b through g. If you enter the pattern `tty[a-z]*`, Wabi finds file names such as `ttya`, `ttyb20`, or `ttyzxt23`, if they exist in the specified device directories.

➢ *To enter an alternate COM device directory*

1. **Open Windows Control Panel.**
2. **Open Wabi Configuration Manager.**
3. **Open the Ports tool.**
   The Port Selection dialog box is displayed.

4. **Select a COM port.**

5. **Choose the Connect button.**
    The COM Port Connections dialog box is displayed.

6. **Choose the Advanced button.**
    The Advanced COM Port Options dialog box is displayed.

7. **Select the COM Device Directories field.**
    The field becomes active.

8. **Type the name(s) of the directory or directories in which COM devices are located.**
    Separate multiple entries with commas; do not use spaces.

9. **Choose OK to save your settings and exit the dialog.**
    Alternatively, choose Cancel to exit the dialog box without changing settings.

    When you choose OK, Wabi validates your entry. If the entry is valid, the directories are searched each time you assign a device to a COM Port.

➤ *To enter an alternate COM device file pattern*

1. **Open Windows Control Panel.**

2. **Open Wabi Configuration Manager.**

3. **Open the Ports tool.**
    The Port Selection dialog box is displayed.

4. **Select a COM port.**

5. **Choose the Connect button.**
    The COM Port Connections dialog box is displayed.

6. **Choose the Advanced button.**
    The Advanced COM Port Options dialog box is displayed.

7. **Select the COM Device File Patterns field.**
    The field becomes active.

8. **Type one or more file patterns.**
    Separate multiple entries with commas; do not use spaces.

9. **Choose OK to save your settings and exit the dialog.**
    Alternatively, choose Cancel to exit the dialog box without changing settings.

    When you choose OK, Wabi validates your entry. If the entry is valid, Wabi searches for serial device files using the specified file-naming patterns.

➤ *To restore advanced COM port options defaults*

1. **Open Windows Control Panel.**
2. **Open Wabi Configuration Manager.**
3. **Open the Ports tool.**
   The Port Selection dialog box is displayed.
4. **Select a COM port.**
5. **Choose the Connect button.**
   The COM Port Connections dialog box is displayed.
6. **Choose the Advanced button.**
   The Advanced COM Port Options dialog box is displayed.
7. **Choose the Defaults button.**
   Default device directory and file pattern settings are restored.
8. **Choose OK to save your settings and exit the dialog.**
   Alternatively, choose Cancel to exit the dialog box without changing settings.

COM Ports and Printing

Wabi lets you print both to COM ports and LPT ports. However, when you print to a COM port, you bypass UNIX's print facility. This allows you to access a printer directly, but you lose the benefits of UNIX print spooling. Also, your printer must be physically connected to your workstation's serial port. For these reasons, it is generally best to use an LPT port for printing.

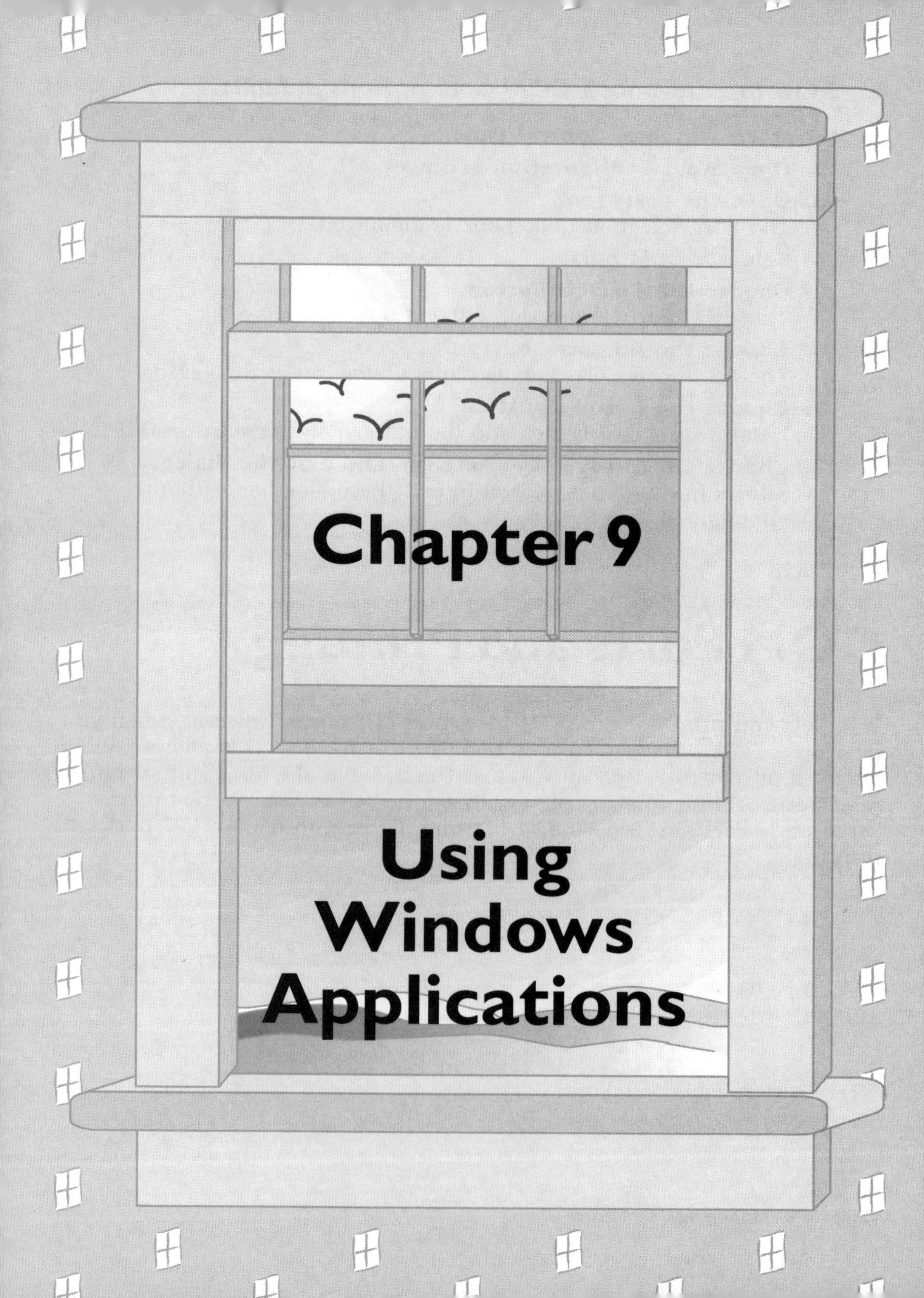

Chapter 9

Using
Windows
Applications

Now comes the moment for which we've all been waiting—the whole point of Wabi software, and the point of this book—Microsoft Windows applications running side-by-side with X Window applications. An integrated desktop, where the applications you want to run are more important than operating systems.

> *Now which of you is Hedgehog and which is Tortoise?*
> *because, to save my spots, I can't tell.*
>
> *– Rudyard Kipling, Just So Stories; "The Beginning of the*
> *Armadilloes," 1902*

In This Chapter

Installing Windows Applications

Installing a Windows application requires that you place the application in a directory on your system or on a network file server. This is generally done by using the application's install or setup program through the Microsoft Windows Program Manager.

Most Microsoft Windows applications are distributed on diskettes or CD-ROM discs in a compressed format. What this means is that you must install them using their own setup or install program; simply copying them to disk will not work.

Before you install an application, consider these important points:

- You are responsible for adhering to the terms of the software license of each application you use under the Wabi program.

- You should use the Run command in the File menu of Program Manager to install all Windows applications (except for Microsoft Windows itself).

- Before you begin installing an application, be sure to read the *Wabi Release Notes* or supplementary guide you received with your version of the Wabi program. It may contain important information about installing particular applications. Also be sure to read Appendix A, "Application Notes," in this book, for application-specific tips.

- Some application installation windows fill the screen, preventing you from using other windows on your desktop. For this reason, you should plan to be unable to use your system for other work while you install an application. See the "Windows Troubleshooting" on page 326 about possible workarounds.

- In general, you should not install applications in drive `C:`, even if the application provides drive `C:` as the default location for installation. Drive `C:` is connected to `$HOME/wabi`, which contains Wabi program files that should be kept separate from application files. You should use drive `C:` only for files of which users must have their own copy, and for applications that must access a simulated hard drive for their copy protection schemes to work.

  You can install an application in any other location you like. The only limitations are that you must have adequate space in the directory in which you install the application, and you must have permission to write to the directory. If you intend to store the files you create with the application in the same directory as the application, make sure the extra space required for these files is available in the directory.

  Installing applications on drives other than `C:` gives you the freedom to move the application to other file systems. If you remap the drive to the new location, the application's setup information, such as the command to run it, will remain valid. For example, if you map drive `F:` to `/home/me/myapps` and install Microsoft Office in `F:\msoffice`, you could later move `msoffice` to `/files/msapps/msoffice` and remap `F:` to `/files/msapps`. The command path to Microsoft Word, for example, would be `F:\msoffice\winword\winword.exe` for both locations.

- Many installation programs tell you to reboot your computer after installing the application. This is not necessary under Wabi. You need only exit and restart the Wabi program.

- Wabi provides application integration with your X Window desktop. However, the degree of integration varies with each UNIX platform. See "Integrating Applications With OpenWindows" on page 229 for more information about integration in the OpenWindows environment.

Wabi does not support Adobe Type Manager (ATM®) fonts. If your application includes a disk containing Adobe Type Manager or ATM fonts, do not install that disk.

The Run Command

You install Window applications under Wabi by using the Run command from the Program Manager File menu. (This command is also on the Windows File Manager File menu.) To install an application, open the File menu and choose Run. The Run dialog box is displayed, as shown in Figure 9-1.

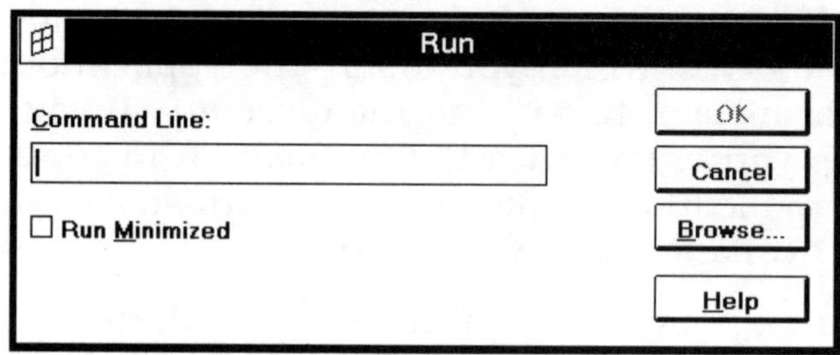

Figure 9-1   Run Dialog Box

The Command Line field in the Run dialog box is where you tell the Wabi program the location of the application files and the name of the application installation program.

The location includes the drive letter, which depends on whether you are installing from diskette, the network, or CD-ROM. It may also include a directory path on the diskette, network, or CD-ROM.

The name of the application's installation program depends on the application you are installing. Many applications use SETUP or INSTALL as the name of the program that starts the installation process. If the application includes both SETUP and INSTALL programs, INSTALL is likely used for DOS systems, and SETUP for Microsoft Windows systems. See the application's documentation for the command to begin installation.

Installing From Diskettes

If you are installing an application from diskettes, the drive letter will be A: or B:, depending on the diskette drive you are using. If there is one diskette drive, it is usually A:.

The command that you use to install a typical application from diskette is often:

```
a:\setup
```

When you type this command in the Run dialog box and choose OK, the Wabi program passes control to the application's installation program. What you see next depends on the installation program. Follow the instructions presented by the installation program, inserting program disks as required throughout the installation process.

➢ *To install a Windows application from diskette*

1. **Determine the directory in which you want to install the Windows application.**
   If necessary, assign a Wabi drive to the directory (see page 162 for instructions). Remember, you should install applications on a drive other than the C: drive.

2. **Choose the Run command from the File menu in Windows Program Manager or File Manager.**
   The Run dialog box is displayed.

3. **In the Command Line field, enter the diskette drive letter and the name of the installation program.**
   For example:

   ```
   a:\setup
   ```

4. **Choose OK.**
   The application's setup program starts, displaying additional instructions.

5. **When prompted for a location in which to install the application, indicate an assigned Wabi drive (and path name, if necessary).**

   Most applications provide a default path name on the C: drive; you should *not* accept this default. Instead use the drive and directory name on which you decided in Step 1.

   For example, if you connected Wabi drive D: to $HOME/winapps, and want to install the application in $HOME/winapps/mailapps, enter D:\mailapps. The application is placed in your $HOME/winapps/mailapps directory.

6. **Follow the instructions in the application's installation dialog box(es) to complete the installation.**

   If your diskette drive does not provide an eject button, you can eject diskettes by clicking in the Wabi window and pressing Meta+E (on Sun keyboards).

Installing From CD-ROM

If you are installing an application from CD-ROM, you must first make sure the CD-ROM drive is accessible from the operating system. See "CD-ROM Drives" on page 176 for information about using CD-ROM drives in the Wabi program.

When you have assigned a Wabi drive letter to the CD-ROM directory, you can install the application by using the Run command in Program Manager, as described in "The Run Command" on page 212.

➤ *To install a Windows application from CD-ROM*

1. **Determine the directory in which you want to install the Windows application.**
   If necessary, assign a Wabi drive to the directory (see page 162 for instructions). Remember, you should install applications on a drive other than the C: drive.

2. **Open Wabi Configuration Manager and assign a Wabi drive to the CD-ROM directory.**
   See "CD-ROM Drives" on page 176 for information about accessing CD-ROM drives.

3. **Choose the Run command from the File menu in Windows Program Manager or File Manager.**

   The Run dialog box is displayed.

4. **In the Command Line field, enter the CD-ROM drive letter and the name of the installation program.**

   For example, if the CD-ROM directory is connected to drive `M:`, and the installation program is `SETUP`, enter:

   ```
   m:\setup
   ```

5. **Choose OK.**

   The application's setup program starts, displaying additional instructions.

6. **When prompted for a location in which to install the application, indicate an assigned Wabi drive (and path name, if necessary).**

   Most applications provide a default path name on the `C:` drive; you should *not* accept this default. Instead use the drive and directory name on which you decided in Step 1.

   For example, if you connected Wabi drive `D:` to `$HOME/winapps`, and want to install the application in `$HOME/winapps/mailapps`, enter `D:\mailapps`. The application is placed in your `$HOME/winapps/mailapps` directory.

7. **Follow the instructions in the application's installation dialog box(es) to complete the installation.**

Installing From a Network Server

Because Wabi runs in a networked UNIX environment with a distributed file system, it is easy to share applications over the network. You do not need any additional software for file sharing as you would on a PC because UNIX already provides that function. You simply connect a Wabi drive to a directory on the network server where you want to install the application, and specify this drive and directory when prompted for the installation location.

Most Wabi-certified applications can be used in both standalone and network environments and provide a way to install to a network file server. The method used for a network installation varies from application to application. Some installation programs require a switch on the command line, which instructs the installation program to place the files on a network server so that users can then install the application from that location to their own workstations. Other application installation programs offer a server installation option you can select in a dialog box.

Some applications let users run the application from the network server without installing all the application files to their workstations. In this case, the installation program copies the minimum files needed to run the application on to the workstation.

Before you install an application to a shared network location:

- Refer to the application's manuals for specific information about installing on a network. Some applications include on the installation diskettes a README file describing network installation.

- Connect a Wabi drive to the network directory, and make sure the **Network Drive** option is selected on the drive.

- If users will be using the application in a workgroup arrangement (for example, working on shared reports, spreadsheets, and so on), you should probably enable file sharing with the **Sharing Enabled** option (see page 164). Look through the application's documentation to see if you should not use file sharing.

  The DOS program SHARE.EXE enables file sharing in the Microsoft Windows environment, so look for a discussion about using SHARE.EXE. If there are no warnings against using SHARE.EXE, select the **Sharing Enabled** option on the Wabi drive where the shared files are stored.

  Remember, Wabi software doesn't actually *use* SHARE.EXE (it's a DOS program, after all); rather, Wabi translates DOS-based SHARE.EXE requests made by Windows applications and passes them to a UNIX-based file sharing mechanism (see "File Locking and File Sharing" on page 169 for a complete explanation). The reason you want to check your application's documentation for compatibility with SHARE.EXE is simply to make sure that the application can be run in a shared environment; some do not allow it.

- Make sure that everyone allowed to install the application has a license to use it. For most applications, this requirement can be fulfilled by purchasing a single-user copy for each user, or by purchasing a "license pack" for multiple users.

Some Wabi-certified applications are created for single-user, single-tasking, nonprotected environments, and do not function well in a network environment. In addition, sharing may be prohibited by the application's software license agreement. You are responsible for adhering to the terms of the software license of each application you use under the Wabi program.

➤ *To install a Windows application on a network server*

1. **Refer to the application's documentation for specific information about installing on a network.**
   Some applications include a README or similar file on the installation diskettes describing network installation.

2. **Start Wabi on your computer.**

3. **Connect a Wabi drive to the server directory where you want to install the application.**
   See "Wabi Network Drives" on page 174 for instructions on connecting Wabi drives.

4. **Select the Network Drive option for the drive.**
   This option is selected with the Wabi Configuration Manager Drives tool.

5. **Select the File Sharing option for the drive if users will be working on shared files stored on this drive.**
   This option is also selected with the Wabi Configuration Manager Drives tool.

6. **Choose the Run command from the File menu in Windows Program Manager or File Manager.**

7. **In the Run dialog box, enter the command needed to install the application onto a network server.**
   Refer to the application's documentation for the command you need to run, along with any necessary switches. Enter the drive letter plus the full directory path to the command. If the path is long, or if you're not sure what it is, choose the Browse button and search for the directory and command on the server.

8. **Choose OK in the Run dialog box.**

   The installation or workstation setup program starts.

9. **Follow the program's instructions to place the application files on a network server.**

   After you install application files in this way, other users will be able to install the application under Wabi, as described in the next section.

Installing From a Network Server Through a Wabi Drive

Once an application has been installed on a network server, as described in the previous section, other Wabi users can install the application on their computers through a Wabi drive.

You are responsible for adhering to the terms of the application's software license. Each user who installs an application, whether from a drive or from diskette, must be licensed to use the software.

The method for installing an application from a Wabi drive is the same as installing from diskette—you use the Run command from the File menu in Program Manager. However, the drive you specify is a Wabi drive through which you access the directory where the application is located.

You can use the preconfigured drive R: and specify a complete path name to the directory. You can also use Configuration Manager to connect a different Wabi drive letter to the directory containing the files. In either case, you enter in the Run dialog box (shown in Figure 9-1) the Wabi drive letter and the path to the application files.

For example, if the application files are located in directory path `/usr/apps/install/hg20`, you could enter the following in the entry field of the Run dialog box:

```
R:\usr\apps\install\hg20\setup
```

You could also assign drive letter F: to /usr/apps/install/hg20 and enter:

```
F:\setup
```

 The type of slash character you use depends on whether a UNIX or a DOS path name is involved. The backslash (\) is used in DOS path names. The forward slash (/) is used in UNIX path names. The Wabi program accepts both types of slash characters, but you should use one type within a command line.

➢ *To install a Windows application to a workstation from a network server*

1. **Make sure you can access the network server directory in which the application files are installed.**
   You may need to contact your system administrator to obtain such access.
2. **Start Wabi on your computer.**
3. **Choose the Run command from the File menu in Windows Program Manager or File Manager.**
4. **In the Run dialog box, enter the command needed to install the application from the network.**
   Refer to the application's documentation for the command you need to run, along with any necessary switches. Enter the drive letter plus the full directory path to the command. If the path is long, or if you're not sure what it is, choose the Browse button and search for the directory and command on the server.
5. **Choose OK in the Run dialog box.**
   The installation or workstation setup program starts.
6. **Follow the program's installation instructions.**

Running Windows Applications

Generally, you can use Microsoft Windows applications in the Wabi environment the same as in the Microsoft Windows environment.

You can start applications several different ways:

- From within Program Manager, by opening an icon or by using the Run command

- Using Microsoft Windows File Manager, by using the Run command or by opening an executable file

- Using OpenWindows File Manager, by opening an executable file, or a document file created by the application

- From a UNIX command window, by using the `wabi` command along with some parameters

Starting Applications From Program Manager

When you install a Microsoft Windows application, the application's installation program usually creates a program item for the application. This program item, represented by an icon, is stored in a program group, which contains one or more program items. Often, an application's install program also creates a program group, in which program items for one or more executable files or documents are created. For example, an application may create a program group containing program items for the application, an application setup program, a README file, and a help file.

Using Program Item Icons

Running an installed application from Program Manager by using an program item icon is straightforward: Open the icon representing the application you want to run, and the application starts. Applications can be opened by double-clicking on the program item with the mouse, or by selecting the program item and pressing Enter.

You can *minimize*—that is, reduce to an icon—any Windows application, including Program Manager itself. Icons for minimized applications are automatically placed in the upper-left corner of your desktop. This is different from Microsoft Windows under DOS, in which minimized icons are placed in the lower-left corner of the screen. You can restore a minimized application by opening its icon, or by single-clicking its icon and selecting Restore from the window control box. Refer to Table 3-2 on page 51 for a list of window controls you can use.

> ### To start a Windows application from a program item icon

1. **Install the Windows application.**
   See "Installing Windows Applications" on page 210 for instructions.
2. **In Program Manager, locate the icon representing the application.**
3. **Open the application icon.**
   Either double-click on the icon, or select it and press Enter. Wabi starts the application.

Using the Run Command

When the Wabi program is already running Program Manager, you can start an application by using the Run command from the Program Manager File menu. The command you enter is the same command you would use to run the application on a PC, except that the drive letter indicates a path on your UNIX system.

➤ *To start a Windows application with the Run command*

1. **Install the Windows application.**
   See "Installing Windows Applications" on page 210 for instructions.

2. **Choose the Run command from the Windows Program Manager or File Manager File menu.**
   The Run dialog box is displayed.

3. **Type the full path name of the application you want to run n the Command field.**
   Alternatively, choose the Browse button to search your directories for the executable file. When you find the executable, select it. The file name is displayed in the Command field.

4. **Choose OK to accept your entry and run the application.**
   Wabi starts the application.

Starting Applications From Microsoft Windows File Manager

You can use Microsoft Windows File Manager to start applications just as you would in the Microsoft Windows environment: Open a program file or a document file associated with an application. In the Wabi environment, however, you cannot open files with .COM, .PIF, or .BAT extensions because they are not Windows executables. Only Windows executables with .EXE extensions will run in the Wabi environment.

Starting Applications From OpenWindows File Manager

When you install applications under Wabi software in the OpenWindows environment, Wabi automatically creates a *binding* for the application and its associated files. Similar to the Associate function in Microsoft Windows, the OpenWindows binding is an association between an application and the file types with which it works. This binding enables you to open a document file with the OpenWindows File Manager, and have Wabi automatically start the application associated with—or bound to—the document file type. See "Integrating Applications With OpenWindows" on page 229 for more information about the binding process and using the OpenWindows Binder program.

Starting Applications From the UNIX Command Line

You can start a Windows application from the UNIX command line at the same time you start Wabi. Depending on how you do this, you can start Wabi so that it runs just the application, or the application and Program Manager together. Unlike Microsoft Windows under DOS, in which a program shell, like Program Manager, is always started, Wabi lets you run just the Windows application, without a program shell.

You can start Windows applications directly from the UNIX command line with either of two Wabi command-line options:

- The `wabi` command with the `-s` command line switch; that is:

  `wabi -s` *application_name*

  This command starts the Windows application, but does not start Program Manager—in effect, you see the application, but you don't see Wabi.

- The `wabi` command with just the application name; that is:

  `wabi` *application_name*

  This command starts the application and Program Manager.

The -s option is recommended when you want to include an application in a UNIX desktop menu (see "Configuring Desktop Menus," later in this chapter). Refer to "Wabi Command-Line Options" on page 134 for more information about the -s option.

Note that you can access Program Manager or Wabi tools such as Configuration Manager by starting them just as you would any other Windows application. For example, the command line below starts Wabi Configuration Manager:

```
wabi -s w:\wbin\config.exe
```

➤ To start a Windows application from a UNIX command line

This method starts your application when the Wabi program starts, with Program Manager and Wabi tools available to you.

➡ **Enter the following command at a UNIX command prompt:**

```
wabi application_name
```

You can use either a DOS path enclosed in quotes, or a UNIX path (without quotes). If the directory containing the application program is not in the path in your $HOME/wabi/autoexec.bat, you must include a full path name.

For example, suppose you have installed Microsoft Excel in your $HOME/excel directory. The Wabi drive H: is connected to your home directory. To start the Excel program, you could enter either of the following commands:

```
wabi 'h:\excel\excel.exe'
```

or

```
wabi $HOME/excel/excel.exe
```

or if H:\EXCEL is in the PATH statement of your AUTOEXEC.BAT,

```
wabi excel.exe
```

Program Manager runs minimized and opens Excel.

The application startup command and optional file name must be the last arguments on the command line.

➤ *To run a Windows application from the UNIX command line without running Program Manager*

This method starts your application when the Wabi program starts, without starting Program Manager.

⇒ **Enter the following command at a UNIX command prompt:**

```
wabi -s application_name
```

You can use either a DOS path enclosed in quotes, or a UNIX path (without quotes). If the directory containing the application program is not in the path in your `$HOME/wabi/autoexec.bat` file, you must include a full path name.

For example, suppose you have installed Microsoft Excel in your `$HOME/excel` directory. The Wabi drive `H:` is connected to your home directory. To start the Excel program, you could enter either of the following commands:

```
wabi -s 'h:\excel\excel.exe'
```

or

```
wabi -s $HOME/excel/excel.exe
```

or if `H:\EXCEL` is in the `PATH` statement of your `AUTOEXEC.BAT`,

```
wabi -s excel.exe
```

Excel is started, but Program Manager is not.

If you want to use Wabi tools, you can also use this method to start them. For example, to start Wabi Configuration Manager, enter:

```
wabi -s 'w:\wbin\config.exe'*
```

The Wabi process that is already running will start Wabi Configuration Manager.

Starting Applications With a Data File

With any of the application startup methods, you can specify a file name
to open with the application, if the application startup command allows it
(as most do). Just include the file's full name as an argument to the
startup command. If the directory containing the file is not on your path
in your `AUTOEXEC.BAT` file, you must include the full path to the file.

The `wabi` command supports additional switches allowing you to display
Wabi on a remote system, and to display Wabi with smaller or larger
system fonts. These switches, which are described in "Wabi Command-
Line Options" on page 134, must be specified before an application
startup command. The application startup command and optional file
name must be the last arguments on the `wabi` command line.

➤ *To open a file when starting a Windows application*

⮕ **Add the name of the file as an argument to any of the
application startup commands described in this chapter.**
You should always use a complete path for the file name.

If you are starting the application from within Program Manager,
add the file name in DOS format, including drive letter, to the
command you enter in the Command field of the dialog box. For
example, the Wabi Release Notes icon uses the command:

```
write w:\wbin\readme.wri
```

If you are starting the application from the UNIX command line,
and use a DOS path for the file to open, include the drive letter
and file name within the quotes along with the startup
command. If you use a UNIX path, do not use drive letters, but
be sure to use accurate capitalization. If you want, you can use a
UNIX path for the command, and enclose a DOS path and drive
in quotes for the file name.

For example, to start the Excel program and open a file named
`sched.xls` in your `h:\excel\files` directory, you could enter
any of the following commands:

```
wabi  -s  'h:\excel\excel.exe h:\excel\files\sched.xls'
wabi  -s  $HOME/excel/excel.exe $HOME/excel/files/sched.xls
wabi  -s  $HOME/excel/excel.exe 'h:\excel\files\sched.xls'
```

When the Excel window opens, it displays the `sched.xls` file.

The application startup command and optional file name must be the
last arguments on the `wabi` command line.

Configuring Desktop Menus

You can add a Wabi command, or the command to start a Windows
application or open a document, to your OpenWindows Workspace menu.
For example, you could add Microsoft Word for Windows to the menu;
when you choose the Word command from the Workspace menu, Wabi
starts and opens Microsoft Word.

To add a command to your OpenWindows Workspace menu, you must
modify your `~/.openwin-menu-programs` file. For example, to add
Microsoft Word to the OpenWindows Workspace menu, you might add a
command like the following:

```
"Word..."  exec  $WABIHOME/bin/wabi  -s  g:\word\winword.exe
```

Refer to your Solaris documentation for complete information about
adding commands to your Workspace menu.

➤ *To configure your OpenWindows Workspace menu to include
a Windows application*

1. **Locate your `.openwin-menu-programs` file.**
   You may need to ask your system administrator for privileges to
   this file. In some cases, this file is shared by many users, and
   you will not be allowed to edit it at all.

2. **Open the file in the text editor of your choice.**
   For example, from a UNIX command prompt you could enter:

   ```
   textedit .openwin-menu-programs &
   ```

3. **Add the menu name and executable name for the application you want to add to the menu.**

   Add the name in the location in which you want it to appear in the menu—that is, if you want it to appear at the top of the menu, add it to the top of list, etc. Use the following format:

   "*menu_name...*" `exec` *wabi_path* `[-s]` *application_path*

   where:

   - *menu_name* (must be enclosed in quotes and followed by an ellipsis (...)) is the name you want displayed on the menu.
   - *wabi_path* is the location of the Wabi program (by default, `$WABIHOME/bin/wabi`).
   - The `-s` switch is optional.
   - *application_path* is the name and location of the application.

   For example, if you wanted to run Microsoft Word, which is located in this example in `g:\word\winword.exe`, you could enter the following statement:

   ```
   "Word..." exec $WABIHOME/bin/wabi -s g:\word\winword.exe
   ```

4. **Save the `.openwin-menu-programs` file and exit the text editor.**

5. **Enable the new menu entry by entering the following command at a UNIX command prompt:**

   ```
   source .openwin-menu-programs
   ```

Integrating Applications With OpenWindows

When you install a Microsoft Windows application under Wabi, it can be integrated in several ways with your X Window environment. This section describes such integration in the context of OpenWindows, the windowing environment on which Solaris is based.

 As with many other topics in this book, Wabi concepts are explained in the context of the Solaris operating environment. Other operating environments may provide fewer or more integration features.

At the most basic level, Wabi integrates itself with OpenWindows in such a way that you can open a Windows application by double-clicking on the application's executable or document icon in OpenWindows File Manager or Mail Tool. If Wabi is not already running, it starts transparently, and then opens the Windows application or file. If Wabi is already running, it simply opens the application or file. Similarly, you can also configure your OpenWindows Print Tool so that you can print files created by Windows applications by dragging and dropping.

Using OpenWindows Binder

In the OpenWindows environment, you can associate a document file with the Windows application that created it by *binding* the document file name extension to the application's executable file. This is similar to the Microsoft Windows Associate command (on the File menu in Windows Program Manager and File Manager). Binding an application to a file name extension makes it possible to:

- Double-click on the icon for a file created by an application to start the application and open the file

- Drag and drop document icon on various targets, for example, the OpenWindows Print Tool, to print the file

For example, in OpenWindows, files with a `.TXT` extension are associated by default with the OpenWindows Text Editor tool; when you double-click on a `.TXT` file, the `textedit` program starts.

Under OpenWindows, the binding of document extensions to executables is managed through the OpenWindows Binder application. When you install a Windows application, Wabi automatically creates bindings that associate one or more file extensions with the application. These bindings also tell OpenWindows to start Wabi before starting the application.

There are several important points to consider when binding Windows application files in the OpenWindows environment:

- You can use the Binder program to change any binding that Wabi has made.

- If you remove an application from your Wabi environment, you should manually remove the binding of file types to the application with the Binder program.

- If you move or reinstall an application to a different location, you must manually update the bindings with the new path.

- Wabi does *not* associate `.TXT` files with the Microsoft Windows Notepad. It is assumed that OpenWindows users prefer to use Text Editor when working with text files. However, if you prefer, you can bind `.TXT` files to Notepad with Binder.

- If you are upgrading from Wabi 1.*x*, applications that you previously installed will not be integrated into your OpenWindows environment because OpenWindows integration was introduced in Wabi 2.0. If you want to integrate them, you can use the Binder program to bind applications to their associated file extensions, or you can reinstall the applications and have Wabi create the bindings for you.

- The binding contains drive- and path-specific information. Therefore, if you run Wabi on two different systems, be sure to use a consistent set of drive mappings when you install your Windows applications. If you have two different drive mappings on two different systems, the File Manager and Mail Tool integration will not work on both systems.

Conflicting Bindings

Within the OpenWindows environment, applications create files with unique extensions. However, some Microsoft Windows applications use the same file extensions as some OpenWindows applications, so there may be conflicts between file types already bound to OpenWindows applications and the file types that are added when you install Windows applications.

For example, the extension .DOC is used by Microsoft Word and also by the desktop publishing application, FrameMaker. If you have FrameMaker installed in OpenWindows and then install Microsoft Word into your Wabi environment, Wabi changes the binding of .DOC from FrameMaker to Word. When you restart File Manager, all .DOC files will have a Word icon; if you double-click them, Word starts instead of FrameMaker. If you want to use FrameMaker, you must either start it and open FrameMaker .DOC files from FrameMaker, or change the binding back to FrameMaker with Binder.

Refer to your Solaris documentation for complete information about using the Binder tool.

OpenWindows File Manager Integration

When you install a Windows application under Wabi, Wabi automatically creates a binder association for documents created by that application. After installing the Windows application, restart the OpenWindows File Manager to allow the binder association to take effect. You can then start the application from OpenWindows File Manager by double-clicking the application's icon. You can also double-click the icon of a file created with an application to start the application and open the file.

If you use OpenWindows File Manager's Large Icon View, the icons you see look like the familiar Microsoft Windows icons. However, in OpenWindows, icons can use only two colors, so the icons do not have the same colors as in the Wabi environment. If you use OpenWindows File Manager's Small Icon View, the icons you see are File Manager's small default icons.

OpenWindows Mail Tool Integration

If you restart Mail Tool after you install a Windows application under Wabi, you can double-click attachments in messages to start the application associated with the attachment. For example, if you have installed Microsoft Word in your Wabi environment and you receive a Microsoft Word document as a mail attachment, you can double-click the attachment to start Word and open the document.

OpenWindows Print Tool Integration

To use OpenWindows Print Tool to print files created by a Windows application, you must first create a binder association between Print Tool and the Windows application's print command.

➤ *To configure a Window application to use print tool*

For this procedure, let us assume that you have installed Microsoft PowerPoint to your `h:\apps` directory (your `$HOME/apps` in UNIX).

1. **Read the application's documentation to find the command-line option to print a file.**
   Many Windows applications use the `/p` or `-p` option. For example, to print a PowerPoint slide (`slide.ppt`) you would use:

   ```
   powerpnt.exe /p slide.ppt
   ```

2. **Start the OpenWindows Binder tool.**
   You can select Binder from your OpenWindows Workspace menu
   or enter the following command in a Command Tool or Shell
   Tool:

   ```
   binder &
   ```

   Binder starts and displays a list of application and file types.

3. **Scroll down the list of application and file types and select
   the file type you want to print.**
   For example, to print PowerPoint slides, which have the `.ppt` file
   extension, select the entry `ppt-file`.

4. **Open Props and choose Icon.**
   The Binder: Properties window shows information about that
   entry, including its icon and foreground and background colors.

5. **Choose the [+] button in the Properties window.**
   Additional information about the file type is displayed. The
   Application field contains a command used to edit files of this type.

6. **Copy the text in the Application field and paste it in the Print
   Method field.**
   For example, for PowerPoint, the Application field contains a
   command similar to the following:

   ```
   wabi -s h:\\apps\\ppt\\powerpnt.exe $FILE
   ```

7. **Edit the Print Method field to insert the command-line
   argument that tells the application to print the file.**
   For PowerPoint you would change the entry to:

   ```
   wabi -s h:\\apps\\ppt\\powerpnt.exe /p $FILE
   ```

8. **Choose the Apply button in the Binder Properties dialog and
   dismiss the window.**

9. **Choose Save in the Binder main window, then exit Binder.**

10. **Restart Print Tool.**
    See the next section for information about printing files.

Once you have created a Binder association between your Windows
application and Print Tool, you can print files created by that application
by dropping their icons on the Print Tool icon.

> ### To print Windows application files with Print Tool

1. **Create a Binder association between the Windows application
   and Print Tool, as described above.**

2. **Open OpenWindows File Manager and find a file with the
   extension associated with the application, or open Mail Tool
   and find a message with an attached file with this extension.**

3. **Drag the file icon and drop it onto the Print Tool icon.**

4. **The associated Microsoft Windows application starts and
   displays its Print dialog.**
   Some applications display their main window, load the file, and
   open a Print dialog. Some applications display only the Print
   dialog. Some applications just print the file to the default printer.

5. **Use the Print dialog as you normally would to print the file.**
   The file is printed on the printer that the application is currently
   set up to use, which is usually either the default printer or the
   printer last used. This may not be the same printer that is
   currently selected in Print Tool.

Using Multimedia Features

On newer SPARCstations and *x86* computers running the Solaris operating environment, Wabi 2.1 supports the audio and video features of Microsoft Windows and Wabi certified applications.

Your computer must include the necessary hardware before you can use these features:

- SPARCstation 5, SPARCstation 10, and SPARCstation 20 ship with both sound cards and microphones, so they are properly equipped to play and record sound in the Wabi environment.

- The SPARCstation 4 does not ship with a sound card or microphone, but can be upgraded to include them.

- A computer based on a 386, 486, or Pentium processor can also use multimedia in the Wabi environment if it is equipped with a 16-bit sound card.

 Multimedia features such as MIDI (Musical Instrument Digital Interface), and AVI (Audio-Visual Interface) for video laser disks and music compact disks are not yet supported.

Audio Features

You can play, record, and edit waveform (.WAV) files by using the Sound Recorder located in the Accessories group or by using a sound tool provided by an application you have installed. You can also use the Control Panel Sound tool to assign system events to waveform sounds. Another program in the Accessories group, Media Player, also lets you play waveform files.

You can embed sound objects in documents when you use an application that supports it, as do most of the certified applications.

 Audio support is not provided when you use the Wabi program remotely. You can hear sound only on the machine on which the Wabi program is actually running.

Controlling Audio Input/Output

By default, Wabi takes input from the microphone and sends output to
the speaker. You can change the input and output settings by using the
Audio Control program in the Solaris environment, or by editing your
`wabi/windows/system.ini` file. When you use Audio Control, the change
applies only to the current Wabi session. When you edit `system.ini`, the
change applies to your subsequent Wabi sessions.

- **Using Audio Control** – You can start Audio Control from a
  Command Tool window by entering the command:

  ```
  /usr/openwin/bin/audiocontrol &
  ```

  You can also start Audio Control from Audio Tool, the Solaris
  sound recording and editing program. When you choose the
  Volume control in Audio Tool, the Audio Control window opens.

  The play, or output, options you can choose are Speaker,
  Headphone, or Line Out. The Line Out option sends sound through
  your workstation's output jack to a device such as a tape
  recorder.

  The record, or input, options you can choose are Microphone and
  Line In. The Microphone option lets you record through a
  microphone connected to your workstation's microphone jack.
  The Line In option lets you record sound from a device (such as
  a radio or tape player) connected to your workstation's input
  jack.

  Audio Control settings are not saved for subsequent sessions.

  Please refer to your *Solaris User's Guide* or the
  `audiocontrol(1)` man page for a description of Audio Control.

- **Editing SYSTEM.INI** – When Wabi starts, it uses the settings in
  `SYSTEM.INI` for its initial audio settings. If you want to specify
  the input and output settings for Wabi to use each time, edit
  your `SYSTEM.INI` file to add the following section to the file:

  ```
  [solarwav]
  input=
  output=
  ```

To use the microphone for input, set `input=mike` or
`input=microphone`. To use a line in, set `input=line`. This
allows you to record sound from a source, such as a tape
player, that you have connected to your workstation.

You can send sound output to speakers, headphones, or to an
output jack to another device, using `output=speaker`,
`output=headphone`, or `output=line`. You can send output to
multiple ports by using the | symbol between them. For
example, to send sound to speakers, headphones, and line out,
use `output=speaker|headphone|line` in your `SYSTEM.INI` file.

To change the settings temporarily while sound is playing, use
Audio Control.

Controlling Audio Volume and Balance

You can use the slide controls in Audio Control in your Solaris
environment to control the volume and balance of the sound produced by
a program running in either your Wabi environment or X Window
environment.

Video Features

You can play Audio-Visual Interface (`.AVI`) files if you have installed the
Microsoft Video for Windows driver. Applications that use the driver
usually install it when you install the application. To determine if the
Video for Windows driver is installed, open the Control Panel **Drivers** tool.
The driver has been installed if the entry `[MCI] Microsoft Video for
Windows` is present in the **Installed Drivers** list.

You can play `.AVI` files with the Microsoft Windows Media Player, located
in the **Accessories** group. Most applications support linked or embedded
video objects by playing them through Media Player. However, some
applications provide their own video players, which should also work in
the Wabi environment.

You can play `.AVI` files when you run the Wabi program remotely, but
performance may be degraded, resulting in slight pauses between
video frames.

Using Remote Database Access

Several Wabi-certified applications can access databases on remote DBMS servers. The supported DBMS servers are Oracle7 and Sybase SQL Server 10 databases running on Solaris 2 systems in TCP/IP networks.

Applications that can access data from servers are:

- Lotus 1-2-3 version 5.0
- Lotus Approach™ 3.02
- Microsoft Access 2.0
- Microsoft Excel 5.0
- Paradox 5.0
- Quattro® Pro 6.0

These applications connect through the Wabi Winsock interface, using additional specialized software: an ODBC (Open Database Connectivity) driver and data source software.

ODBC drivers enable applications to connect to remote databases. Oracle and Sybase ODBC drivers from Intersolv have been tested with the Wabi program and found to be compatible. You can purchase a driver from Intersolv individually or get Intersolv's complete DataDirect ODBC Driver Pack 2.0 for Windows.

Data source software provides TCP/IP connectivity over Winsock to the DBMS server. You can obtain this software from the DBMS vendors, Oracle and Sybase. Oracle's data source product is SQL*Net TCP/IP 1.1. Sybase's data source product is Open Client Net-Library 10.0.2.

Lotus 1-2-3 also needs a proprietary component, the Lotus DataLens driver (DLODBC), an interface to the ODBC driver. The DataLens driver is available on the Lotus Data Access Tools 2.0 for Windows disks, which you can obtain from Lotus.

For each application, follow these general steps to set up the application to access remote databases:

- Install the application fully or by using a custom install option, and be sure to include the options the application needs for remote database connectivity.

- Install the Oracle and/or Sybase data source software.

- Install the Intersolv ODBC drivers for Oracle 7 and Sybase System 10.

- Run the ODBC Administrator utility in Control Panel to configure the data sources for Oracle7 and Sybase System 10.

- Verify the connection to the server.

When you have completed these procedures, you can use the application's database query facilities to access the remote databases.

Installing Applications for Remote Database Access

With the exception of Lotus 1-2-3, each application will install the files it needs for remote database access if you do a full installation. Table 9-1 tells you how to install the additional software that Lotus 1-2-3 needs, and also provides pointers on getting the files you need for the other applications if you do not want to do a full installation of all the application's files.

Table 9-1   Remote Database Connectivity Application Notes

Application	Notes
Lotus 1-2-3, version 5.0	When you install Lotus 1-2-3, choose the **Customize Features** install option. After you specify the drive and path for the `123r5w` directory (and `lotusapp` directory if you don't already have one), a Customize dialog box opens. Click the **Shared Data Access** tab and select the database drivers you want to install. Be sure to choose the SQL Server driver. When you continue with the installation, you will be prompted for the name of your SQL server. Next, you must install drivers from the Lotus Data Access Tools disks. Notes on the procedure are included below.

Lotus Data Access Tools 2.0	Insert disk 1 and run the install program. Choose the **Customize Features** install option. In the Customize dialog box, click the **DataLens Drivers** tab and select `ODBC Data Sources`, `ORACLE`, and `SQL Server`. Enter the name of your SQL server when prompted. Complete the installation and restart Wabi when prompted.
	
	After installation is complete, edit the Lotus DataLens Registration File, `lotus.bcf`, which is located in `x:\lotusapps\datalens`, where *x:* is the drive where you installed the DataLens drivers.
	
	Insert the following lines into your `lotus.bcf` file to add driver records for Oracle and Sybase:
	
	`DN="ODBC_SYBASE" DL="DLODBC"`
	`DD="DataLens Driver for ODBC Data Sources"`
	`DB="SYBASE" AC=UI,PW;`
	
	`DN="ODBC_ORACLE" DL="DLODBC"`
	`DD="DataLens Driver for ODBC Data Sources"`
	`DB="ORACLE7" AC=UI,PW;`
	
	Note: When you connect to the remote database servers, you should use these driver records instead of the ones provided by default in `lotus.bcf`.
	
	Next, install the Oracle and/or Sybase software and Intersolv ODBC drivers.

Application	Notes
Lotus Approach 3.02	When you install Lotus Approach, choose the **Customize Features** install option. After you specify the drive and path for the approach directory (and `lotusapp` directory if you don't already have one), a Customize dialog box opens. Click the **PowerKeys** tab and select `ODBC`, `Oracle SQL`, and `SQL Server`. Continue with the installation. Next, install the Oracle and/or Sybase software and Intersolv ODBC drivers.
Microsoft Excel 5.0	When you install Microsoft Excel, choose the **Complete/Custom** install option. When selecting which components to install, select **Data Access**. The **Data Access** component installs Microsoft Query software and several ODBC drivers, including the SQL Server Driver. Continue with the installation. When installation is complete, you should install Oracle and/or Sybase software and Intersolv ODBC drivers.
Microsoft Access 2.0	When you install Microsoft Access, choose the **Complete/Custom** install option. When selecting which components to install, select **ODBC** support. Next, install the Oracle and/or Sybase software and Intersolv ODBC drivers.
Novell Paradox 5.0	When you install Paradox, install the IDAPI engine. Use the IDAPI Configuration Utility to add new drivers and aliases for Oracle and Sybase. Next, install the Oracle and/or Sybase software, and Intersolv ODBC drivers.
Novell Quattro Pro 6.0	When you install Quattro Pro, install the IDAPI engine and the DataBase Desktop. Use the IDAPI Configuration Utility to add new drivers and aliases for Oracle and Sybase. Next, install the Oracle and/or Sybase software and Intersolv ODBC drivers.

Installing Oracle SQL*Net TCP/IP

The SQL*Net TCP/IP Version 1.1 software for Microsoft Windows includes three diskettes, which are labeled as follows:

- Install V3.0.9.4.0
- SQL*Net TCP/IP V1.1.7.7B
- Required Support Files V7.012.1.0

➤ To install Oracle7 Software

1. **Insert the Install diskette and run the** `ORAINST.EXE` **program from Program Manager to start the Oracle Installer.**

2. **Follow the Oracle Installer's prompts for your language, company, and Oracle home path name.**
   Install diskettes as prompted.

3. **In the Vendors dialog box, select** `Sun PCNFS 5.0 via winsock` **for the TCP/IP vendor.**

4. **In the TCP/IP Services dialog box, accept the default path for the NFS services file, which is probably** `C:\NFS\SERVICES`. The Oracle Installer expects this file because the Vendor selection was `PC-NFS 5.0 via winsock`. The `SERVICES` file does not exist in the Wabi environment. Note that accepting the default causes a temporary error, which the next step works around.

5. **In the error dialog box that opens when Oracle Installer cannot find the** `C:\NFS\SERVICES` **file, choose OK to accept a sample file.**

6. **Exit Oracle Installer.**

7. **Edit your** `AUTOEXEC.BAT` **file.**
   Add the *x*:`\ORAWIN\BIN` directory to your `PATH` statement, where *x*: is the drive where you installed the Oracle files.

If you need help with the installation, refer to "Installing SQL*Net TCP/IP for Windows" in the document *Setting Up SQL*Net TCP/IP for Windows Version 1.1*, which you received with the SQL*Net TCP/IP diskettes. The Oracle Installer program also includes on-line help.

Installing Sybase Open Client Net-Library

The Sybase Open Client Net-Library software includes several diskettes, but only the following diskettes are needed for establishing remote database access in the Wabi environment:

- Net-Library for PC/MS Windows
- Open Client/C Developers Kit for PC/MS Windows (1)
- Open Client/C Developers Kit for PC/MS Windows (2)

➤ To install Sybase Open Client software

1. **Insert the Net-Library disk and run the SETUP_10.EXE program from Program Manager.**
   Follow the installation program's prompts. For detailed information, see the *SYBASE Open Client/Server Product Installation Guide for Microsoft Windows* manual.

2. **In the Net-Library Driver Selection dialog box, select Windows Sockets.**

3. **In the Windows Socket Driver Information dialog, enter the server machine name and port number of the computer running the Sybase database.**
   Contact your system administrator for the server machine name and port number.

4. **Specify the server name or accept the default server name, SYBASE.**

5. **When the installation program prompts you to modify the AUTOEXEC.BAT file, select No.**
   The CALL command that the installation program would add cannot be executed in the Wabi environment. Later, you must edit your AUTOEXEC.BAT file to include the statements contained in the WSYBSET.BAT file.

6. **When installation is complete, eject the Net-Library diskette.**

7. **Insert disk 1 of the Open Client /C Developers Kit and run the `SETUP_10.EXE` program from Program Manager.**
   Follow the installation program's prompts to complete the installation.

8. **When the installation is complete, edit your `AUTOEXEC.BAT` file and insert the contents of `x:\SQL10\BIN\WSYBSET.BAT`.**
   The lines should be similar to the following:

```
set  PATH=%PATH%;  x:\SQL10\BIN;  x:\SQL10\DLL
set  SYBASE=x:\SQL10
set  DSQUERY=SYBASE
set  INCLUDE=%INCLUDE%;  x:\SQL10\INCLUDE
set  LIB=%LIB%;  x:\SQL10\LIB
set  USER=username
```

   x: is the drive where you installed the Sybase SQL10 files, such as `G:`.

Installing Intersolv DataDirect ODBC Drivers

Even if the application you want to use includes its own ODBC drivers, you should install ODBC drivers from Intersolv. These drivers have been tested in the Wabi environment more extensively than those provided with applications.

The Intersolv driver pack includes three diskettes, labelled Intersolv DataDirect ODBC Driver Pack for Windows.

➤ *To install Intersolv ODBC Drivers*

1. **Insert disk 1 and run the `SETUP.EXE` program from Program Manager.**

2. **In the DataDirect ODBC Driver Pack Setup dialog box, specify the directory where you want to install the drivers, then choose the Select button.**

3. **In the next dialog box, choose Clear All, then select INTERSOLV Oracle 7 and INTERSOLV Sybase System 10.**

4. **Follow the installation program prompts to complete the installation.**
   If you are prompted to install files that will overwrite existing ones, choose to install the new ones.

5. **Read the Driver Pack release notes; follow any instructions applicable to the Oracle 7 and Sybase System 10 drivers.**

6. **Configure data sources for the drivers.**
   The installation program prompts you to do this. You can either proceed as prompted, or run the ODBC Administrator later from the Control Panel, as explained in the next section.

Configuring Data Sources for Oracle7 and Sybase System 10

You must configure data sources by using the ODBC Administrator. Before attempting to do so, see the "Oracle Drivers" and "Sybase System 10 Driver" chapters in the *INTERSOLV DataDirect ODBC Drivers Reference*.

➢ *To configure a data source for Oracle7*

1. **Start the Control Panel and open the ODBC icon to start the ODBC Administrator.**

2. **In the Data Source dialog box, enter a data source name, which is a string that identifies the Oracle data source.**
   A data source name, `Oracle7 Tables`, may already be entered by default. You can accept this name or enter one of your own.

3. **Enter a description of the data source.**
   For example, you might enter Oracle server.

4. **Enter the Server Name, the SQL*Net connection string designating the server and database to be accessed.**
   Refer to the *INTERSOLV DataDirect ODBC Drivers Reference* to determine what this should be. The rest of the entries in the dialog box are optional. See the on-line help and reference manual for more information.

➤ **_To configure a data source for Sybase System 10_**

1. **Start Windows Control Panel and open the ODBC icon to start the ODBC Administrator.**

2. **In the Data Source dialog box, enter a data source name, which is a string that identifies the Sybase data source.**
   A data source name, `Sybase System 10`, may already be entered by default. You can accept this name or enter one of your own.

3. **Enter a description of the data source.**
   For example, you might enter Sybase server.

4. **Enter the Server Name that contains the System 10 tables you want to access.**
   This is the server name you entered when installing the Sybase Net-Library software. The rest of the entries in the dialog box are optional. See the on-line help and reference manual for more information.

Verifying Connection to Oracle and Sybase Servers

After you install the Oracle and Sybase software and configure your system, verify the connection to the servers by using the utilities provided with your Oracle and Sybase package.

➤ **_To verify connection to Oracle 7 servers_**

➡ **Run the program _x_:\ORAWIN\BIN\NETTEST from Program Manager.**
   NETTEST verifies that your SQL*Net software has been installed correctly and that you can connect to the server. NETTEST reports information about both successful and failed connection attempts. If the connection is successful, NETTEST displays a "Logon Successful" message.

➤ *To verify connection to Sybase servers*

➠ **Run the program *x*:\SQL10\BIN\WSYBPING from Program Manager.**

WSYBPING verifies that your Net-Library software has been installed correctly and that you can connect to the Sybase server. WSYBPING reports information about both successful and failed connection attempts. If the connection is successful, WSYBPING displays the message "SYBASE network address is alive!"

Accessing Remote Databases

Refer to your application's documentation and on-line help for information about using the application's remote database access facilities.

When you try to connect to a remote database, your application may offer several choices of ODBC drivers and data sources with similar names. You may find it confusing to determine what choice you should make to connect to a remote server. With all the applications, we recommend you use the Oracle7 and Sybase System10 ODBC drivers from Intersolv, even if the application provides others. These recommended data sources and drivers have tested well in the Wabi environment. Other data sources and drivers have not been tested or have not performed reliably.

Notes About Lotus Applications

In Lotus 1-2-3, when you connect to the Oracle7 or Sybase 10 database, you should use the ODBC_ORACLE or ODBC_SYBASE data source names, which you added to the lotus.bcf file, as described on page 240.

In Lotus Approach, you connect to the remote database server by opening a file. In the Open dialog box, select ODBC Data Sources(*) in the List Files of Type list box. This brings up a list of data sources, including those for Oracle7 and Sybase System 10. The data source name matches the name you specified when configuring the data sources in the ODBC Administrator in "Configuring Data Sources for Oracle7 and Sybase System 10" on page 245. Select one of these two data sources.

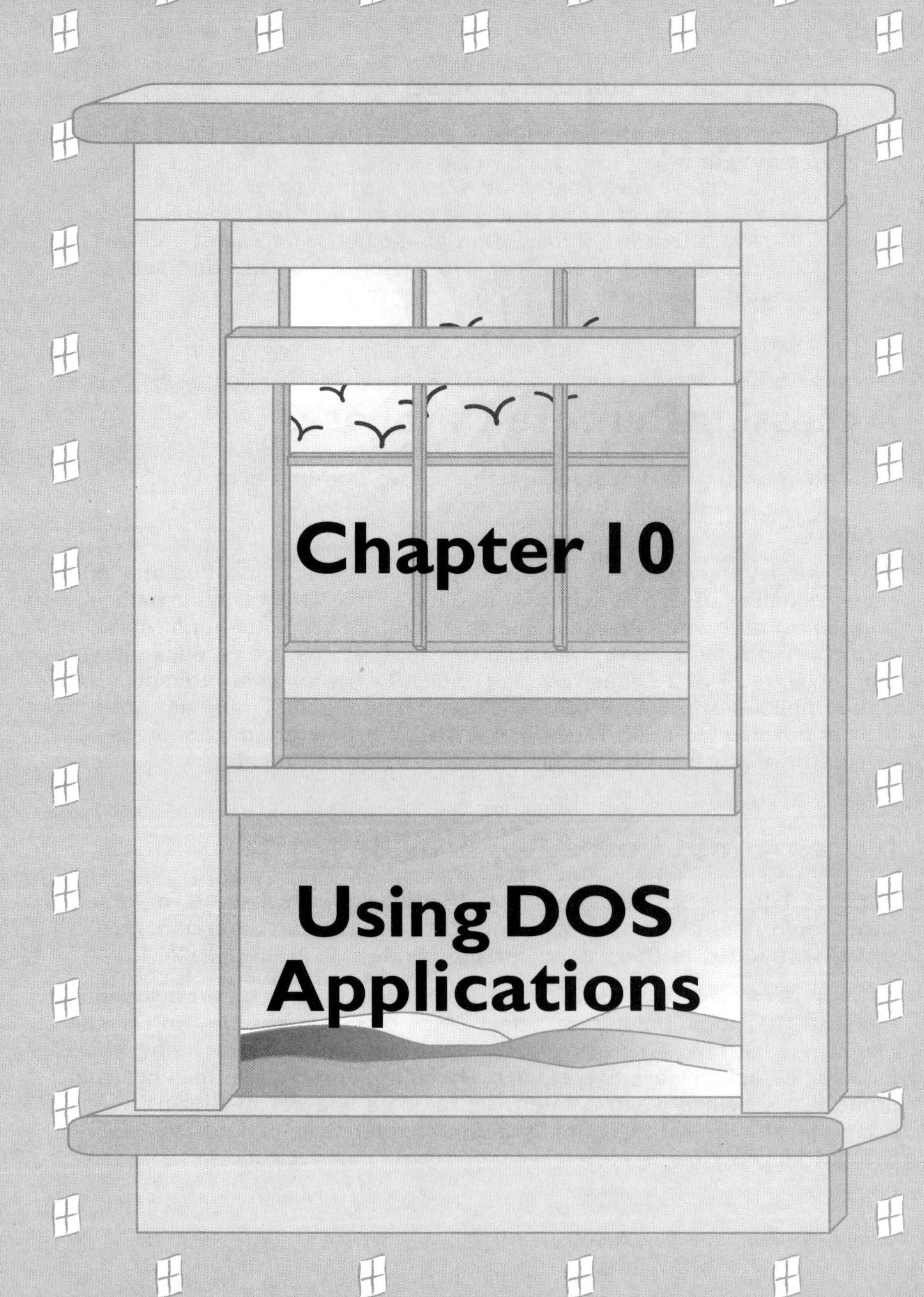

Chapter 10
Using DOS
Applications

There are times when—believe it or not—some people *need* DOS; times when big, graphical operating environments like Microsoft Windows or OpenWindows won't do; times when the lowest (and most popular) common PC denominator, DOS, is the only thing that works.

Whatever is popular is wrong.

– Oscar Wilde, to students at Royal Academy, London, 1883

In This Chapter

About DOS Under Wabi

In general, there are two occasions when you may want to use DOS for running certain applications from Wabi:

- You want to run a straight DOS application, like WordPerfect® 6.*x* for DOS.

- You want to run a Windows application that does not work under Wabi (see "Supported Applications" on page 6).

Wabi 2.1 cannot run DOS on its own; some sort of DOS emulation is planned for later releases of Wabi, but none exists now. Therefore, if you want to run DOS applications from Wabi, or to run regular Microsoft Windows under DOS on UNIX (theoretically compatible with all Windows applications, but *slow*), you need to use some sort of DOS emulation product.

There are several DOS emulation products for the UNIX platform available today. Some advantages and disadvantages of using these products with Wabi are explained in Chapter 1, in the section titled "Solutions For Running Unsupported Applications" on page 10. In particular, see Table 1-2 on page 11 for a comparison of Wabi features and the features provided by various emulation products.

Technically, whatever DOS emulator you use runs outside of Wabi—that is, the emulator and Wabi are run as separate UNIX processes. The question then arises, why use Wabi to run the DOS emulator? The main advantage to using Wabi to manage your DOS emulation tasks, rather than working with the emulator entirely in UNIX outside of Wabi, is that you can use the facilities of Windows Program Manager under Wabi to organize your DOS applications graphically. That is, as with Microsoft Windows under DOS, you can create program items and program groups for your DOS applications.

For example, you could create a program item for WordPerfect 6.x for DOS; click on its icon to start WordPerfect in the emulator. You could even create program items for unsupported applications; choosing such items would start an emulator, which could start Microsoft Windows, which would then start the application.

It's even easier to run DOS applications under Wabi than it is under DOS-based Windows, because you don't need to create PIF files. The emulator is really running your DOS applications directly in DOS, rather than through Windows, so a PIF file is unnecessary.

Preparing to Use DOS Applications

To use DOS applications with the Wabi program, there are two sets of tasks you must perform to prepare your Wabi environment. The first set of tasks is done one time only; the second set is done for each DOS application you want to run.

- **One-time tasks**
  - Install a DOS emulator if you do not already have one installed; follow the installation instructions included with your emulator.
  - Connect the DOS emulator to the Wabi program through the DOS tool in Wabi Configuration Manager; see "Configuring DOS Emulator Connections" on page 254 for instructions.

- **Tasks done once for each DOS application**
  - Start the DOS emulator.
  - Install the DOS application from the DOS session, following the DOS application's instructions.
  - Create a program item and, optionally, a program group in Wabi.

After you have performed these tasks, you do not need to start the DOS emulator before starting a DOS application; Wabi starts and passes command-line parameters to the DOS emulator for you.

Installing a DOS Emulator

You do not use the Wabi program to install a DOS emulator. You should install the emulator, using the instructions provided with it, outside of Wabi. Also be sure to note the path and command needed to start the emulator, along with any parameters you might want to use under Wabi.

Before you use the emulator with Wabi, verify that it is correctly installed by running it directly from UNIX.

Drive mappings (for emulated hard drives, or virtual drives) that you use in the DOS emulator must match the drive mappings you use in the Wabi program (except for drive C:, and possibly D:, which are likely to be permanently assigned by the DOS emulator). If the drive letters do not connect to the same file system or directory on the host computer, the emulator may not work correctly. See Chapter 6, "Managing Drives," for more information about drive mappings.

As noted above, you must coordinate the drive mappings that you assign in Wabi with the drive mappings you assign in your DOS emulator. For example, if Wabi drive G: is assigned to the UNIX directory named /home/room, the DOS emulator drive G: must also be assigned to /home/room. If drives are not mapped identically in both programs, an error will occur if an application running under the DOS emulator tries to access a drive through Wabi.

Before you run a DOS application through the DOS emulator under Wabi, make sure all drive mappings in both the DOS emulator and Wabi are consistent.

The DOS Emulator Drive C:

With most DOS emulators, the emulator's C: drive cannot be mapped to a Wabi drive because it is usually a special file that the Wabi program cannot access. For example, SunPC's C: drive is in a nonstandard format. Most DOS emulators create one or two special drives which, while existing in the UNIX file system, contain an internal structure meant to duplicate a DOS/FAT file system. This makes it possible for programs that require their files to remain in specific sets of clusters on a DOS disk—like Windows permanent swap files and some copy-protected programs—to work normally under UNIX.

You should store any files you want to use in both the Wabi program and the DOS emulator in your home directory. Make sure both programs connect the same drive (H:, for instance) to your home directory. If you want to use the Wabi program and your emulator to run applications installed in your DOS emulator's drive C:, you should:

- Start the DOS emulator.

- Map a DOS emulator drive to your home directory if you don't already have one.

- Copy the application directories and files from drive C: to the drive connected to your home directory.

- Start the application from the drive connected to your home directory to make sure the application runs correctly.

- When you are sure the application runs correctly, delete the application files from drive C:.

  Note that this may not work with certain applications or files.

Configuring DOS Emulator Connections

The Wabi program must know the UNIX command used to start your DOS emulator. You specify this information by using the DOS tool in Wabi Configuration Manager. The DOS Emulator Connection dialog box (Figure 10-1) lets you specify your DOS emulator's UNIX path name, startup command, and startup parameters. Once your DOS emulator is functional under the Wabi program, you can use it to install and run DOS applications.

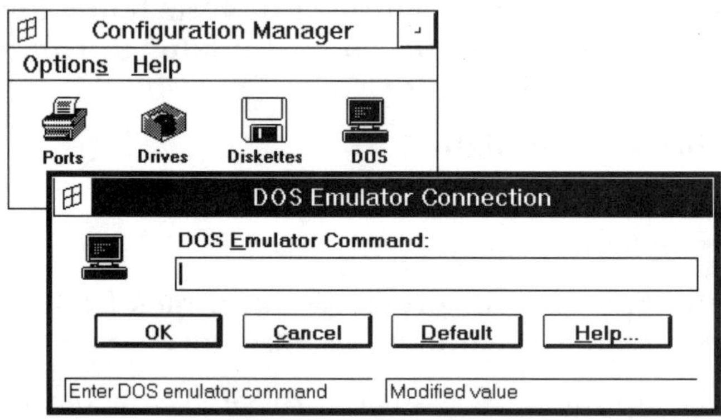

Figure 10-1 DOS Emulator Connection Dialog Box

In the DOS emulator command, there are three variables you can include for parameters that enable Wabi to start DOS applications running under the emulator. Table 10-1 lists these parameters and their purposes.

Table 10-1 DOS Emulator Startup Variables

Variable	Purpose
%d	Used with the emulator's -display option (-display is an option with most X-based DOS emulators). Wabi replaces %d with a display name. Including %d with the -display option makes the DOS session appear on the same display screen as Wabi. When you start Wabi with -display, the same remote host display name is substituted for %d in the DOS emulator command. If you do not start Wabi with the -display option, %d is replaced by the name specified by the DISPLAY variable in your UNIX environment. See "Displaying Wabi On a Remote System" on page 135 for more information about -display.
%f	Passed as a parameter to the DOS emulator option that starts a DOS program. Including %f, preceded by the appropriate command-line option, allows you to start a DOS application through Wabi by using the Windows Run command, or by double-clicking a Windows program item icon. The emulator option you use with %f is specific to the emulator; for example, the emulator may use -c or -s. (Some emulators don't require any option.) Wabi replaces %f with the name of an executable DOS program. Wabi uses the name of the executable file that you specify when you create a program item for the application, or when you run the application through the Windows Run command.
%c	Related to %f, %c lets you specify additional command-line parameters. For example, including %c lets you specify an argument such as a file name or some other parameter. %c must be used in combination with %f. Wabi replaces %c with the remainder of the DOS command line that follows the executable command.

For example, suppose you want to run a DOS application called CLEANUP.EXE on a file called PRICE.LST, using a hypothetical /X option, and you are using the SunPC emulator. Suppose now that, under DOS, the command line you would normally use to do this would be:

```
CLEANUP.EXE  PRICE.LST  /X  /Y
```

In Wabi Configuration Manager, the emulator command would include the emulator name, and the %f and %c variables. For example:

```
sunpc -c %f %c
```

When Wabi passes this command to the emulator, %f is replaced by CLEANUP.EXE, and %c is replaced by PRICE.LST and the /X option.

➤ *To configure your DOS emulator startup command*

1. **Open Windows Control Panel.**

2. **Open Wabi Configuration Manager.**

3. **Choose the DOS tool.**
   The DOS Emulator Connection dialog box is displayed.

4. **Enter a path name, startup command, and optional variables for your DOS emulator.**
   This should be the command you would use to start the emulator directly under UNIX.

5. **Choose OK to save your settings and exit the dialog.**

Starting DOS Sessions

After configuring your DOS emulator connection, you can start DOS sessions just as you would in the Microsoft Windows environment under DOS. By default, The Windows Main group includes an MS-DOS Prompt program item (Figure 10-2). When you open this program item in the Wabi environment, the DOS emulator starts.

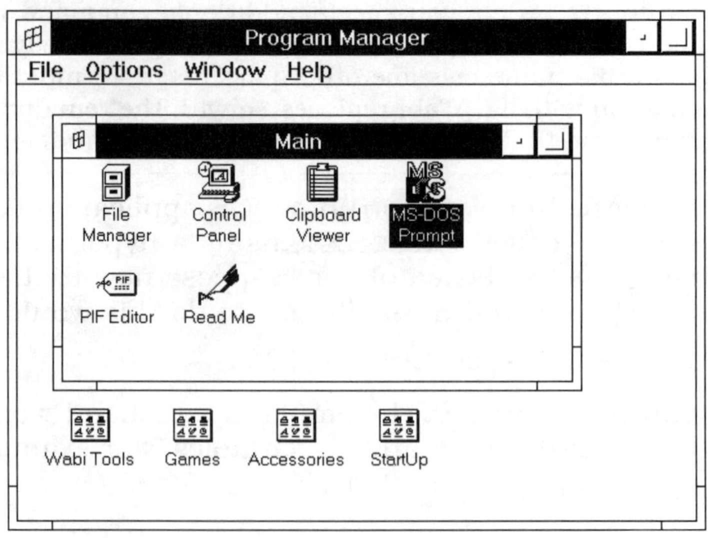

Figure 10-2 MS-DOS Prompt Icon in the Main Group

Wabi 2: Opening Windows

The DOS emulator starts in its own UNIX process in its window, so you still have access to the Wabi window, your Windows applications, and your UNIX desktop. Note, however, that with this implementation, you cannot use the Windows task-switching mechanisms to switch to the DOS session—that is, the familiar Windows Alt+Tab (to switch among Windows tasks) or Ctrl+Esc (to display Windows Task Manager) do not recognize the DOS session as a Windows task. To switch to the DOS session, you must use the mechanisms provided by your X Window environment.

> ### To start your DOS emulator under Wabi

1. **Open Windows Program Manager.**
2. **Open the Main program group.**
3. **Open the MS-DOS Prompt program item.**
   You can either double-click on the icon for the program item, or select the icon and then press Enter.

Installing DOS Applications

After you install your DOS emulator, you can use it to install DOS applications. You can start the emulator from the UNIX operating system, or you can open the MS-DOS Prompt program item in the Windows Main program group. Once you are running a DOS session, proceed to install the DOS application as indicated in the application's installation instructions.

You should not install any applications in Wabi's C: drive or the DOS emulator's C: drive. Also, you should configure drives for both programs so they use the same UNIX directories, and install applications in those drives. If you want Wabi to access files already stored in your DOS emulator's drive C:, follow the instructions in "The DOS Emulator Drive C:" on page 253.

➤ *To install DOS applications under Wabi*

1. **Configure your DOS emulator for use with Wabi, as explained in "Configuring DOS Emulator Connections" on page 254.**

2. **Start the DOS emulator.**

3. **Install the DOS application from within the emulator, just as you would under DOS.**

   Use the installation instructions provided with the application.

After a DOS application has been installed through your DOS emulator, you can create a Windows program group and program item for it so you can start the application easily from within Wabi. Microsoft Windows applications create their own program groups and items when you install them, but DOS applications do not because they are not designed to run under Windows.

You can create program groups and items for DOS applications the same way you create them for Microsoft Windows applications, using the New command in the Windows Program Manager or File Manager File menu.

When you choose New from the File menu, the New Program Object dialog box is displayed (Figure 10-3).

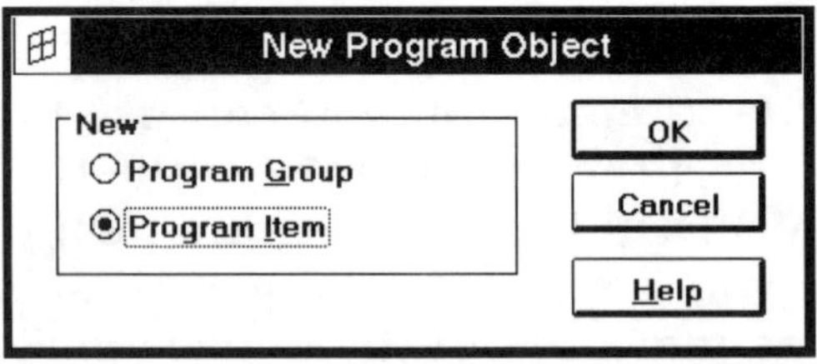

Figure 10-3 New Program Object Dialog Box

You use the New Program Object dialog box to specify whether you want to create a new program group or a new program item.

- To create a program group, choose Program Group and enter a group description in the Program Group Properties dialog box that is subsequently displayed.

- To create a program item, choose Program Item and enter program item information in the Program Item Properties dialog that is subsequently displayed (Figure 10-4).

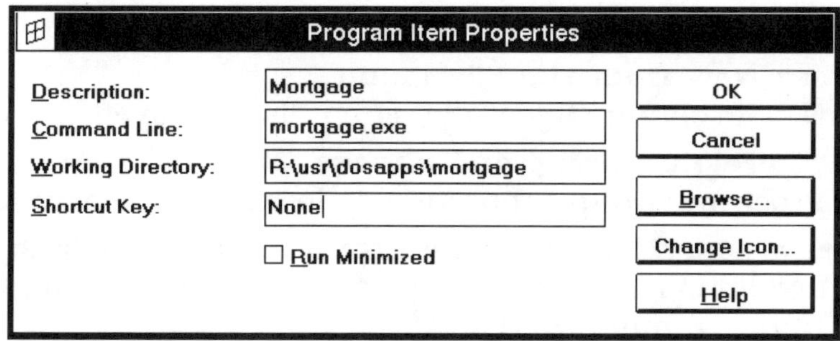

Figure 10-4 Program Item Properties Dialog Box

For DOS applications, the command you enter in the Command Line field is the same command you would use to start the application in DOS. It must be in DOS format and include the Wabi drive location, and may include parameters or switches. Do not include the DOS emulator command. When you start the application from the icon, the Wabi program detects that the application requires DOS, starts your DOS emulator, and passes the command you enter here.

Microsoft Windows applications generally have icons associated with the executable files, but DOS executables do not. When you create a program item for a DOS application, the Program Manager uses a generic icon indicating that the program is a DOS program. However, you can use a different icon if you like. The Change Icon button opens a dialog box that lets you select a different icon image to represent the application when it is minimized or displayed in a group window.

DOS applications used with a DOS emulator through Wabi do not need a Program Information File (PIF).

➤ *To create a program group in Windows*

1. **Open Windows Program Manager.**
2. **Choose New from the File menu.**
   The New Program Object dialog box is displayed.
3. **Select Program Group and choose OK.**
   The Program Group Properties dialog box is displayed.
4. **Enter a description for the group in the Description field.**
   The text you enter here is displayed beneath the group icon when the group is minimized.
5. **Enter a file name in the Group File Name field (optional).**
   By default, Windows creates a group file name based on your entry in the Description field; fill in this field only if you want to use a different name to store the group file on disk.
6. **Choose OK to accept your entries and exit the dialog.**
   A group window with the description you specified opens. You can now create program items for applications in this group.

➤ *To create a program item in Windows*

1. **Open Windows Program Manager.**
2. **Select or create the program group in which you want to place a new program item.**
3. **Choose New from the File menu.**
   The New Program Object dialog box is displayed.
4. **Select Program Item and choose OK.**
   The Program Item Properties dialog box is displayed.
5. **Enter the appropriate information in the Program Item Properties dialog box.**
6. **Choose OK to accept your entries and exit the dialog.**
   A program item for DOS application appears in the program group you selected in Step 2.

Running DOS Applications

You can use Wabi to start DOS applications the same way you would in "regular" Microsoft Windows under DOS—that is, either with the Windows Program Manager or File Manager File→Run command, or by opening the program item for the application, if one exists.

Using Run to Start Applications

You can start DOS applications under Wabi by using the Windows Run command. To do this, open the File menu in either Windows Program Manager or File Manager, then choose Run to display the Run dialog box (Figure 10-5).

The command you enter in the Run dialog box is the same command you would use to run the application under DOS, except that the drive letter indicates a directory path in your UNIX file system.

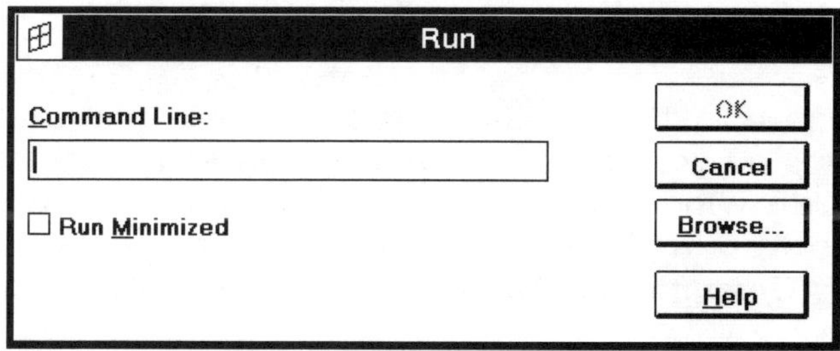

Figure 10-5 Run Dialog Box

Type the DOS command you want to execute in the Command Line field—do not, however, specify the name of your DOS emulator here. When you choose OK, Wabi detects that the application requires DOS, then automatically starts your DOS emulator, which loads and runs the DOS application.

Using Program Items to Start Applications

Perhaps the easiest way to use a DOS application under Wabi is to create a program item for it (as described in "Installing DOS Applications" on page 257). You can then open the program item (that is, start the application with which it is associated) by double-clicking on an icon representing the application. When you open the program item, Wabi detects that the item is a DOS application, then automatically starts your DOS emulator program, which runs the DOS application.

Running Windows From a DOS Emulator

If you want to run an unsupported Windows application under Wabi—remember that an application does not need to be Wabi-certified in order for it to run—your only recourse is to run Windows through a DOS emulator, if possible, and then run the application from there.

Windows under DOS is considerably slower than under Wabi. Also, depending on your emulator and its configuration, you may not be able to run Windows in 386 Enhanced Mode, and consequently be unable to run applications requiring this mode. See "Solutions For Running Unsupported Applications" on page 10 for more information.

To run Windows under an emulator from Wabi, use either the Windows Run command, or create a program item for the application under Wabi. On the command line for the application enter:

```
WIN [application_name] [file_name] [options]
```

Refer to your *Microsoft Windows User's Guide* for more information about Windows command-line options and parameters.

➤ *To start a DOS application under Wabi*

The instructions in this procedure assume that you have configured your DOS emulator and DOS application as described earlier in this chapter.

➡ **Open the program item representing the DOS application.**
Either double-click the icon for the program item, or select the item and press Enter.

The DOS emulator starts and loads the DOS application.

or

1. **Choose the Run command from the File menu in either Windows Program Manager or File Manager.**
   The Run dialog box is displayed.

2. **Enter the desired command in the Command Line field.**

3. **Choose OK to accept your entry and execute the command.**
   The DOS emulator starts and loads the DOS application.

Chapter 11

Managing
Colors

Windowing environments—whether Microsoft Windows or X Window—just aren't the same without color. As users of notebook computers with monochrome LCD screens know, navigating through menus, using toolbars, and figuring out what the heck various icons mean is far more difficult in black and white. On the flip side, a bad color scheme is worse than no color scheme at all.

Why do two colors, put one next to the other, sing? Can one really explain this? no. Just as one can never learn how to paint.

– Pablo Picasso. *Arts de France, no. 6, 1946*

In black and white, the ideas behind the art are communicated more directly. Meaning transcends form.

– Scott McCloud, *Understanding Comics*, 1993

In This Chapter

About Colors Under Wabi

Many popular color-display devices are able to generate thousands or even millions of different colors, but can display only 256 or fewer colors at a time. Because of this, the colors available for display at a given time must be defined and listed, or allocated, in a place where the window system can look them up.

To this end, colors are identified by RGB values, which are numbers that indicate the amounts of red, green, and blue light needed to produce the color. Microsoft Windows and X Window both use a table of RGB values stored in memory to determine what colors are available for use. Microsoft Windows calls its table of colors a *color palette*, and X Window calls it a *colormap*.

Each entry in the table is called a *color cell*, and specifies the RGB values for a particular color. Each pixel on a display is assigned a number corresponding to a color cell, and the RGB value stored in the color cell determines the color displayed by the pixel.

Microsoft Windows and X Window each use a color table that is hardware-dependent, so the color tables vary from one display type to another. Both window systems also let applications provide their own color tables, and here is where color handling in the two systems differs markedly.

A good source of detailed information about X Window color handling is the *Xlib Programming Manual* (Adrian Nye; O'Reilly & Associates, Inc., 1995.).

Microsoft Windows Color Allocation

Microsoft Windows tries to match the colors in an application's color palette, called the *logical palette*, to colors already allocated in the default palette. Windows uses one of two methods for handling this. The method chosen depends on the particular display type.

- For some displays, Microsoft Windows uses a single color palette, one that cannot be changed. If an application requests a color that is not in the palette, Windows either uses the closest color it can find in the palette, or approximates the color by making a pattern composed of pixels of different colors (a process called *dithering*). For example, a light yellow might be approximated with a checkerboard pattern of bright yellow and white. Usually, if the color is for a line, Windows uses the closest color. If the color is for filling a shape, Windows dithers the color.

- For other displays, Microsoft Windows uses a palette manager, which can change colors in the default palette. If an application requests a color that is not in the palette, and an unallocated color cell exists, the color is added to the palette. If no more unallocated color cells are available, Windows either matches the logical palette color to the closest color it can find in the default palette, or dithers it.

Because all windows running in Microsoft Windows use the default palette, Windows allocates colors for the active window first, to make sure its colors are correct. The inactive windows could potentially show some colors that are not exactly what the application requested. However, for the most part, colors in inactive windows are close to what is intended.

X Window Color Allocation

X Window color handling is more complex, and varies with the display type and the capabilities of the X server, a program that controls all aspects of the display for X applications. It usually supports several color handling methods, called *visuals.*

- The X server has a default visual, the method used to handle color when an X application does not request a specific visual. Wabi uses the X server's default visual whenever possible.

- On the most common types of color display, 8-bit or 8-plane, the usual default is a visual called `PseudoColor`, which is therefore the visual that Wabi uses most often.

  8-plane displays generally have one hardware colormap, into which the X server loads a default colormap when it first starts up. The default X colormap is changeable, so X applications can change individual color cells in the default colormap to allocate colors they need.

- X applications can also provide their own colormaps, called *virtual colormaps*, which are loaded into the hardware colormap. The X server can maintain more than one virtual colormap at the same time, but only one can be used in the hardware colormap at any given instant. This means that if the active application swaps in its own colormap, all other (inactive) applications' windows must use this same colormap. As a consequence, the color cells assigned to pixels might now contain colors completely different from those intended, resulting in undesirable color schemes for the inactive windows.

  As you change focus from one window to another, colors flash as each application's colormap is loaded and used by all running applications.

To minimize color flashing, only color-intensive X applications use virtual colormaps. The Wabi program is a color-intensive X application by virtue of the many color-intensive Windows applications it runs, so color flashing can be a problem, but you can alleviate it by controlling certain aspects of the Wabi colormap.

The Wabi Colormap

When the Wabi program uses `PseudoColor` visuals, it creates a virtual colormap but tries to retain as many as possible of the colors already allocated in the default colormap. This reduces the number of colors that might be changed for other X applications that are running.

When Wabi starts, it uses the current default colormap as the starting point for creating a virtual colormap. First, the Wabi program changes some of the color cells in the default colormap to provide a range of colors needed for the Windows applications you may subsequently run. It allocates 49 colors—7 shades of each of the 7 solid colors (red, green, blue, cyan, magenta, yellow, and gray). In addition, it allocates 15 more colors—5 shades of each of the primary colors (red, green, and blue). Some of these additional reds, greens, and blues may be duplicates of the 49 shades of solid colors, so the total number of colors allocated may be something less than 64 colors. On an 8-plane display (which has 256 colors in its colormap), this leaves the majority of colors in the default colormap unchanged. Wabi then copies the changed default map into its own virtual colormap. Finally, the Wabi program frees half of the color cells it allocated in the default colormap so that they can be allocated by other X applications.

Wabi Color Variables

Wabi uses several variables that influence how the Wabi colormap is created, and how Wabi interacts with the default X colormap. One variable, `Technicolor`, affects Wabi on all display types. The other variables depend on `Technicolor` being set to `0`, and apply only when Wabi is using the 8-bit `PseudoColor` visual. You set these variables in your `WIN.INI` file. (See "Setting Wabi Color Variables" on page 275 for more information.)

The `Technicolor` Variable

The Wabi `Technicolor` variable allows you to make a trade-off between color flashing when you switch focus among different X windows (an unpleasant effect referred to as *technicolor*) and flexibility in allocating and changing colors in Microsoft Windows applications running in the Wabi environment.

- **`Technicolor=1`** – If you want applications running under Wabi to be able to allocate all the colors they want, you can set `Technicolor=1`, and put up with color flashing in inactive X windows. When `Technicolor=1` is set, Wabi uses a standard X colormap as its colormap. This often causes color flashing on 8-bit displays when you switch between Wabi windows and other X windows.

- **`Technicolor=0`** – If it does not matter to you if applications in Wabi get the exact colors they want, set `Technicolor=0`, and color flashing will be minimized as Wabi tries to share colors with other X applications. When `Technicolor=0` is set, Wabi allocates colors from the default X colormap and then copies them to the Wabi colormap, as described on the previous page, in an attempt to share as many colors as possible.

The default value is 0 (color flashing off), unless there is more than one hardware colormap for the display screen. If there is more than one hardware colormap, it is assumed one will be available for Wabi, and the value defaults to 1.

If your X server has more than one hardware colormap, but the colormaps are normally already in use by other X applications when you start Wabi, you can set `Technicolor` to 0 to alleviate color flashing.

If your X server has one colormap, as is the case with most 8-bit displays, you may set `Technicolor` to 1 to give Wabi, and the Windows applications running under it, the most flexibility in allocating and changing color. If you need the color flexibility and find that color flashing is annoying, try maximizing the Wabi window when you use the Windows application. This prevents the mouse pointer from drifting into other X application windows and causing their colormaps to be swapped in.

Other Wabi Color Variables

The other Wabi color variables affect Wabi only when it uses 8-bit `PseudoColor` visuals (on 8-bit and 24-bit displays) and `Technicolor` is set to 0. You can see if Wabi is using 8-bit `PseudoColor` by running the X program `xwininfo`, which should be present on most UNIX systems with X Window.

➤ *To determine if Wabi is using 8-bit `PseudoColor`*

1. **Start Wabi.**
2. **Enter the following command in a UNIX command window:**

   ```
   xwininfo
   ```

   The `xwininfo` program starts.
3. **Select the Wabi window when prompted.**
   Information about the Wabi window is displayed.
4. **Look for the following lines:**

   ```
   Depth:8
   Visual Class: PseudoColor
   ```

   If you see these lines, you can use the variables listed in Table 11-1.

If xwininfo is not available, use the xdpyinfo command. This displays information about your X server, including the visuals that are available.

➤ *To use the xdpyinfo command*

⇒ **Enter the following command in a UNIX command window:**

```
xdpyinfo | grep class
```

If you see the class , you can use the variables in Table 11-1.

Table 11-1 describes the various Wabi 8-bit PseudoColor variables. Remember, these variables:

- Are set in your WIN.INI file (see page 275)
- Only work when Technicolor=0 (also set in WIN.INI)
- Only work when you are using 8-bit PseudoColor visuals (8-bit PseudoColor visuals are also supported on 24-bit displays)

Table 11-1   Variables for 8-Bit PseudoColor Visuals

Variable	Description
PercentFree=n	Specifies how much of the default X colormap Wabi should free up after allocating its colors. The range of acceptable values is 0 through 100, with a default of 50, which means Wabi frees 50% of the color cells.
	Setting PercentFree higher could reduce color flashing as you activate and deactivate the Wabi window, because the other X windows use most of the colors that were in effect when they started. However, setting PercentFree to 100 means Wabi frees all the color cells it allocated, which leaves the same number of free color cells as there were before Wabi started. This may cause flashing as the default X colormap and the Wabi colormap are swapped in and out.
	Setting PercentFree lower reduces the chance that other X applications will find insufficient free color entries available. If an X application does not find enough free color cells, it may display incorrect colors, return an error message, or detect that the default X colormap is too full and swap in its own virtual colormap. This causes more color flashing when you move the mouse out of the X application's window.

Variable	Description
`SolidColorCount=`*n*	Defines how many shades of each of the seven colors (red, green, blue, cyan, magenta, yellow, and gray) are allocated. The total number of shades allocated is equal to seven times the value specified for `SolidColorCount`. The range of acceptable values is 1 through 16, with a default of 7. Set this variable higher to let Wabi allocate more colors so that applications running under Wabi don't find it necessary to allocate new colors. Set this variable lower if most colors have already been defined by X applications before Wabi starts, or if you will be manually defining all your colors anyway (through a "paint" program, for example).
`RedCubeCount=`*n* `GreenCubeCount=`*n* `BlueCubeCount=`*n*	These three variables define the dimensions of the red, green, and blue components of the color cube. The color cube comprises the additional reds, greens, and blues that Wabi adds to its colormap. These variables allow you to alter the number of reds, greens, and blues, respectively, that will be used in the Wabi colormap. The range is 4 through 9, with a default of 5. You can adjust these variables if you find that Windows applications you run need more colors of a particular shade. These variables have no effect on color flashing.

Variables for 24-Bit Displays

Wabi does not directly support 24-bit TrueColor displays. However, some X servers that run on 24-bit displays can simulate an 8-bit `PseudoColor` device. The Wabi program uses an 8-bit `PseudoColor` visual on 24-bit displays that support `PseudoColor`, so all the variables described above apply to such 24-bit displays as well as 8-bit displays.

One additional variable, `UseRootWindow`, may be useful if you find Wabi has problems drawing to your 24-bit display. `UseRootWindow=`n tells whether Wabi can draw to and read from the root window (the "background" window of your X Window desktop). The default value is `1` (yes), unless the Wabi colormap and the default colormap are of different sizes, in which case the default is `0` (no).

Most users will never need to set `UseRootWindow`. This variable should not be set unless you need it, because it may cause problems, especially on 8-bit displays. You should only consider using it if you are using a 24-bit display and Wabi appears to be having problems drawing to the screen (windows and icons do not look right, for example).

If you are experiencing such problems, experiment with `UseRootWindow` to see if it alleviates them. If this does nothing, or makes the drawing worse, remove the variable entirely.

Setting Wabi Color Variables

To set Wabi color variables, edit your `$HOME/wabi/windows/win.ini` file and add them. None of the variables appear in `win.ini` as shipped in the Wabi program.

If you want the variables to affect your running of Wabi on any display you use, set the variables in the `[ColorMap]` section in win.ini. For example, if all displays you use are 8-bit, set the variables in the `[ColorMap]` section.

If you run Wabi on more than one display and you want the variables to affect Wabi only on a particular display, create a section whose title is the display name and set the variables in that section. For example, to apply the variables to Wabi only when you display it on the display `jethro:0.0`, create a section called `[jethro:0.0]`.

The Wabi program reads the `[ColorMap]` section first, and then the `[host:0.0]` sections, so that variables set in `[host:0.0]` sections supersede variables set in the `[ColorMap]` section for the specified displays. If you set the same variables in both sections, the `[host:0.0]` variables are used for those displays. This may be helpful if you use multiple displays and one of them is 24-bit, for example. You could set variables specific to the 24-bit display by creating a `[host:0.0]` section, and set variables for all 8-bit displays in the `[ColorMap]` section.

➤ *To add Wabi color variables to WIN.INI*

1. **Open your `$HOME/wabi/windows/win.ini` file in your preferred text editor.**
   You can edit the file from within Windows or from UNIX. If you edit the file from within Windows, you will need to restart Wabi for your changes to take effect.

2. **Locate the `[ColorMap]` section.**

3. **Add the desired entries, one per line.**
   You must add `Technicolor=0` for any other variables to work.

4. **Save the file and exit the text editor.**

5. **Start (or restart) Wabi.**

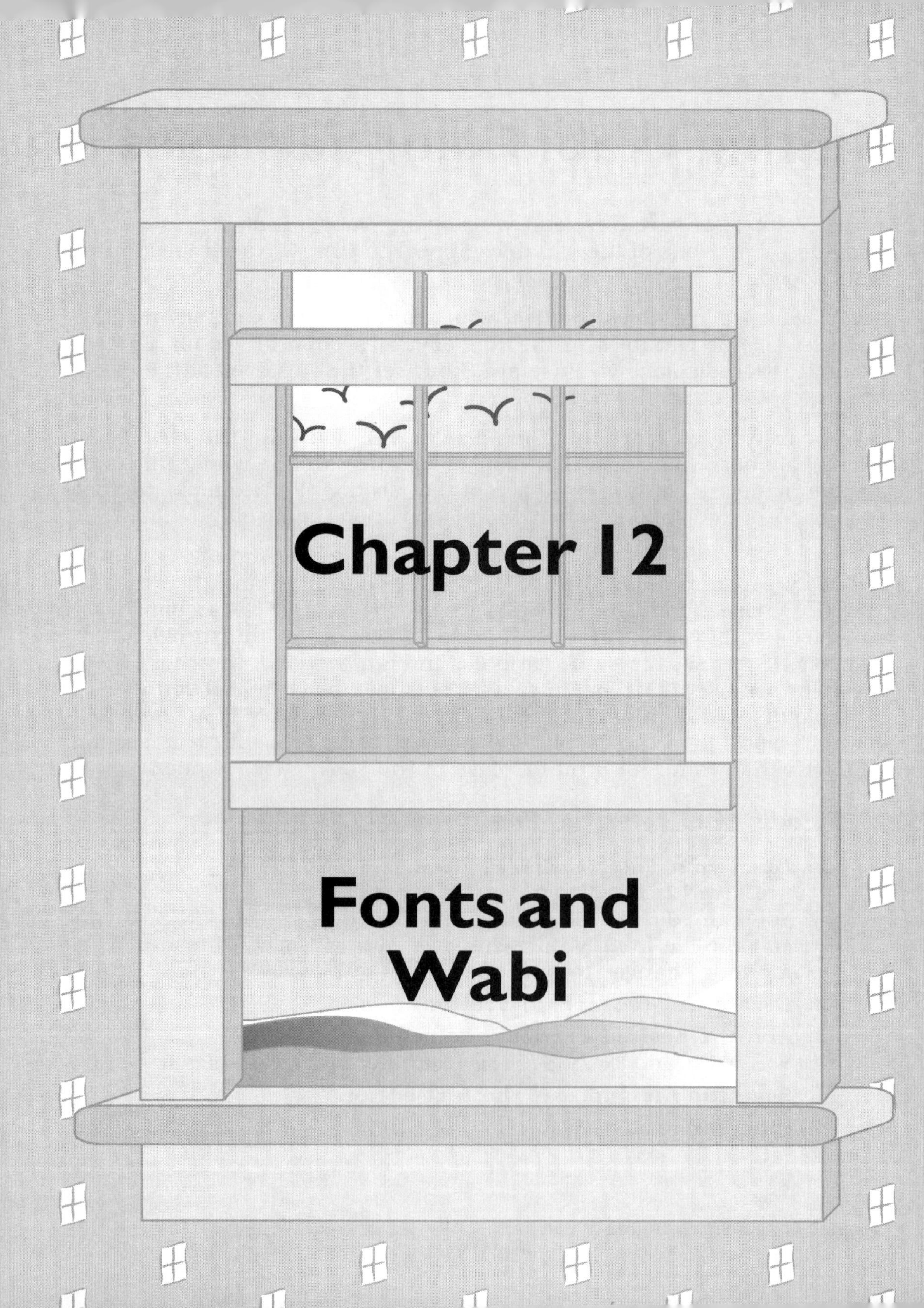

Chapter 12

Fonts and
Wabi

One of the most important developments in the evolution of graphical user interfaces is bitmapped displays. Rather than forcing users to work with fixed-width, fixed-size, text-only characters, displayed in a rigid row/column format, bitmapped displays allow any combination of graphical and textual elements. This makes possible every visual interface component to which we've grown accustomed: windows, pull-down menus, and perhaps most significant, the display of variable-width, scalable type, in a variety of faces and styles.

The question of when to introduce lined paper needs careful thought; lines help the child to control the direction and size of script, but they also constrain the spontaneity of a natural writing style.

– David Crystal, *The Cambridge Encyclopedia of Language:* "Learning to Write," 1987

In This Chapter

Topic	Page
About Fonts Under Wabi	*278*
Font Display Types	*278*
Wabi Font Processing	*280*
Wabi Font Server	*281*

About Fonts Under Wabi

Wabi software translates between the on-screen fonts displayed by Microsoft Windows and those displayed by X Window.

Fonts used in Microsoft Windows applications are described in font resource files, usually stored in `C:\WINDOWS\SYSTEM` with file name extensions such as `.FON` and `.TTF`. These files contain either the actual images of fonts and detailed numeric information about them, or precise information about how to create the font images.

The X Window System cannot use the Microsoft Windows font images or font information directly because it expects font information in a different form. The Wabi program must convert the font information so that the X server can use it to display the desired fonts.

On X Window systems using the X11R5 protocol (or a more recent version), the Wabi program uses the Wabi font server, `wabifs`, which speeds up the conversion process so that the X server can display the fonts faster.

Font Display Types

Three font display types are relevant to applications running in Microsoft Windows and in the Wabi environment: bitmap fonts, outline fonts, and vector fonts.

- **Bitmap fonts** – Bitmap fonts are stored as graphic images of characters, with each point size of a typeface stored as a separate font. Generally, in Microsoft Windows, the fonts used in dialog boxes and in an application's screen displays are bitmap fonts. Bitmap fonts can be scaled (displayed in smaller and larger point sizes), but a scaled bitmap font may display with poor resolution.

A bitmap font displayed on the screen is not the same font used by a printer. Most WYSIWYG ("what you see is what you get") applications running in the Microsoft Windows or Wabi environment only use bitmap fonts that can be matched to a printer font on the printer you are currently set up to use. The font used by the printer, while not the same as the bitmap font shown on the screen, usually looks nearly identical. For example, if you use the font Courier 10 in your document, you see a bitmap Courier 10 on the display. When you print your document, you see the printer's version of Courier 10.

- **Outline fonts** – Outline fonts are produced from stored information about the shape, or outline, of the font. Outline fonts scale better because the information about the shape is independent of the size. In both Microsoft Windows and X Window environments, different font sizes are created by calculating the new size and reproducing the exact shape of a character in the new size. TrueType fonts and many X Window fonts, including those used by Adobe PostScript, are outline fonts.

  Outline fonts can be used both on the screen and on the printer. If you are using a printer that can handle outline fonts in either Microsoft Windows or Wabi environments, the outline information is passed to the printer and the printer creates the raster images. If you are using a printer that cannot handle outline fonts, Microsoft Windows or Wabi creates the raster images and sends them to the printer. In either case, the fonts are the same printed and on the screen.

- **Vector fonts** – Vector fonts (or plotter fonts) are stored as lists of vectors to be drawn in sequence to generate each character. Although they are easily scalable, their appearance is poor compared to outline fonts.

Wabi does not support third-party font utilities like Adobe Type Manager and Bitstream® FaceLift™.

Wabi Font Processing

Each time you start the Wabi program, it creates a list of available fonts from the `[fonts]` section in `win.ini`, which includes bitmap fonts shipped with the Wabi program, TrueType, bitmap, and vector fonts installed with Microsoft Windows, and any fonts installed with your applications. This list of fonts is made available to applications, just as in Microsoft Windows.

When you select a font name, the Wabi program finds the font information and determines how to display it. The method for displaying the font varies depending on whether the font is a TrueType, bitmap, or vector font, and whether the Wabi font server (see next page) is running.

- **Vector fonts** – Vector fonts are the easiest to display. For each character to be displayed, Wabi simply draws the list of vectors, or lines, that make up the character. Because line drawing is fast, Wabi is able to draw these characters itself, without help from the X server. Bitmap and TrueType fonts, however, are more complicated to produce.

- **Bitmap and TrueType/with the Wabi font server** – If the font server is running and Wabi is asked to display characters using a bitmap or TrueType font, Wabi simply passes the font information to the Wabi font server. Wabi passes the text to be displayed to the X server. The X server obtains any necessary font images or information from the Wabi font server and displays the text.

- **Without the font server**
  - **TrueType** – If the font server is not running and the font requested is\TrueType, Wabi creates bitmap images of the TrueType font. The Wabi program can then draw characters by painting these bitmaps onto the screen, using the X server's normal functions.
  - **Bitmap** – If the font server is not running, and the requested font is a Microsoft Windows bitmap font, the font's raster images, or bitmaps, are already created, so the Wabi program uses them to draw the characters on the screen.

Wabi Font Server

The Wabi font server uses the X Font Service Protocol, a method introduced in the X11R5 release of the X Window System for separating font handling from the X server's other duties. (Note, however, that not all X11R5 servers support the Font Service Protocol.)

If the X server is the X11R5 release and supports the Font Service Protocol, Wabi starts its font server, `wabifs`, when you start the Wabi program. When Wabi selects a font in the available fonts list, it passes the font information to `wabifs`, which takes over font processing for the request and interacts with the X server.

If the X server is the X11R4 release or does not support the Font Service Protocol, Wabi creates bitmap images of the fonts on the X server, which then displays them.

When the Wabi font server is running, you see two UNIX processes rather than one. The main process is called `wabiprog`, and the font server process is called `wabifs`. The processes work together closely.

With the Wabi font server running, the Wabi program can send text rather than bitmapped images to the X server no matter what font you are using. Even if you are using a TrueType font that your X server does not know about, Wabi can act as though the X server knows about the font. The Wabi program passes the Windows font data to the Wabi font server, which converts the font information to a form the X server can use. The font server passes the converted font information to the X server, which then displays the characters on the screen in the specified font.

Font processing is most efficient when the Wabi font server is running. There is no performance difference between TrueType and Microsoft Windows bitmap fonts. If the font server is not running, all fonts take longer to display because the Wabi program must create the font images and pass them to the X server.

If you have a problem with fonts and cannot tell where the problem lies, you can take a step towards isolating it by starting Wabi without the font server to see if the symptoms change. See "Starting Wabi Without the Font Server" on page 136 for instructions.

Chapter 13
Network Notes

Wabi lets your Windows application access your UNIX network facilities in various ways. In addition, Wabi provides some basic PC network interface support.

Information networks straddle the world. Nothing remains concealed. But the sheer volume of information dissolves the information. We are unable to take it all in.

– Günther Grass, in New Statesman & Society, 1990

In This Chapter

Topic	Page
About Wabi Networking	*284*
Wabi and UNIX Networking	*284*
Wabi and Windows Sockets	*285*
Networking for Email Applications	*285*
Network-Aware Applications	*286*
Novell NetWare File Systems	*286*

About Wabi Networking

The Wabi program provides an environment that combines UNIX and PC networking. A computer running UNIX is very likely connected to a TCP/IP network, and probably uses distributed file system software, like NFS, which allows the computer to access directories on remote computers as if those directories were on a local hard drive. A personal computer running DOS and Microsoft Windows is often connected to a PC network, through one of several PC network products using one of several networking interfaces. The Wabi program uses the TCP/IP network and a distributed file system to provide some of the services of a PC network, such as shared file systems and devices. The Wabi program also supports the Windows Sockets networking interface to allow certified applications, such as Lotus Notes, to communicate through the network directly.

Wabi and UNIX Networking

Wabi uses the TCP/IP network and distributed file system capabilities of the UNIX host to which it is connected or on which it is running. This process is mostly transparent to the applications running in Wabi.

For example, the printers and drives to which you connect through Wabi Configuration Manager are often residing on a network. To a Windows application running under Wabi, the printer seems to be connected locally to a port on a PC, but in reality, it may be in another wing of the building, connected to a remote print server. Wabi can make any drive, local or remote, appear to an application as either local or remote, as you prefer—that is, remote drives can be configured to appear local, or local drives can be made to appear remote, depending on your needs. You use Wabi Configuration Manager to configure drives as local or remote. See "Wabi Network Drives" on page 174 for instructions.

You can connect a Wabi drive to any file system that can be accessed through your UNIX operating system. For example, if you can access a NetWare® file system from your operating system, you can access it through a Wabi drive. See "Wabi Drives" on page 162 for details.

Wabi and Windows Sockets

Windows Sockets is a network interface protocol that allows Microsoft Windows applications to exchange data over a network. Windows Sockets, or Winsock, is based on the sockets interface, a network interface used by most UNIX operating systems, and is tailored for the Microsoft Windows environment. In the Wabi environment, Winsock is internal to the Wabi program, so you won't see a `WINSOCK.DLL` in your windows directory, as you would on a DOS-based PC.

Applications can make Winsock calls, and Wabi carries them out using TCP/IP. The Wabi program's Winsock capability is always available to applications, and no configuration is necessary. Note that the Wabi program runs only the client version of applications that use Winsock.

The Wabi program is not guaranteed to support every application that uses the Winsock network interface. Only certified applications, such as Lotus Notes, are supported for Winsock. See "Using Remote Database Access" on page 238, for information about using supported applications featuring remote database connectivity through Winsock.

Networking for Email Applications

Wabi-certified electronic mail applications do not use a PC network interface to exchange messages. When Microsoft Mail and Lotus cc:Mail™ clients, for example, run in "regular" Microsoft Windows under DOS, they use a distributed file system provided by the PC networking software under which they are running. When they run in the Wabi environment, they use the distributed file system provided by the UNIX operating system. Therefore, Wabi Configuration Manager does not present any network options that affect electronic mail programs.

Network-Aware Applications

Some Windows applications that run under Wabi, while not actually communicating over a network, are "network-aware." Such applications take steps to prevent problems caused by multiple users having access to the same files: locking files when open, creating temporary files for each user, storing times in Greenwich Time for accurate time stamps across time zones, and so on. Network-aware applications may need to know if they are using a local or network drive. "Wabi Network Drives" on page 174, explains how to work with network drives under Wabi.

Novell NetWare File Systems

The Wabi program does not support the Novell® NetWare API. This means you cannot run a NetWare client to use NetWare's file and print services directly from the Wabi environment. The Microsoft Windows NetWare client requires DOS-based drivers in order to communicate with the NetWare server.

However, you can set up the NetWare server and your operating system to allow the Wabi program to access files on the NetWare server in the same way it accesses UNIX file systems. You can purchase an add-on NetWare Loadable Module (NLM) from Novell, Inc. to provide name space support on your NetWare server for UNIX NFS-based distributed file systems. Once the NLM is loaded, you can add an NFS name space to a NetWare volume so that the UNIX operating system can see the files on the volume. Then, in the Wabi environment, you can map a drive letter to the mount directory in the UNIX file system and see the files.

You can also access files on a NetWare server that does not have the NLM
for NFS if your operating system is equipped with IPX/SPX streams
drivers and a "netware" file system type. If your system has devices
named something like `/dev/ipx` and `/dev/spx`, it has IPX/SPX streams
drivers. If your system has either additional parameter values on the
`mount` command or an entirely new command for mounting NetWare
volumes, it has software that provides a NetWare-type file system.

If your operating system does not provide IPX/SPX streams drivers and a
NetWare-type file system capability as part of its core, you may be able to
obtain the necessary software as an extension to the operating system,
possibly as custom software or from a third-party vendor.

Chapter 14
Tips and Tricks

Because Wabi does its work in both the Microsoft Windows and X Window worlds, it provides unique capabilities for working with data and features in either or both environments.

> *...and in these degrees have they made a pair of stairs to marriage...*
>
> – William Shakespeare, *As You Like It*, 1623
>
> *I really feel HI-TECH... Now if I can only program it to stop burning the Pop-Tarts!!*
>
> – Bill Griffith, *Zippy the Pinhead* (speaking of his new VCR): *"Beta Than Ever,"* 1987

In This Chapter

Cut, Copy, and Paste

You can cut, copy, and paste text and graphics between applications running in the Wabi environment just as you do in Microsoft Windows. Generally, applications use menu commands (e.g., Edit→Cut) or accelerator keys (e.g., Ctrl+X) to cut, copy, and paste. You should use the same methods when using the applications in the Wabi environment.

You can also copy and paste text between Windows applications running in Wabi and X applications running on your X desktop. You should follow each application's normal methods to cut, copy, and paste. For example, some UNIX desktops support the use of keyboard keys and menu commands to cut, copy, and paste. You can use the special keys or commands in the X applications to copy text, and then paste it into a Windows application in Wabi by using that application's paste method. You cannot use the UNIX desktop special keys to paste into the Windows application.

You cannot copy and paste graphics from Windows applications to X applications, and vice versa, because they use incompatible graphics formats.

> ### To copy and paste from Windows applications to X applications

1. **Click in the X application window to set the insertion point for pasting.**

2. **Copy the text in the Windows application by using the application's normal method for copying.**
   For example, select the text and press Ctrl+C or choose the Copy command from the Edit menu.

3. **Click the title bar of the X application window to make it the active window.**
   In some X applications, if you click in the work area of the window, the copied text is lost because Wabi interprets this as a new text selection and erases the contents of the clipboard.

4. **Paste the text into the X application window by using the application's normal method for pasting.**
   The text is pasted at the insertion point you set in the first step.

➤ *To copy and paste from X applications to Windows applications*

1. **Copy the text in the X application by using the application's normal method for copying.**

2. **Click the title bar of the Windows application to make it the active window.**

3. **Click in the work area of the Windows application to set the insertion point.**

4. **Paste the text by using the application's normal method for pasting.**
   For example, press Ctrl+V or choose the Paste command from the Edit menu. The text is pasted at the insertion point.

Remote Display

Because Wabi is an X Window application, you can take advantage of X's ability to redirect display output to remote terminals. This feature is described in detail in "Displaying Wabi On a Remote System" on page 135. Briefly, however, the steps required to redirect Wabi display output are listed below.

➤ *To display Wabi output on a remote system*

1. **Set the remote system to allow access to its display.**
   Enter the following command at the UNIX command line on the remote system:

   ```
   xhost  +remote_host
   ```

2. **Start Wabi on your system with the** `-display` **option followed by the remote host name and** `:0`
   For example, to display on a remote system named `myscreen`, enter:

   ```
   wabi -display myscreen:0
   ```

   Screen output is sent to the remote system with the specified host name.

Window Focus and Raising

Window managers on X Window desktops often let you choose your window focus policy. You can configure your X desktop so that you must click on a window to activate it, or so that you can move your mouse into a window to activate it. In addition, you can also specify whether you want a window to be raised to the top when activated. Each UNIX vendor's desktop has its own terminology for these desktop properties and its own utility for changing them.

In Microsoft Windows, you must click in a window before you can type into it. When you do, the window automatically rises to the top, overlaying other windows. Wabi's behavior matches that of Microsoft Windows.

Wabi windows use the click-to-focus mode even if you set your X Window desktop to use the follow-mouse mode, because it is the only mode Microsoft Windows applications can use. You should configure your X Window desktop to use the click-to-focus mode so that all your windows behave the same way.

Virtual Window Managers

In the X Window System, virtual window managers create several logical views of your desktop, and let you designate specific windows to "stick" so that they appear in all logical views. Other windows stay in the logical screen in which you place them. When you run the Wabi program with some virtual window managers, conflicts can occur between the Wabi window manager and the virtual window managers. Two virtual window managers with which Wabi is known to have conflicts are `olvwm` (OPEN LOOK Virtual Window Manager) and `tvwm` (Tom's Virtual Window Manager). You can use Wabi with `olvwm` or `tvwm`, but Wabi windows will always follow you to the current view rather than remaining on the logical screen where you've placed them.

When running the Wabi program in the Common Desktop Environment (CDE), HP-VUE, or SCO Panorama™ window environment, any Microsoft Windows application you start is displayed in the workspace where you first started the Wabi program (if it is still running in this workspace).

Resolving Key/Mouse Conflicts

Some Microsoft Windows applications may have conflicts with the OPEN LOOK Window Manager (`olwm`) over some key/mouse combinations. For example, the Alt+LeftMouse button combination is sometimes used by applications for specific functions, whereas `olwm` uses the combination for menu selections.

If you are using `olwm` (as OpenWindows does by default) and you want the application to have control of Alt+LeftMouse, try typing these two commands at your UNIX prompt before you start the Wabi program:

```
echo "olwm.Modifier.WMGrab: " | xrdb -merge
xrdb -edit $HOME/.Xdefaults
```

ODBC

Wabi 2.1 software provides support for several ODBC-compliant applications. ODBC (Open Database Connectivity) configuration is a complex task in any operating environment. Wabi ODBC support is explained in detail—with much application-specific information—in Chapter 9, in the section "Using Remote Database Access" on page 238.

Working With File Formats

File and directory structures differ in many ways between DOS and UNIX. Fortunately, Wabi manages these differences transparently, so you don't have to worry about them. The major differences between DOS and UNIX file systems, and the way Wabi handles them, are described in detail in Chapter 3, in the section titled "What's in a Name?" on page 73.

Provided below are some additional tips and comments about working with DOS and UNIX files under Wabi.

Files Created With Applications

The files you create with an application running in the Wabi environment are the same as files created with the same application running in the DOS environment with Microsoft Windows. If you run an application in both environments, you can create a file with an application in one environment, and edit the same file in the other environment.

Text Files

Simple ASCII text files can be used in both the UNIX and DOS environments, but there are a few slight differences in file format. For example, the UNIX operating system interprets the DOS end-of-line character as a ^M (Ctrl+M), so if you view a DOS ASCII file in a UNIX text editor, it may have a ^M at the end of each line.

Text File Conversion Between UNIX and DOS

On some platforms, Wabi software includes two UNIX text file conversion utilities. (Some platforms already provide these utilities, so they are not included in the Wabi package.) You run these utilities from a UNIX command prompt, and you can use them to convert simple ASCII text files created with tools such as a text editor, vi, or the Microsoft Windows Notepad, back and forth between UNIX and DOS formats. This allows you to view and print ASCII text files in either environment. These two utilities are described in Table 14-1.

Table 14-1 UNIX/DOS Text Conversion Utilities

Utility	Description
`unix2dos`	Converts text files created with UNIX-based tools, such as vi or a text editor, to a common DOS format.
`dos2unix`	Converts text files created with DOS-based tools, such as the Microsoft Windows Notepad, to a common UNIX format.

➤ *To convert a DOS text file to a UNIX text file*

➡ **Use the `dos2unix` command.**

The `dos2unix` command takes the following form, where *originalfile* is the DOS file and *newfile* is the UNIX file:

`dos2unix` *originalfile newfile*

The original DOS text file is converted from DOS format to UNIX format. The converted file is given the name represented by *newfile*. (The original file still exists.) If the original file and the new file are the same, `dos2unix` rewrites the original file after converting it.

➤ **To convert a UNIX text file to a DOS text file**

➥ **Use the** `unix2dos` **command.**
Similar to the `dos2unix` command, the `unix2dos` command takes the following form, where *originalfile* is the UNIX file and *newfile* is the DOS file:

`unix2dos` *originalfile   newfile*

The original UNIX text file is converted from UNIX format to DOS format. The converted file is given the name represented by *newfile*. (The original file still exists.) If the original file and the new file are the same, `unix2dos` rewrites the original file after converting it.

File Names in UNIX and DOS

The DOS operating system limits file names to a format using 8 characters, a period, and up to 3 characters in a file name extension (commonly known as the 8.3 convention). Also, DOS recognizes only a single case, so it doesn't matter whether you type a name in uppercase or lowercase. The UNIX operating system accepts file names up to 128 characters and distinguishes between uppercase and lowercase. The only UNIX file name that matches the DOS file name format is all lowercase and no more than 8 characters plus 3 extension characters.

A file created in the UNIX system and named with a long descriptive file name such as `QuarterlyReport.doc` cannot be handled by DOS. The Wabi program must map UNIX file names that use uppercase or are longer than the DOS 8.3 naming convention to names acceptable in both DOS and UNIX environments because Microsoft Windows applications expect the DOS file name format.

A detailed explanation of the different file naming conventions used in UNIX and DOS, and how Wabi manages those differences, is provided in "What's in a Name?" on page 73.

The Wabi program creates names that may be hard to recognize because
they may include tildes (~), and may sometimes not include the DOS file
name extension. For example, if you have files named `ORANGE.TXT`,
`Red.doc`, and `GREENERY.ZIP` in the directory `$HOME/ColorFiles`, they
might be mapped to names like `orang~5z`, `red~~~s2.doc`, and `green~26`.
Note that these names follow the 8.3 convention, but not the all-
lowercase convention.

 See Table 3-7 on page 75 for some examples of how Wabi software
might map different file names.

This mapping may sometimes cause a problem if the file extension is
omitted. For example, if an application you run in the Wabi program
looks for files with a particular file extension, it may not be able to find
them. If you run into such a problem, you run the `wabimakelower` utility
to map mixed-case file names to lowercase names, as described below.

➤ *To map file names to lowercase*

If you find the Wabi program's mapping of file names using
uppercase to be a problem, you can run the `wabimakelower`
program to create symbolic links to file names that include UNIX
uppercase characters. This program works only on file names
that fit the DOS 8.3 convention but include uppercase
characters. To run the program:

➠ **Enter the following command:**

```
wabimakelower directory
```

where *directory* is a directory containing files whose names you
want to map.

For example, for the files named `ORANGE.EXE`, `Red.doc`, and
`GREENERY.ZIP` in the directory `$HOME/ColorFiles`, use the
command:

```
wabimakelower $HOME/ColorFiles
```

The program creates symbolic links `orange.exe`, `red.doc`, and
`greenery.zip`, with the original files as their targets. This
enables you to see recognizable file names in your applications
and when browsing directories in the Wabi program.

DDE, OLE, and Packager

Dynamic Data Exchange (DDE), Object Linking and Embedding (OLE), and Object Packaging are Microsoft Windows-based data exchange features supported under Wabi, though not all Windows application actually implement these features.

- **DDE** – Allows one Windows application to request and exchange data and commands with another application. For example, a macro running in Microsoft Word for Windows could query a Novell Quattro Pro spreadsheet for the value of a particular range of cells. More important, when the value of that cell range changes, the Word document can be automatically updated via the DDE link with Quattro Pro.

- **OLE** – A more advanced implementation of the DDE concept, in which data from one application is embedded as an *object* in another application. As with DDE, the data in the embedded OLE object can be automatically updated to reflect changes in the object's source application. Unlike DDE, you can double-click on an OLE object in one application to automatically launch its source application. In some cases, this allows you to edit the OLE object *in situ*. For example, when you edit a Microsoft Draw OLE object from within Microsoft Word for Windows, it appears as if you are still in your Word document—the menu bar changes, and some different tools are at your disposal, but the rest of your document appears just as it does in Word.

- **Object Packager** – Lets you insert embedded or linked objects as icons in documents. Such objects can include executables or data. For example, you could insert an icon for a Windows sound clip in `.WAV` format in a document; when someone double-clicks on the icon, the sound clip plays. Alternatively, you could configure the object so that, when double-clicked, a wave file editor is launched.

Wabi software fully supports each of the above features. You use these features under Wabi exactly as you would in the Microsoft Windows environment. Refer to your *Microsoft Windows User's* guide for instructions on using DDE, OLE, and Object Packager.

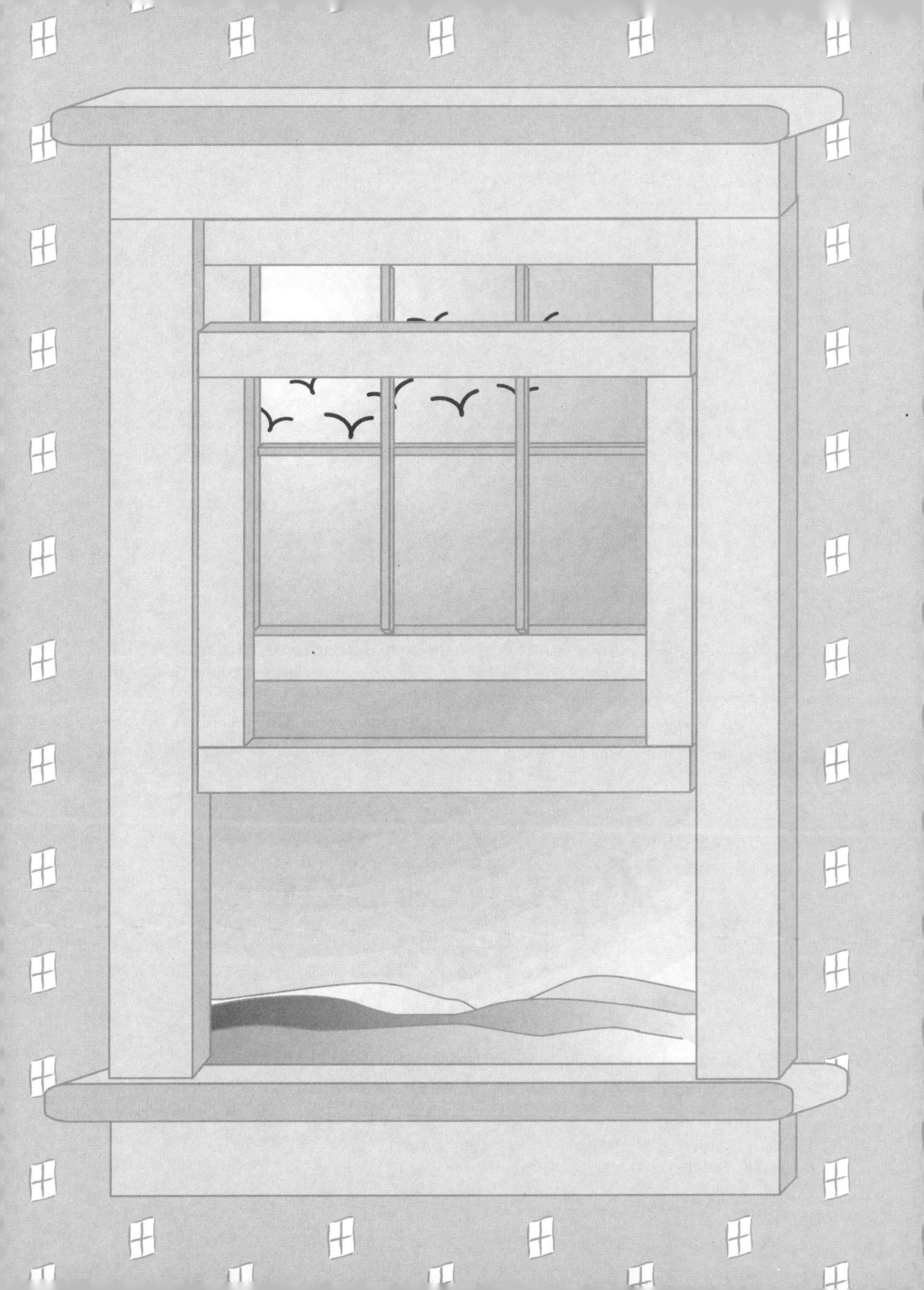

Appendix A
Application
Notes

Windows applications, whether for the Microsoft Windows or X Window environment, draw upon a variety of shared, external configuration files, program libraries, device drivers, and hardware devices, among other components. These components, alas, do not always interact in ways that you might expect. Indeed, the Microsoft Windows API is not fully documented, and its interactions with DOS, and much less with UNIX and X Window, are not completely understood.

Paradoxically, it is smart to realize that one is confused —as opposed to being confused without knowing it.

– Marvin Minsky, *The Society of Mind*, 1986

In This Appendix

 The application notes in this appendix apply specifically to Wabi 2.1 software from SunSoft, Inc. Other Wabi manufacturers (see "Wabi Operating Environments" on page 17) may have other application notes. Also, these notes are as up-to-date as possible, but given the rapid pace of software evolution, some of these notes may no longer be accurate. Be sure to consult the Wabi `README.WRI` file for the version of Wabi you are using. A program item for this file is installed by default in the Wabi Tools program group.

Microsoft Windows for Workgroups 3.11

Wabi 2.1 software supports Microsoft Windows for Workgroups (WFWG) 3.11 software in a limited capacity. Specifically, all components except for those that require Windows networking are supported. Table A-1 describes the features and limitations of Wabi 2.1 WFWG support.

Table A-1   Wabi 2.1 Window for Workgroups 3.11 Support

Feature	Comments
Mail	WFWG Mail is functionally similar to Microsoft Mail, and can use Microsoft Mail post offices. WFWG Mail works under Wabi 2.1 if you connect a Wabi drive to the post office and then add the following lines to your `MSMAIL.INI` file (located in your `WINDOWS` directory): `[Microsoft Mail]` `ServerPath=`*post_office_server_path* `Login=`*MSMail_username* For example, if you connect drive `Z:` to the post office, the *post_office_server_path* is `Z:\maildata`. *MSMail_username* is the name you use for your Mail account. Refer to your WFWG documentation for information about the differences between Workgroup Mail and Microsoft Mail. In particular, see the WFWG Resource Kit, Vol. 1.

Wabi 2: Opening Windows

Feature	Comments
Schedule+	WFWG Schedule+ replaces the Windows Calendar program and lets you schedule appointments with other WFWG users. To use Schedule+, you must first set up WFWG Mail.
ClipBook Viewer	The WFWG ClipBook Viewer replaces the Windows Clipboard Viewer. ClipBook lets you store multiple pages of clipboard information, so you can work with more than one piece of information at a time. This functionality is supported under Wabi 2.1 ClipBook also lets you share clipboard pages with other WFWG users over a network. This sharing is not supported by Wabi because it requires Windows networking.
Hearts	Hearts is a networked game that lets you play with up to three other players. Wabi does not support such network play; you can, however, play as a single user, against three computer-generated opponents.
File Manager	The WFWG File Manager can act as a file and print server, and can mount file systems from other machines on a WFWG network. These features require a Windows network, and are therefore unsupported in Wabi 2.1. The WFWG File Manager network features are disabled, making it basically the same as the Windows 3.1 File Manager.
WINCHAT WINPOPUP NETWATCH WINMETER	These programs require a Microsoft Windows network, and are therefore not supported under Wabi 21. Similarly, other network products that require Microsoft Windows network components are not supported under Wabi software.

Adobe PageMaker 5.0

If you will be using a PostScript or HP LaserJet III printer with Adobe PageMaker® 5.0, Adobe recommends that you install the `PostScript Printer` or `HP LaserJet III` printer driver provided with the PageMaker setup program.

If you installed Microsoft Windows 3.11 or Microsoft Windows for Workgroups 3.11, you do not need to install the PostScript driver provided with PageMaker. However, you should always install the LaserJet III driver from Adobe and use it instead of the HP LaserJet III (Wabi) driver.

➤ To install the Adobe PostScript Printer and/or HP LaserJet III driver

You can install these drivers either during or after your PageMaker installation:

1. **Run the `aldsetup.exe` program from Program Manager.**
2. **Select any PostScript and/or LaserJet printer in the Select Printer Devices dialog.**
   For example, select `Adobe LaserJet II Cartridge v52.3`. To select more than one printer, press the Control key and click the mouse button on the printers you want to install.
3. **Choose OK to continue with the installation.**
   When installation is complete, the Must Install Drivers message box tells you to install the PostScript or LaserJet III driver from the last disk of the set. When you click OK in this box, the installation program starts the Microsoft Windows Control Panel so you can install the drivers.
4. **Choose OK to start Windows Control Panel.**
   Control Panel starts and the Printers dialog opens.
5. **Choose the Add button.**
6. **Select the first item in the List of Printers, `Install Unlisted or Updated Printer`.**
7. **Choose Install.**
   You are prompted to specify the location of the printer driver file.

8. **Specify the location of the desired printer driver file.**

   a. **If you are installing from diskettes, insert the last disk in the PageMaker set in the drive, and enter the diskette drive letter in the Install Driver dialog.**

   b. **If you are installing from a network location, enter the network path to the PageMaker installation files.**

9. **Select `PostScript Printer` and choose OK in the Add Unlisted or Updated Printer dialog.**

   `PostScript Printer` is added to the list of Installed Printers. The older version that was installed with Microsoft Windows 3.1 remains in the list as `Postscript Printer` (note the lowercase "s"), and uses the same `pscript.drv` file. You can remove one of the entries if you like.

   If you want to install the HP LaserJet III driver, repeat Step 6 through Step 9, choosing the appropriate HP LaserJet III printer instead of `PostScript`. If the Wabi version of the HP LaserJet III printer is already connected to LPT1, you will be asked if you want to use the current printer port, or a new one. You can replace the Wabi version of the HP LaserJet III if you like, or keep both drivers by using a new port.

10. **Choose Close to exit the Printers dialog box.**

Use the PostScript Printer driver when printing PageMaker files to any PostScript printer. Use the appropriate HP LaserJet III driver when printing PageMaker files to a LaserJet III printer.

The Expert Kerning option on PageMaker's Utilities:Additions menu is not supported under Wabi because it relies on Adobe Type Manager, which is also not supported.

Borland Paradox 4.5 and 5.0

If you use Paradox in a shared environment, all Paradox users should have read and write access to files in Paradox's network control file directory and any Paradox .LCK file. To ensure this, each Paradox user must change the default file creation privileges before starting the Wabi program by entering the following command:

```
umask 000
```

This command must be issued each time you start a Wabi session from a new UNIX shell.

If you start the Wabi program from a desktop menu, edit the entry for Wabi in your desktop menu file to add the umask command before the wabi command. Your entry should be similar to the following:

```
umask 000 ; /wabihome /bin/wabi
```

wabihome is the location where the Wabi system files are installed.

After you use this command, all files you create with applications running in the Wabi program (not just those in the network control file directory) will have read and write access for all users.

If two or more people will be accessing the database, each user should disable attribute caching on the network file system from which he or she is accessing the database. To do this, mount the file system with the -o noac command-line switch.

Corel Draw! 4.0

- On Solaris for x86 systems, to use the Alt+PrintScreen feature of CorelCapture, press and hold the Alt key and press the PrintScreen key twice.

- To delete a graphic image, use the Delete key rather than the Edit→Cut menu command.

- When you switch from Chart view to Data Manager view, you should minimize the window and restore it to display the new view completely.

Harvard Graphics 3.0

You cannot use the conference feature in Harvard Graphics® because it requires NetBIOS to be loaded. The Wabi program does not yet support NetBIOS.

Intuit Quicken 3.0

When you install Intuit Quicken® 3.0, after you insert the second diskette and choose OK, you may see the following error:

```
Error in Application
Disk I/O Error
Access Denied (5).
```

To work around this problem, you can do one of the following:

➧ **Insert the second diskette, wait 30 seconds, and then choose OK.**

   or

➧ **Change the Diskette Timeout value in the Wabi Configuration Manager Diskette Connections dialog box from 30 seconds to 5 seconds. Then wait 5 seconds before you choose OK to install the second diskette.**

- Do not install Quicken 3.0 to the R: drive. Map a drive in Wabi Configuration Manager to the location in which you want to install Quicken 3.0.

- The "CD-ROM deluxe edition" of Quicken 3.0 is not supported in the Wabi program.

Lotus cc:Mail Client 2.0 and 2.03

The Wabi program supports only the cc:Mail client, which allows you to send and receive mail from an existing post office that is accessible to your computer. The post office administrator must add a mailbox for you before you can use cc:Mail.

➤ *To install the cc:Mail Windows client software into your Wabi environment*

1. **Use the Wabi Configuration Manager Drives tool to connect the** M: **drive to the server directory containing the cc:Mail post office database directory.**
   This directory is the parent directory of ccdata.

2. **Use the Run command on the Windows Program Manager File menu to run the `setup.exe` program, either from the cc:Mail Workstation Setup Disk or from the post office.**

   To run it from disk, enter `A:\setup`. To run it from the post office, enter `M:\ccmail\setup.exe`.

3. **Follow the instructions in the cc:Mail Workstation Installation window to install the client software on your computer.**

When you start cc:Mail from the Wabi program, you are prompted for your login name and password. Obtain these from your post office administrator.

- If you want to use cc:Mail in Notes, you must install cc:Mail before you install Notes.

- On Solaris 2.4 for SPARC systems, make sure you do not have Solaris patch 101945 version 17 through 23 installed. This range of patch versions can cause cc:Mail to hang. (As of this writing, patch version 29 is the one you want.) See your Wabi release notes for more information about current patches.

Lotus Notes Client 3.0c and 3.3

Make sure you install the Solaris patches relevant to Lotus Notes before you install Lotus Notes. See your Wabi release notes for more information.

- The Wabi program supports only the Lotus Notes client. You can use the Notes client locally without a server, or you can connect a Notes client to an existing Notes server through the TCP/IP Windows Sockets network interface.

- If you want to use cc:Mail in Notes, you must install cc:Mail before you install Notes.

➢ **To install the Notes client into your Wabi environment**

1. **If you are installing from the network, use the Wabi Configuration Manager Drive Connections dialog to connect a drive to the directory containing the Lotus Notes installation files.**

2. **Use the File→Run command in Windows Program Manager to run the Lotus Notes installation program for Windows clients, `instwin.exe`.**
    If necessary, use the Browse button to locate the file on diskette or the network.

3. **In the Main Menu dialog, choose Install Workstation software on this system.**

4. **Follow the installation program's instructions until installation is complete.**

➢ **To set up your Notes workstation in the Wabi environment**

1. **Start Notes.**
    The Notes Workstation Setup dialog is displayed

2. **Specify the type of connection to your Notes server.**

    a. **If you will be connecting to a Notes server, select Network connection (via LAN).**

    b. **If you will be running Notes locally, select No connection to a server.**

3. **Choose OK.**

4. **Enter your Notes user name and password.**
    These are assigned by your Notes server administrator.

5. **Enter your Home server name.**
    If you are not sure what the server name is, ask your Notes server administrator.

6. **In the Network type list, select TCP/IP.**

7. **Choose OK.**

8. **Enter the password given to you by your administrator.**
    The workstation files are copied to your system.

- On RISC platforms, when designing a form in a Lotus Notes database and adding keyword values for a field in the form, press Ctrl+J instead of Return to advance to the next line.

- If you are designing a form in a Lotus Notes database and save changes by using the right mouse button, the next time you edit the form, the entire form becomes highlighted up to your current cursor position. You can deselect it by clicking elsewhere. To avoid the problem completely, use a different method to save your changes.

Lotus SmartSuite 3.1

- Recording in ScreenCam is not supported because it requires a Windows video driver, which is not available in the Wabi environment.

- If you install SmartSuite on a network server and elect to use license management, you must change permissions for the license directory and files before users can run SmartSuite applications. The license directory must be writable by users. By default, the licenses are stored in a subdirectory `lotshare/application/license.`*number.*

➤ *To change file permissions on the license directory*

➡ **Enter the following command at a UNIX prompt:**

```
chmod a+w /serverdir/lotshare/*/*
```

where *serverdir* is the server directory in which SmartSuite is installed.

Microsoft Access 2.0

If you want to share a Microsoft Access® database, make sure all users have read and write access to the database file (*file*.mdb) and the locking file (*file*.ldb).

If there is no locking file, Access will create one the first time it is accessed through a network drive. You must change the locking file's permissions by entering the following command:

```
chmod 666 file.ldb
```

Microsoft Mail Client 3.2

The Wabi program supports only the Microsoft Mail Windows client, which allows you to send and receive mail from an existing post office that is accessible to your computer. The post office administrator must create a mailbox for you before you can use Mail.

➤ *To install the Microsoft Mail client software into your Wabi environment*

1. **Use the Wabi Configuration Manager Drives tool to:**

    a. **Connect any Wabi drive to the parent directory of the maildata directory on the server, and**

    b. **Connect the M: drive to the maildata directory.**

2. **Use the Run command on the Windows Program Manager File menu to run the setup.exe command, either from diskette or from the post office.**
    To run the command from diskette, enter A:\setup. To run it from the post office, use the Browse button to find the setup.exe program in the mailuser subdirectory.

3. **Follow the instructions in the setup program for installing the client software on your computer.**
   When you start Microsoft Mail from the Wabi program, you are prompted for your mailbox name and password. Obtain these from your post office administrator.

- If you do not have an existing post office, you must set one up from a PC onto your network (LAN) as described in the Microsoft Mail documentation.

  If your PC LAN software is NFS-based, before you set up the post office you must set file creation privileges on the destination PC network drive to allow read, write, and execute permission for user, group, and other. For more information about file creation options, see your PC network documentation for the procedure for connecting drives. After the file creation privileges are modified, you can set up the post office on the drive.

- If your Microsoft Mail post office has already been set up on an NFS file system, you will have to change the permissions for the `maildata` directory and the files and directories within it.

  On NFS file systems, new files are created with `rwxr-xr-x` permissions, so only the owner has write permission. As a result, the Microsoft Mail setup program creates files and subdirectories with `rwxr-xr-x` permissions, so only the user who set up the post office has write permission. When Microsoft Mail sends mail, it creates temporary files in various subdirectories within the `maildata` directory, so all users must have read, write, and execute permission to the `maildata` directory and its subdirectories.

> ### To correct the directory and file permissions in the `maildata` subdirectory

1. **Log in with the user name used to create the post office.**
2. **Change to the `maildata` directory for your post office.**
3. **Enter the following command to recursively change permissions:**

```
find . -user $USER -exec chmod 777 {} \; -print
```

If you add more user accounts later, new files are created with `rwxr-xr-x` permissions, so you must use this same procedure to change permissions on the new files.

- If you try to open a shared folder and get a message that the folder is "busy," it is likely that the file permissions on the shared folder must be changed from `rwxr-xr-x` to `rwxrwxrwx`. The owner of the shared folder must change permissions on the folder in `maildata/folders/pub` to make the folders accessible to all users.

> **To give all users access to shared folders that you own**

1. **Log in with your user name.**
2. **Change to the `maildata/folders/pub` directory for your post office.**
3. **Enter the following command to recursively change permissions:**

```
find . -user $USER -exec chmod 777 {} \; -print
```

On Solaris 2.4 for SPARC systems, make sure you do not have Solaris patch `101945` version `17` through `23` installed. This range of patch versions can cause Microsoft Mail to hang. (As of this writing, patch version `29` is the one you want.) See your Wabi release notes for more information about current patches.

Microsoft Office 4.3c

The CD-ROM version of Microsoft Office 4.3c includes some additional accessory programs that are not available on the diskette version. Some of these programs include multimedia features that cannot be used in the Wabi environment. If you use them, you may see error messages or perhaps cause Wabi to hang. Programs known to have problems are the Microsoft Multimedia Catalog and Microsoft Bookshelf.

WordPerfect 6.0a and 6.1

When you install WordPerfect 6.0a or 6.1 from diskettes, the installation procedure attempts to run a DOS batch file, `WP{INS}2.BAT`, which deletes temporary installation files. You may see the message: "Running a DOS session requires a DOS emulator, which does not come with Wabi." Even if you have a DOS emulator, the files may not be deleted. If these files are not deleted no harm is done, and WordPerfect runs normally. However, you can delete the files to free over 300 Kbytes in your directory.

> ### ➤ *To delete WordPerfect's temporary installation files*

➠ **Enter the following commands at a UNIX command line:**

```
cd  $HOME/wabi/windows
rm  wp\{ins\}*
```

The WordPerfect 6.0a and WordPefect 6.1 Coaches are not supported under Wabi software.

Appendix B
Trouble-
shooting

Computer systems always work in a consistent, predictable manner... except when they don't.... The key is often how well you recover from error, rather than trying to prevent every possibility for error. When a computer program is able to recover from an error—or at least not go down in a ball of digital flames—we say that it recovered *gracefully*. Given the complexity of what it does, Wabi software is actually quite graceful. Nonetheless, the interaction of Microsoft Windows and Wabi has so many crannies and combinations that they cannot all be catalogued. The goal of this appendix is to help you sort out most of the problems you may encounter.

> *While certain bugs were bartered as curiosities, others were exploited as valuable collector's items.*
>
> – Derek Pell, *Doktor Bey's Bedside Bug Book*, 1978
>
> *Given a peeler made on the moon, a good repair person would know how to fix the moonmade gadget without waiting for a diagram to be flown in from out there.*
>
> – Franklynn Peterson, *How to Fix Damn Near Anything*, 1977

In This Appendix

Wabi Troubleshooting

The problems discussed in this section apply to general Wabi usage.

- Table B-1 – Wabi General Usage Problems and Solutions
- Table B-2 – Diskette Drive Problems and Solutions
- Table B-3 – Wabi Drive Problems and Solutions
- Table B-4 – CD-ROM Drive Problems and Solutions
- Table B-5 – Printing Problems and Solutions
- Table B-6 – COM Port Problems and Solutions

Table B-1   Wabi General Usage Problems and Solutions

Symptom	Possible Cause	Solution
Can't start Wabi.	Startup command not in path.	Use the full path name for the `wabi` command. This path is specific to your operating system. Or, edit your user profile for the UNIX shell you use (for example, `.cshrc` for the C shell) to include the Wabi `bin` directory in your search path.
	Not enough swap space or memory.	Make sure your system has at least the minimum requirements specified in your installation instructions. If you need to run several programs concurrently, you may need more memory and swap space.
	Too many other UNIX programs running.	Quit some of the running programs and start Wabi again.
Can't access Wabi man page.	Wabi man page directory not in `MANPATH`.	See "Wabi man Page" on page 143 for more information.
Can't display to remote system.	System not open to external displays or no display identified.	See "Displaying Wabi On a Remote System" on page 135 to make sure you've followed the correct procedure.

Table B-1   Wabi General Usage Problems and Solutions (Continued)

Symptom	Possible Cause	Solution
Can't install Microsoft Windows program from diskette.	Incorrect diskette drive specified or diskette drive not configured.	See "Installing Windows From Diskette" on page 115.
Can't install Microsoft Windows program from Wabi drive R:.	Drive or path incorrect or inadequate permissions to directory.	Use the **Browse** button to find the correct path to the Microsoft Windows files. Make sure you have read permission to the directory and files. See "Installing Windows From Wabi Drive R:" on page 117.
Can't access Program Manager.	Windows software incorrectly installed.	You must use the Wabi Microsoft Windows Install Tool to install Microsoft Windows. See "Installing Microsoft Windows" on page 114 for more information.
Can't change settings from Control Panel.	Some Control Panel functions are not valid under the Wabi program.	Use operating system utilities to perform some functions of Control Panel. See page 126 for more information about the Control Panel.
Icons missing from Main group.	Some Windows components cannot be used in Wabi, so they are not installed.	See "Windows Main Program Group" on page 125.

Table B-2   Diskette Drive Problems and Solutions

Symptom	Possible Cause	Solution
"Device Not Ready (Abort, Retry, or Ignore)" error.	Diskette may not be seated properly in the drive.	Remove diskette and reinsert it. Try to access the diskette again.
Can't access drive A: or B:.	Another program is controlling the drive.	Eject the diskette with a command from the other program, reinsert the diskette, and try accessing it through Wabi again.

Symptom	Possible Cause	Solution
Can't access drive A: or B:. (*cont.*)	Invalid device name specified in Wabi Configuration Manager Diskette Connections dialog.	Specify a raw diskette device file. See your UNIX documentation for information about diskette devices.
	Inadequate file permissions to device file or directory.	You must have read and write permission to your UNIX system's device files and directories. Use the UNIX `chmod` command to change permissions if necessary.
Can't locate diskette devices.	Wabi is searching the wrong directory for the diskette devices, or is using an incorrect file name pattern.	Determine the location and names of the raw diskette device files in your operating system, then specify the directory and a file naming convention in the Advanced Diskette Drive Options dialog box, as explained on page 158.
Diskette will not eject with special keys (e.g., Meta+E).	Wabi window does not have input focus.	Place mouse pointer in Wabi window, click to make it the active window, and then press keys.
Can't format DOS diskette.	Not supported under Wabi program.	You can use preformatted diskettes or format them on a PC running DOS. Your operating system may also provide a way to format DOS diskettes, so refer to your operating system user's manual.

Table B-3   Wabi Drive Problems and Solutions

Symptom	Possible Cause	Solution
Can't connect a drive to a local directory.	Inadequate file permissions.	You must have at least read permission to any directory you want to access. Use the UNIX `chmod` command to change permissions.
	Incorrect path assignment.	If you entered the path name manually, make sure the path is a directory, not a file.
Can't connect drive to remote directory.	Inadequate file permissions.	You must have at least read permission to any directory you want to access. Contact your system administrator or the directory owner.
Remote directory not in Available Directory Paths.	Remote file system not mounted.	You must be able to access the directory from the operating system before you can access it in Wabi. • If your UNIX system automatically mounts remote file systems, open a UNIX command window and use the `cd` command to change to the directory to which you want to connect. This mounts the file system. • If your UNIX system does not automatically mount remote file systems, see your UNIX manuals for procedures to make remote file systems accessible. • You can also type the directory name directly in the Directory Path field in the Wabi Drive Connections dialog box. (See page 167 for more information.) Once the file system is accessible from the operating system, open the Drives icon in Configuration Manager and connect a drive to the directory.

Table B-3   Wabi Drive Problems and Solutions (Continued)

Symptom	Possible Cause	Solution
Can't change connection for Wabi drives `C:`, `R:`, or `W:`.	Permanent Wabi drive connections cannot be changed.	There is no way to change the `C:`, `R:`, or `W:` connections. If you want to change the `C:` connection because you do not want your user `wabi` directory in your home directory, do *not* simply move or copy your existing `wabi` directory to another location, because the numerous symbolic links will not be preserved. Instead, try the following procedure: • Exit Wabi. • Rename your existing `wabi` directory to `wabi.old`. • Create a directory named `wabi` in the desired new location. • Create a symbolic link named `wabi` in your home directory, with the new directory as the target. • Restart Wabi. The Wabi program creates a new `wabi` directory, placing it in the new location. If you added any files to your original `wabi` directory, move them from `wabi.old` to the new directory, and then delete `wabi.old`.
Drive errors when using a DOS Emulator.	Dissimilar drive mappings.	Assign the same drive letters to the same path names in both the DOS Emulator and Wabi. See page 162 for more information.

Wabi 2: Opening Windows

Table B-4   CD-ROM Drive Problems and Solutions

Symptom	Possible Cause	Solution
Can't mount CD-ROM.	CD-ROM not in format supported by operating system.	The Wabi program can only use CD-ROMs that your operating system can use. See your operating system documentation for information about CD-ROMs.
Can't run application off CD-ROM.	Application detects network environment.	Some applications on CD-ROM will not work in Wabi because they determine the drive is a network drive. There is no way to use such applications. See page 174 for more information.

Table B-5   Printing Problems and Solutions

Symptom	Possible Cause	Solution
Can't print.	Invalid native printer name or print command.	Make sure you can print to the same printer outside Wabi, using a UNIX print command such as `lp` or `lpr`. If you can print in UNIX, try resetting Wabi's printer connection (the UNIX printer name and command) to the default value. See "Default Wabi Printer Configuration" on page 182 for instructions. If you cannot print using these defaults, the problem is probably outside Wabi.
	Printer not configured correctly in operating system.	If the printer is not configured correctly, you cannot print outside Wabi with a UNIX print command. If this is the case, see your system administrator or your UNIX system documentation for help with configuring the printer.
	Printer port connected to wrong printer.	Check the Wabi Printer Output Connections setting to make sure the port is connected to the UNIX printer you want to print on. See page 185 for more information.

Table B-5   Printing Problems and Solutions (Continued)

Symptom	Possible Cause	Solution
Can't print large graphics files.	Out of space in `/tmp`.	The `/tmp` directory could become filled with temporary printing files if it does not have enough free space, so you may have to increase the space allotted `/tmp`. On some systems, the `/tmp` directory is simulated inside the system's swap space rather than existing as separate disk space. To find out if your system uses disk or swap space for `/tmp`, enter the command: `df -k /tmp` If the first word on the output line is swap, the `/tmp` directory is simulated in swap space. You can increase the space allocated to `/tmp` by increasing your system's swap space. See your operating system documentation for the procedure to do this.
Desired Windows printer driver not listed in List of Printers.	Printer not officially supported.	If it is a PostScript printer, you should be able to use one of the listed printer drivers. The printer's documentation may list other drivers you can use, or tell you what printer is emulated. If it doesn't, contact the printer vendor, who might suggest other drivers to use. You might also contact Adobe Systems, Inc. (the developer of PostScript) for advice, or customer support from your UNIX vendor.
		If it is not a PostScript, Epson, HP LaserJet III, or text-only printer, its native driver will not work with Wabi. Note that most printers provide Epson or LaserJet emulation, and can use the Epson or HP printer drivers.

Wabi 2: Opening Windows

Table B-5   Printing Problems and Solutions (Continued)

Symptom	Possible Cause	Solution
Desired UNIX printer not listed in the Native Printer Name list.	Printer not configured in operating system.	See your system administrator or your UNIX system documentation for help in setting up a printer in the operating system.

Table B-6   COM Port Problems and Solutions

Symptom	Probable Cause	Solution
Can't assign COM1, device busy.	Serial port is being used by another device, such as a mouse or terminal, or by a UNIX `tip` connection.	Try using a different COM port, if you have one that is not in use.
Can't access COM2.	Serial port not configured at operating system level.	See your operating system documentation for information about configuring serial ports.
	Insufficient permissions on serial device file.	Use the command `chmod 666` *device* to set the permissions so that all users have read and write permission to the device.
Can't connect COM port to serial device.	Inadequate permissions to device file or directory.	You must have read and write access to your UNIX system's device files and directories. Change permissions in the operating system by using the `chmod` command.
No devices shown in COM Port Connections device driver list.	Invalid device directories or file patterns.	Locate the device files in your operating system. Make sure the COM device directories and COM device file patterns that Wabi uses to find COM devices are set correctly. See page 204 for more information.

Windows Troubleshooting

The problems discussed in this section apply to Microsoft Windows and Windows applications.

- Table B-7 – Windows Application Installation Solutions
- Table B-8 – Windows Applications Solutions

Table B-7   Windows Application Installation Solutions

Symptom	Possible Cause	Solution
Application will not fully install.	Not certified to run in Wabi program.	Only certified applications are sure to install correctly. Uncertified applications may use nonstandard installation procedures or data compression methods that Wabi has not been designed to translate.
Application does not install correctly.	Special installation procedures required.	See the Release Notes or supplementary manual you may have received with the Wabi program.
Application installation fails with error: "ACMSETUP Caused a General Protection Fault in Module MMSETUP.DLL."	Some Microsoft applications' setup programs alter the `system.ini` file incorrectly.	With a DOS or UNIX text editor, edit `$HOME/wabi/windows/system.ini` and insert a blank line before each section title. Section titles are enclosed in square brackets. (Note that UNIX editors display blank lines in DOS text files as `^M`. You do not need to remove them.) Save the file, restart the Wabi program, and reinstall the application.

Symptom	Possible Cause	Solution
Application installation program covers the screen, blocking other application windows.	Application was not designed for the X Window desktop.	Some applications do not let you change this, but you can try the following: • Try reducing the size of the window by restoring it. To restore, click on the Wabi logo in the upper-left corner of the window, if it's visible, then choose Restore in the pull-down menu. (Alternatively, press Alt+Spacebar, R.) This does not work for all installation programs. • If your keyboard has a key or key combination that raises windows, such as a Front key, try pressing it once to make the installation window go to the back so you can see other windows. It may take Wabi several seconds to respond to key strokes if the application installation is loading your computer heavily. This does not work with all installation programs.

Table B-7   Windows Application Installation Solutions (Continued)

Symptom	Possible Cause	Solution
Application installs very slowly.	Application uses nonstandard compression routines. Most files must be decompressed at installation. If an application uses standard Windows routines, it installs quickly because Wabi translates to UNIX routines to decompress. If an application does not use standard routines, Wabi must execute the compression one instruction at a time.	If you find an application installation intolerably slow, try the following: • Obtain the application on CD-ROM if possible. CD-ROM files are not compressed, so Wabi does not have to decompress them, making installation faster. • Check the application documentation for an installation option to perform a partial installation that just decompresses the files. If there is such an option, do the partial installation, and store the decompressed files in a network directory where other users can use them to do the second half of the installation. • Investigate the possibility of all the users on the network referencing a single copy of the application, so you only have to install the application once. Remember, however, that if you share a single copy, you *must* have a license for each user of the application. You are responsible for adhering to the terms of the software license for every application you run under the Wabi program.

Wabi 2: Opening Windows

Table B-8   Windows Applications Solutions

Symptom	Possible Cause	Solution
Application does not start.	Incorrect executable name or directory path.	Make sure you have entered the correct path name.
Application not fully functional.	Application function not compatible with Wabi or X Window System.	See the Release Notes or supplementary manual you may have received with the Wabi program for information about the application.
"Not enough memory" or "Out of memory" message from application.	Application encountered an unrecoverable error.	This error message is often generated when applications cannot perform some function for an unknown reason. Memory shortage is seldom the actual cause. Contact Wabi support.

DOS Troubleshooting

The problems discussed in this section apply to DOS applications and emulators.

- Table B-9 – DOS Application Problems and Solutions

Table B-9   DOS Application Problems and Solutions

Symptom	Possible Cause	Solution
DOS emulator will not start.	DOS emulator not installed on system.	You must install the DOS emulator onto your UNIX system before you can use it through the Wabi program.
	The Wabi program cannot locate the DOS emulator program.	Specify a full path name in the startup command, even if the emulator's directory is on your UNIX path. See page 254 for more information.
	Improperly configured startup command string.	Make sure you can start the emulator from a UNIX command line first. Use this UNIX command as the basis for your startup command string, with variables inserted as necessary. See page 254 for more information.
Installed DOS program does not appear in any group.	No icon created for this application.	You must create a program item for a DOS application. See page 257 for more information.
DOS application won't install or run.	DOS emulator not installed or not configured correctly.	See the DOS emulator documentation to make sure you have installed and configured the emulator correctly. See page 254 for information about connecting it to the Wabi program.

Table B-9   DOS Application Problems and Solutions (Continued)

Symptom	Possible Cause	Solution
Can't start DOS application by opening its icon.	Missing placeholders in DOS emulator startup command or DOS emulator not in UNIX path.	Make sure you have inserted the correct placeholders in the DOS emulator connection. Use a full path in the emulator command if the directory is not in your UNIX path. See page 254.
	The path specified in either the Command Line or Working Directory field in the Program Item Properties dialog may no longer be valid.	If the DOS application files have been moved, or if you have changed the Wabi drive connection to the directory, the Program Item Properties must be changed. See page 257 for information about the Program Item Properties dialog.
Application not fully functional.	Application function incompatible with DOS emulator or X Window System.	See documentation for the DOS emulator for known problems. Also see any supplemental documentation included with your Wabi software.

Glossary

access control list – A list of hosts that can access a given X terminal or workstation for the purpose of running and displaying host-based client programs. For *host-based access control*, this list is maintained in the `/etc/X`*n*`hosts` file, where *n* is the number of the display, usually 0. (Note that an `/etc/X0hosts` file is not included in most default configurations of X11, but must be created by the system administrator.) By default, only the local host may use the display, plus any hosts specified in the `/etc/X`*n*`hosts` list. This list can be dynamically augmented or superseded by the user with the `xhost` client. *See also* **magic cookie**.

active window – In an environment capable of displaying on-screen windows, the window containing the display or document that will be affected by all cursor movements, commands, and text entry until a new window is chosen; also called the **focus window**.

address – (1) A number used by the system software to identify a storage location. (2) In networking, a unique code that identifies a node to the network. *See* **Ethernet Address** and **IP Address**.

Address Resolution Protocol – *See* **ARP**.

ADJUST mouse button – The (usually) center button on the three-button mouse included with many UNIX-based workstations. The ADJUST button can be used to extend a given selection to the current pointer position. For example, if a sentence of text is selected (highlighted), moving the pointer to the end of a subsequent sentence and clicking ADJUST causes both sentences to be included in the selection. *See also* **MENU mouse button** and **SELECT mouse button**.

ANSI – *American National Standards Institution*. The standard command codes for color and character attributes.

ARP – *Address Resolution Protocol.* The Internet protocol used to dynamically map Internet addresses to physical (hardware) addresses on local-area networks. Limited to networks that support hardware broadcast. *See also* **RARP**.

ASCII – *(Pronounced "as-kee.") American Standard Code for Information Interchange.* A 7-bit code for representing a standard set of 128 alphanumeric characters, punctuation, and control characters; used for data communications and in most minicomputers and microcomputers. *Extended* ASCII uses the eighth bit of the byte to represent an additional 128 characters, such as non-English language and graphics symbols.

asynchronous – A communications mode that uses variable time intervals between characters in a message.

authentication server – A machine on a network that has software for verifying user privileges. *See also* **login**.

batch file – Also called a *BAT* file. A DOS or OS/2® ASCII text file containing commands that are executed by the operating system as if each command were entered interactively, one at a time, from the command line. In DOS and OS/2, batch files must be named with a `.BAT` extension. Such files can be run from the command line like any other program. For example, you could create a batch file named `go.bat`, and include in it the following commands:

```
cd \wp
copy *.doc a:
del *.bak
```

Entering `go` at a DOS prompt would then cause the above three commands to be executed sequentially.

baud – A unit of data communications rate that signifies the speed of the transmitted data bits. One bit of data per second equals one baud. 1200 bits of data per second equals 1200 baud. Named after the French engineer, Jean Maurice Emile Baudot.

binary – The base-2 numbering system, consisting of digits 0 and 1. Binary is the basic numbering system used in programming microelectronic devices today. In computing, each binary digit corresponds to one of two conditions; for example, 0 or 1, on or off, true or false, open or shut, yes or no. Much of computing involves stringing together 4, 8, 16, 32, and 64 binary digits to represent *bits* (one digit), *nibbles* (4 digits), *bytes* (8 digits), and *words* (two or more bytes). *See also* **hexadecimal**, **octal**, **one's complement**.

bit – Abbreviation for binary digit. A bit is the smallest information unit in a computer system. The value of a bit is either 0 or 1. Eight bits equal one byte.

bitmap – A grid of **pixels**, in which each pixel is either white or black (for monochrome), or red, green, or blue (for color). The combination of pixels in the grid creates a *bitmapped image*, such as a picture, or an alphanumeric character on a video display. The `bitmap` client allows you to edit bitmaps, which you can use as pointers, icons, and background window patterns.

bit plane – A bitmap in a window, when that window is thought of as a stack of bitmaps.

byte – A sequence of eight adjacent bits operated upon as a unit.

case-sensitive – The differentiating of lowercase letters from uppercase letters. For example, in a case-sensitive system, "ABC" is treated differently than "abc." NFS file systems are case-sensitive; DOS FAT file systems are case-insensitive. Therefore, in an NFS system, you could have two different files, one named "BigBucks" and another named "bigbucks." In the DOS FAT system, however, these two files would be regarded as having the same name. *See also* **FAT**, **NFS**.

character attribute – Display features that affect the appearance of characters on the screen; for example, bold, blink, and underline.

character set – A group of graphics characters stored as a unit in the terminal.

client application – In the X Window environment, a program that receives input and/or displays output on a local X terminal or workstation. Some X client applications run on a remote *client host*—that is, the bulk of the processing performed by the program occurs remotely—with only input/output occurring locally on the display server.

client-server – (1) In networking, a *server* (also called a *host*) is any computer that performs services for other computers on a network. Computers that use any of these services are called *clients*. For example, a computer that provides data file storage and retrieval services is called a *file server. Client-server computing* refers to a network organized in such a way that some machines are clients and others are servers—although some machines may play both roles. Theoretically, any computer on the network can act as a server; conversely, some computers may provide more than one service. (2) In the X Window environment, the relationship between application programs and display devices. Specifically, the server handles user input from the keyboard and mouse, and sends it to a client application running on a remote host. The client, in turn, sends the server the contents of the application window and other program responses for display on the server screen.

clipping region – In the X Window environment, the area of the screen in which client output can be displayed; commonly restricted to one or more client windows.

colorcell – Entries in a **colormap**. Each colorcell contains three values that specify red, green, and blue component intensities. These values are 16-bit unsigned numbers, with 0 specifying the minimum intensity for the given component color.

colormap – The color options in a graphics system, arranged by index number. Typically, the system has a default color map. The index of colors in the colormap can be reallocated, however, depending on the application. There is one colormap in the hardware (often called a *color lookup table (CLUT)*, but many colormaps can be allocated in software (as *virtual* or *private* colormaps) and indexed as appropriate for separate applications. *See also* **colorcell**.

command shell – An operating system-level program that accepts a limited range of commands that can be entered by a user; these commands are converted into machine-level commands required by the given operating system (like DOS or UNIX). From the standpoint of the user, the command shell is the command-line interface seen outside a graphical environment like Sun's OpenWindows or Microsoft Windows. For example, for DOS users, the command shell interface usually includes the following *prompt*:

```
C:\>
```

Users can type in commands at this prompt, and then press the Enter key to execute (that is, *do*) them. Common DOS commands include `copy` (`cp` in UNIX), `del` (UNIX `rm`), and `print` (UNIX `lp` or `lpr`). Common UNIX command shells include the C shell (`csh`) and the Bourne and Korn shell (`ksh`).

connect – Also *mount*. To make a remote file system, printer, or other network resource accessible from your local computer. *See also* **disconnect**, **mount point**.

connections – The disk drives that are redirected to your local computer. In Wabi, these drives are referred to by names such as `N:` and `G:`, but are actually pointers to directories located on one or more machines on the network.

cursor – A movable symbol on the display screen that serves as the contact point between the user and the client program. In the X Window environment, the cursor consists of a *hotspot*, a *pattern* bitmap, a *shape* bitmap, and a pair of colors. Different cursors can be defined for different windows and/or functions; the specific cursor that is displayed depends on the current location of the *pointer*. The cursor is often synonymous with the pointer. In text applications (like a word processing program), however, there is usually a differentiation made between the pointer, which provides navigational control, and the cursor, which is the text-insertion point. For example, the cursor may remain in a paragraph while the pointer is used to navigate pull-down menus at the top of the screen. *See also* **pointer**.

daemon – A UNIX process (or application) that runs in the background on a network server, handling commands delivered for remote execution.

default – A setting that is automatically used by a component in the system or a function in the software when no other setting is entered by the user.

desktop – In windowing environments, the screen background on which program windows, icons, and dialog boxes are displayed. *See also* **dialog box**.

dialog box – In windowing environments, a screen that is displayed in response to a command, into which you can enter data, or from which you can select various options.

disconnect – Also *unmount*. To remove the link between a file system, or other network resource and your computer. *See also* **connect**.

DISPLAY – An environment variable that tells X client programs the names of the display server(s) to which they should connect and send/receive their input/output. The DISPLAY variable can be overridden with the -display command-line option when launching the client application. The default is always screen 0 of display server 0 on the local network node; for example, the terminal through which the user logs in to the network. *See also* **environment variable**.

display device – A set of one or more screens driven by a single X server; usually, the physical display device is the monitor that is attached to a computer. With some systems, it is possible to connect more than one physical display to a single system unit.

Display PostScript – A display language, developed by Adobe Systems, Inc., that translates elementary commands from the operating system and client applications to graphics and text elements on screen. It is the screen counterpart to the PostScript printer language.

domain – A named group of machines on a network.

domain name – The name assigned to a group of systems on a local network that share administrative files. The domain name is required for the network information service database to work properly.

Domain Name System – *DNS*. A hierarchical device-naming system provided by the Internet. DNS provides a mechanism for mapping mnemonic device (such as host) names with their more cryptic numeric IP addresses. *See also* **host**, **IP address**.

download – To transfer data or a file from a remote device, such as an ftp server, to a local device, such as your computer. The opposite of *upload*: Download means sending files from a remote machine to a local machine; upload means sending files from a local machine to a remote machine. Note that upload and download imply the transmission of an entire file, rather than an ongoing conversation between local and remote machines.

dpi – *dots per inch*. A measure of screen resolution; indicates the number of dots or pixels that are printed or displayed in a linear inch.

echo – The character that appears on the screen in response to a typed character; indicates that the computer has received and processed the data sent to it.

environment variable – A configuration setting defined for a particular instance of a command shell or a system as a whole; this setting is used by one or more programs that are subsequently run from that shell or on that system. For example, a common environment variable is `PATH=`*directory_list*. After setting the `PATH` variable in a given command shell, the operating system will automatically "look for" programs and files in the set of directories specified by *directory_list*.

Environment variables can sometimes be set directly from a command line on an as-needed basis, but are more commonly set in a startup command file like `.login`, `.cshrc`, `.profile` (UNIX), or `AUTOEXEC.BAT` (DOS). The specific syntax used to specify environment variables depends on your operating system and/or command shell.

Ethernet – A type of local-area network (LAN) that enables real-time communication between machines connected directly together through cables. Ethernet was developed by Xerox in 1976, originally for linking minicomputers at the Palo Alto Research Center. A widely implemented network from which the IEEE 802.3 standard for contention networks was developed, Ethernet uses a bus topology (configuration) and relies on the form of access known as CSMA/CD to regulate traffic on the main communication line.

Network nodes are connected by coaxial cable (in either of two varieties known as Thin and Thick) or by twisted pair wiring. Thin Ethernet cabling is 5 millimeters (about 0.2 inch) in diameter and can connect network stations over a distance of 300 meters. Thick Ethernet cabling is 1 centimeter (about 0.4 inch) in diameter and can connect stations up to 1000 meters (about 3300 feet) apart.

Ethernet address – A six-part hexadecimal number that identifies a hardware device on an Ethernet network; for example, `2:60:8C:A6:34:29`. Every hardware device designed for Ethernet communications is assigned a unique Ethernet address by the hardware manufacturer; this address cannot be changed by the user.

export – To make a file system available on a network file server so that other machines on the network can connect to it. In some operating systems, sometimes referred to as *share*.

FAT – *File Allocation Table*. Also called *DOS/FAT*. The file system used by the DOS operating system; specifically, a hidden operating system table that stores the names and locations of files stored on DOS disks. DOS/FAT volumes (single logical drives) can be a maximum of 2 gigabytes in size. DOS/FAT files can be a maximum of eight alphanumeric characters, followed by a period, followed by a maximum of three alphanumeric characters. For example:

```
ABCDEFGH.123
12345678.ABC
```

Additionally, the following are special reserved characters that are not allowed in the alphanumeric portions of DOS/FAT file names:

```
. , ; / \ [ ]
: < > | + = "
```

See also **file system**.

file locking – A network service that prevents simultaneous modification of a single region of a file by two or more users. *See also* **lock manager**.

file mapping – Automatic conversion by Wabi of various incompatible file elements between DOS/FAT and NFS file systems; makes transparent file access through Wabi across different operating systems possible. Specifically, Wabi software maps (and preserves the original state of) the following file elements:

- File securities and attributes
- File name length
- Uppercase/lowercase characters
- Special and illegal characters

See also **file system**.

file permissions – Refers to the three types of file access—read, write, and execute—allowed on a file server. As the owner of a file, you can grant all or some of these permissions to individual users, user groups, or users on the network as a whole. Similar permissions can be applied to directories.

file sharing – A software mechanism that prevents simultaneous access or modification to entire files. When a file is opened, the sharing mechanism determines access rights (like read or write) to be granted, and rights to be denied. For example, you may have write access to a particular file, but the sharing mechanism may also detect that another program has put a deny write restriction on the file; you would therefore be unable to modify the file until the deny write restriction is removed. In DOS, the file sharing mechanism is a program called `SHARE.EXE`. There is no direct UNIX equivalent, but similar file locking functions are implemented in the Solaris environment with the `lockd` lock daemon. Compare with **file locking**.

file system – The internal data structure used by an operating system to name, store, and track files on a disk. Different operating systems use different (that is, incompatible) file systems. For example, DOS uses the DOS/FAT system; many UNIX systems use Sun's NFS file system. Wabi software provides a transparent, automatic means by which files can be easily shared between different file systems. *See also* **FAT**, **NFS**.

focus window – The window to which keyboard and mouse input is directed. In general, the keyboard focus belongs to the *root window*, which has the effect of directing input to the window in which the pointer is currently positioned. Some clients, however, may automatically grab the focus, regardless of the current pointer position. Also sometimes called the **active window**.

font – A set of printable characters sharing a common size and design. Fonts may be designed with *fixed-width* or variable-width (*proportional*) character cells. *Bitmapped* fonts are stored as discrete sets of bitmaps in specific sizes. *Scalable* (or *outline*) fonts are stored as mathematical functions describing the outlines of the fonts; such fonts can be sized, rotated, slanted, and filled freely.

font alias – A substitute name for a font; used in a lookup table to automatically substitute one font for another. Font aliases are stored in a font alias file, which must be located in your font directory.

`fonts.dir` file – An index file listing the number and names of the fonts available in a given font directory. `fonts.dir` files can be created by using the `mkfontdir` command.

font directory – A directory or set of directories on the font host that contain font files; these font files are downloaded as needed by a workstation.

font file – A file that contains the definition of a font. Fonts are stored in a variety of formats.

font host – (1) In X Window-based systems, a machine on the network containing font files used by local display servers. Display servers on the network download fonts as needed from the font host. Font files can be quite large; therefore, some networks may have a machine that is dedicated to the task of font serving. Also called a **font server**. (2) In X Window-based systems, a software process that manages the distribution and display of X fonts according to the X *font service protocol. See* **font service protocol**. (3) In Wabi software, a proprietary font server program, named `wabifs`, that interacts with an X11R5-based server via the font service protocol.

font server – *See* **font host**.

font service protocol – An extensible, standardized X Window System communication protocol used between X font servers and X font clients. Designed by Jim Fulton of Network Computing Devices, and introduced in the X11R5 release of the X Window System. The font service protocol provides a standardized format for the exchange of font data between font server and client, and provides an interface through which the font server can resolve disparate font formats.

FTP – *File Transfer Protocol.* An Internet file transfer protocol (and program) that can handle binary and ASCII data. Note that most implementations of FTP require a valid login name and nonblank password to operate. *See also* **TFTP**.

gateway – A computer that provides a link between two dissimilar networks. Typically, a user logs in from a computer running one type of network software to a remote gateway running another type of network software. From the gateway, the user can access other machines on the gateway machine's local network. Gateway software and hardware handle the protocol conversion of data between the two networks.

gateway address – The IP address of a gateway computer. *See also* **netmask**.

glyph – The bitmapped representation of a single character in a specific font.

group ID – A unique number associated with a group name on a file server. Generally, the file server assigns your group ID to any files that you create. *See also* **group name**, **user ID**.

group name – The name assigned to a group of users on a network. Members of a group share common file-access privileges. The group name is mapped to a group ID. For example, "engineering" could be a group name that maps to the group ID 123. A user may belong to several groups. *See also* **group ID**, **user name**.

hard copy – A permanent copy of the displayed data. Hard copy usually refers to a printout or plot.

hexadecimal – A base-16 numbering system wherein the letters A through F represent the base-10 numbers 10 through 15; used as a shorthand for representing all the possible values in a byte. In hexadecimal notation (called *hex* for short), each single hex digit represents four binary digits (bits). Table G-1 shows the equivalencies between decimal, hexadecimal, and binary numbers.

Table G-1   Decimal/Hexadecimal/Binary Equivalencies

Dec	Hex	Binary	Dec	Hex	Binary	Dec	Hex	Binary	Dec	Hex	Binary
0	0	0000	4	4	0100	8	8	1000	12	C	1100
1	1	0001	5	S	0101	9	9	1001	13	D	1101
2	2	0010	6	6	0110	10	A	1010	14	E	1110
3	3	0011	7	7	0111	11	B	1011	15	F	1111

Note that X client applications can accept hexadecimal notation (prefixed by a # character) in all command-line options relating to color.

host – (1) in a network, a computer that primarily provides services such as computation, database access, or special programs. (2) The primary or controlling computer in a multiple-computer installation.

host name – A unique character string used to identify a device on a network; part of the device's domain name.

hub – A device for connecting the nodes in a network.

icon – A small graphical representation of an object, such as a window, program, file, or directory folder.

input device – A hardware device that enables a user to communicate with the computer. Examples of input devices are keyboard, mouse, track ball, light pen, joy stick, or digitizer tablet.

internet; Internet – (1) (*lower-case "i"*) A collection of networks interconnected by a set of gateways or routers that enable them to function as single, large virtual network. (2) (*upper-case "I"*) The largest internet in the world, consisting of large national backbone nets (such as *MILNET, NSFNET,* and *CREN*) and a myriad of regional and local campus networks all over the world. The Internet uses the Internet Protocol (IP) suite. To be on the Internet, the user must have IP connectivity; i.e., be able to **Telnet** to—or **PING**—other systems. Networks with only email connectivity are not actually classified as being on the Internet.

IP – *Internet Protocol.* A subset of the TCP/IP protocol describing software that tracks Internet addresses and routes outgoing and incoming messages.

IP address – *Internet Protocol (IP) Address.* A 32-bit, dot-separated number that uniquely identifies every computer connected to the Internet; for example, `129.555.205.14`. An *internet* is a collection of networks connected in such a way that they can act as a single, virtual network; the *Internet* (with a capital "I") is the largest internet in the world. The Internet provides an addressing scheme for all devices that are connected to it. The Internet also provides the IP Suite (sometimes called TCP/IP), which is the set of rules governing data transfer that is utilized by Wabi software. *See also* **Ethernet address**, **Domain Name Service**, **Internet**, **TCP/IP**.

Kbyte (KB) – *kilobyte.* 1024 bytes of information.

Kermit – A file transfer protocol, developed by Columbia University. Kermit is designed to support file transfer between nearly all types of computer systems. Kermit ensures reliable, error-free transmissions, despite telephone and data line noise.

kernel – The core functional module in the UNIX operating system.

LED – *light-emitting diode.* Semiconductor diodes that emit light when current passes through them; commonly used in computer and other equipment. For example, the lights on or above the CapsLock, ScrollLock, NumLock, and Compose keys on most computer keyboards are LEDs.

lock manager – A daemon (for example, `lockd`) on some NFS servers and all Solaris systems that controls file access and sharing; specifically the simultaneous access of files or regions of files. For example, if User A opens a file, the lock manager enforces rules that determine whether User B can open that file at the same time and, if simultaneous access is allowed, whether User B can modify the file. Most, but not all, NFS implementations provide some sort of lock manager. File locking under Wabi software is controlled by a lock manager. *See also* **file locking**.

login – The process by which you identify yourself to a remote server, usually by entering your user name and password. After logging in, an *authentication server* verifies your user name and password, and allows you access to some or all available server resources, depending on the privileges assigned to you by a system administrator. *See also* **authentication server**, **logout**, **password**, **user name**.

`.login` – A startup script that is run automatically for a user when that user logs in to a UNIX system host. The `.login` script provides a means to automate the setup of the user's general environment, such as defining the `PATH`, `DISPLAY`, and other variables, and launching applications or other scripts. Note that the `.login` script is run only if the user's environment is configured to run a UNIX C shell; if the user's environment is configured for the Bourne shell, a similar script, named `.profile`, is run instead. *See also* **`.profile`**.

logout – To end a user session; depending on your system configuration, the logout process also terminates one or more network connections. *See also* **login**, **mount point**, **NFS**.

magic cookie – *MIT-MAGIC-COOKIE-1.* One of the authentication protocols used by X11/NeWS™ to authenticate client connections. The MIT-MAGIC-COOKIE-1 authorization protocol was developed at the Massachusetts Institute of Technology. At display server startup, a magic cookie is created for the server and the user who started the system. On every connection attempt, the user's client sends the magic cookie to the server as part of the connection packet. This magic cookie is compared with the server's magic cookie. If the two magic cookies match, the connection is allowed; if they do not match, the connection is denied. Magic cookies are also sometimes used on a per-application basis as part of a licensing scheme.

man pages – In most UNIX-based systems, on-line, command-oriented help texts you can access from any UNIX shell prompt. Most operating system commands, and often other scripts and programs, are accompanied by man pages with usage instructions. To access a man page, enter the following command at a UNIX shell prompt:

```
man command
```

where command is the name of the command for which you want to display information. For example:

```
man chmod
```

displays information about the `chmod` command.

menu – A list of options or commands displayed on screen by a program. Users can select a given menu item by clicking on it with the mouse, or by typing a selected letter in the item's name, or by using the cursor (arrow) and Enter keys to respectively highlight and select the item. Menus are generally either *pop-up* or *pull-down* in design. Pop-up menus are displayed at the current pointer position; pull-down menus sometimes make use of a horizontal *menu bar* containing a number of menu names; alternatively, the pull-down menu may be represented by a small *down arrow*. In either case, when the user clicks on a particular menu name or down arrow, the items associated with that menu are displayed in a drop-down list.

MENU mouse button – The (by default) rightmost button on the three-button mouse included with many UNIX-based workstations. Clicking the MENU button displays a pop-up menu at the current pointer position; the specific menu that pops up depends on the current context in the active window. *See also* **ADJUST mouse button** and **SELECT mouse button**.

mkfontdir – A utility is used to create `fonts.dir` files, which are index files that list the number and names of the fonts available in a given font directory. *See also* **`fonts.dir` file**.

modem – A contraction of the words modulator-demodulator. A modem modulates and demodulates signals transmitted and received over a phone line. A modem is used at the host and terminal end of a connecting telephone line.

monochrome – (1) The display of one foreground color and one background color; for example, white on black, black on white, and white on blue. Bitmapped shades of gray are created by dithering black and white pixels. (2) In the X Window environment, a special case of `StaticGray` in which there are only two colormap entries.

mount daemon – A network server-based daemon, called `mountd`, that provides NFS volume-mounting services for users of Wabi.

mount point – A location in an NFS directory structure to which you connect (or *mount*) and assign a local disk drive letter, thus creating a *virtual disk drive*. For example, if your home directory on an NFS-based file system is `/home/yourstuff`, you could define that directory as a mount point, and then assign `G:` as the virtual disk drive to represent that directory from within Wabi. From the Windows File Manager, you could then click on the icon for `G:` to display the files in `/home/yourstuff`. *See also* **NFS**, **virtual disk drive**.

mouse – A small, palm-sized input device used for pointing, selecting text, and drawing. When the mouse is moved across a flat surface, an optical, mechanical, or opto/mechanical mechanism generates electrical pulses that are translated into corresponding movement of a pointer symbol on screen, thereby allowing control over displayed applications. The mouse included with most UNIX workstations has three input control buttons: SELECT, ADJUST, and MENU, arrayed from left to right. The mouse included with most DOS-based PCs like the Microsoft mouse) has two buttons. *See also* **pointer**.

name server – A program run on a remote host that translates a local device name to its associated IP address. Sometimes also refers to the host computer on which the name server software is run. *See also* **domain name service**.

netmask – A number used by software to separate the local subnet address from the rest of given Internet protocol address.

NeWS – *Network extensible window system.* A PostScript-based window system developed and licensed by Sun Microsystems.

NFS – A UNIX-based distributed file system developed by Sun Microsystems that enables computers on a TCP or UDP network to cooperatively access each other's files in a transparent, seamless manner. Furthermore, instead of duplicating a set of directories on all machines on a network, NFS lets you have one common set of directories on one machine that can be shared by all other systems. *See also* **file system**.

NIS – *Network Information Service.* A distributed network database containing key information about the systems and users on the network. The NIS database is stored on a *master server* and all associated *slave servers*.

nobody – The default user name assigned to a user who logs in without specifying a "real" user name. By default, nobody has a primary group ID of –2, and is assigned a minimum number of system privileges, as determined by the system administrator. *See also* **password**, **user name**.

node – Any computer with an active network address.

NTP – *Network Time Protocol.* A set of communications rules governing the transmission of computer system-clock synchronization data across the Internet. *See also* **Internet**, **NTP server**.

NTP server – A computer running the ntpd time server daemon, and connected to a network in such a way that it can provide NTP synchronization services for other machines on the network. *See also* **daemon**, **NTP**.

NVRAM – *Nonvolatile Random-Access Memory.* A type of RAM that retains information when power is removed from the system. *See also* **RAM**.

octal – The base-8 numbering system, consisting of digits 0 through 7. The octal system is used in programming as a compact means of representing binary numbers. Because octal consists of eight digits, and because three bits can take any one of eight different combinations, binary numbers are commonly divided into groups of three bits for conversion to octal. *See also* **binary**, **hexadecimal**, **one's complement**.

olwm – *OPEN LOOK Window Manager.* The executable file for the X Window-based OPEN LOOK window management software package included with the Solaris operating environment; provides functionality for opening, closing, moving, stacking, and resizing windows, and trapping mouse, keyboard, and other input.

one's complement – Also *1's complement.* A number in the binary (base-2) system that is the complement of another number. To derive the one's complement of a binary number, simply reverse each digit. For example, reversing the digits in `0101` produces the one's complement `1010`. *See also* **binary**, **octal**.

OPEN LOOK – A graphical windowing management system derived from the X Window System and trademarked by AT&T; the windowing system included with the Solaris operating enviroment.

OpenWindows – An X Window-compliant graphical desktop environment developed by Sun Microsystems. The OpenWindows environment comprises OPEN LOOK window management software with various DeskSet™ utilities (client applications), such as a Mail tool, Print tool, File Manager, and Calendar. OpenWindows is bundled with the SunOS operating system in the Solaris 2.*x* package.

OPENWINHOME – An environment variable that points to the location of the OpenWindows directories; used by many OpenWindows-based applications. By default, `OPENWINHOME` is set to `/usr/openwin`.

.openwin-init – An OpenWindows desktop configuration script that brings up the user's X desktop. It describes, among other things, screen colors and layout, and which client applications to open. This file is automatically created or modified when you save your desktop workspace with the Save Workspace command on the Workspace Utilities menu.

package – (1) A collection of software grouped for modular installation. (2) A computer application consisting of one or more programs created to perform a particular type of work; for example, an accounting package or a spreadsheet package.

packet – A group of data combined or divided into a fixed-length format (individual packets), which is then transmitted over communications lines. By breaking large amounts of data into fixed-length packets, the data can be transmitted more easily, and provides the possibility for dynamic routing, in which all packets in a single message do not have to be sent along the same route—the most efficient combination of routes may be used instead.

parity bit – In 7-bit data communications, the eighth bit in a byte used for error detection. A parity bit is added to the end of a byte so the total number of 1s is either always even (even parity), or odd (odd parity), and the total number of bits is eight.

password – A character string used to verify a user name when a user logs in to a network server. For example, a user name might be `tarzan`, and the password, `swinging`. In general, though, passwords should not be so easily associated with a user. For example, you should not set your password to be your telephone number, birth date, first name, spouse's name, or similar words that are easy for a would-be snoop to guess.

Most networks require you to enter a password before allowing you any significant access to network resources. Ask your system administrator for information about how to set your password. *See also* **login**, **user name**, **nobody**.

PATH – An environment variable that specifies the names and ordering of directories the operating system should search when attempting to run a program or locate a file. For example, if `PATH=/home/foo`, and an executable named `bar` is located in the `/home/foo` directory, a user could enter the `bar` command from any other directory, and the operating system would be able to locate and run it. If `/home/foo` was not defined in the `PATH`, however, the user would have to either switch first to the `/home/foo` directory or enter the full *pathname* with the command; that is, `/home/foo/bar`. Many application programs reference the `PATH` variable to locate ancillary files without specific user interaction; the `PATH` variable must point to the proper directories for such programs to run. *See also* **environment variable**.

PING – *Packet Internet Groper.* A program used to test accessibility of
destination systems by sending them an *Internet control message
protocol* (*ICMP*) echo request and waiting for a reply. The term is used
as a verb: "PING host X to see if it is up!"

pixel – Short for *picture element.* In a raster grid, the smallest unit that
can be addressed and assigned a color or intensity. The pixel is
represented by some number of bits in the frame buffer, and is
illuminated by a collection of phosphor dots in the CRT that are
struck by the beams(s) of the electron gun. *See also* **raster**.

pixel value – An n-bit value, where n is the number (depth) of bit planes
used in a particular window or **pixmap**. For a window, indexes a
colormap to determine the specific color(s) to be displayed. *See also*
bit plane.

pixmap – A three-dimensional array of bits; specifically, a pixmap is a
two-dimensional array of pixels, where each pixel can be a value from
0 to $2n-1$, and where n is the depth (z axis)—the third dimension—of
the pixmap. Alternatively, a pixmap can be thought of as a stack of n
bitmaps.

pkgadd – An installation utility included with Solaris 2.*x* software; the
required tool for installing Wabi package. `pkgadd` is located by default
in the `/usr/sbin` directory. *See also* `swm`, `swmtool`.

pointer – In the X window environment, the arrow or other marker that
indicates to the window system and to the user which window is
active. The user positions the pointer within a chosen window. The
pointer is also called a cursor, although the term cursor should be
reserved for the text marker that indicates the current input location
for a text character. *See also* **cursor**.

pointing device – A mechanical or electrical device, such as a mouse, used
to manipulate the screen pointer. *See also* **pointer**, **cursor**, and
mouse.

PostScript – A page description language (PDL) published by Adobe Systems Incorporated. PostScript describes the appearance of text and graphics on printed pages. The best-known page-description language, PostScript uses English-like commands to control page layout and to load and scale outline fonts. Because PostScript uses scalable outline fonts, it can create a font of any size, giving the user flexibility in creating documents. PostScript is used in many printers, either as the only print mode or as one alternative among several. *See also* **Display PostScript**.

privileges – A set of one or more permissions granted by a system administrator to a user; allows that user to view, run, add, modify or delete programs, files, and/or system configuration settings.

.profile – A startup script that is run automatically for a user when that user logs in to a UNIX system host. The .profile script provides a means to automate the setup of the user's general environment, such as defining the PATH, DISPLAY, and other variables, and launching applications or other scripts. Note that the .profile script is run only if the user's environment is configured to run a UNIX Bourne shell; if the user's environment is configured for the C shell, a similar script, named .login, is run instead. *See also* **.login**.

protocol – A formal description of messages to be exchanged and rules to be followed for two or more systems to exchange information.

PseudoColor – A class of **colormap** in which screen colors are rendered by using pixel values to index a colormap with separate red, green, and blue values (RGB), which may be changed dynamically.

RAM – *Random Access Memory.* Semiconductor-based memory that can be read or written by the CPU or other hardware devices. The storage locations can be accessed in any order. Note that the various types of ROM memory are also capable of random access; the term RAM, however, is generally understood to refer to volatile memory, which loses its contents when power is removed, and which can be written to as well as read. *See also* **NVRAM**.

RARP – *Reverse Address Resolution Protocol.* The Internet protocol that a diskless host uses to find its Internet address at startup. RARP maps a physical (hardware) address to an Internet address. *See also* **ARP**.

RARP database – A database on a network server containing hardware addresses and their corresponding IP addresses.

raster – When speaking of display or print devices, a set of horizontal lines composed of individual pixels, used to render screen or page images. For example, the images on a typical computer monitor are rendered by projecting an electron beam in a zig-zag pattern that moves down the screen one horizontal line at a time. *See also* **pixel**.

remote host – A nonlocal computer on the network that provides services to other devices on the network. Such services include file serving, computation, client applications, login and authorization, and message routing.

resource – In the X Window System, variables used to customize the appearance or behavior of a client; such variables are compiled in one or more resource files, for example `.Xresources` and `.Xdefaults`. Resources can be defined at the system level and the local level; for all machines, one machine, or a subset of machines; and for specific and general features in one or many client applications. The various resources files that may exist are read and processed by a *resource manager*. Resources can also be applied on a client-by-client, as-needed basis by launching a given client with command-line options that specify the desired resources.

RGB – *Red-Green-Blue*. An *additive* method for defining color in which the primary colors red, green, and blue are combined to form other colors. Adding no color produces black, and adding 100 percent of all three colors produces white. The range of colors that can be displayed on-screen depends on the number of bits that have been assigned to each pixel.

RGB colormap – A lookup table (usually a text file named `rgb.txt`), containing red, green, and blue color intensities, along with a name for each particular color created from these combined primaries; allows you to use a color name, such as "navy blue" instead of having to specify numeric red, green, and blue values.

RISC – *Reduced Instruction Set Computer.* A computer architecture based on a chipset that is designed to perform a limited number of instructions; the architecture upon which SPARC machines are based. Compared to architectures based on *CISC* (*Complex Instruction Set Computer*) chipsets (as used by PCs built around Intel's 80*x*86 processors), RISC architectures are optimized to perform the most common instructions faster. The processing burden required by more complex or less common instructions is handled by software, rather than directly in the RISC hardware.

root menu – *See* Workspace **menu**.

root user – UNIX user name that grants special privileges to the person who logs in with that ID. The user who can supply the correct password for the root user name is given *superuser* privileges for the particular machine.

root window – The window that fills the entire screen during an X session; all windows opened by client applications are stacked on top of the root window. Also sometimes called the *background window.*

router – A system responsible for making decisions about which of several paths network (or Internet) traffic will follow. To do this, the router uses a routing protocol to gain information about the network, and algorithms to choose the best route based on several criteria known as "routing metrics." In the International Standards Organization for Standardization's open systems interconnection (OSI) terminology, a router is a *network layer* intermediate system. *See also* **gateway**.

RPC – *Remote Procedure Call.* A mechanism that allows for client-server computing. The client program calls for procedures that a server application performs on another machine. The RPC protocol provides the set of rules that govern the interaction between the client and server. *See also* **client/server**, **protocol**.

screen saver – A utility program that blanks the screen (or displays an animated bitmap pattern) after a specified period of keyboard inactivity, or (under Solaris) when the user chooses the Lock Screen command from the Workspace Utilities menu. To unlock the screen, the user must enter his or her password. Microsoft Windows also includes a screen saver program, but this should *not* be used under Wabi.

scrollback – A feature that allows a user to view text that has scrolled off the screen.

SELECT mouse button – The (by default) leftmost button on the three-button mouse included with most UNIX-based workstations. Clicking the SELECT button selects an object, initiates a menu command, activates a button, or inserts a text insertion cursor at current pointer position. Double-clicking on an icon opens or launches the application with which the icon is associated. *See also* **ADJUST mouse button** and **MENU mouse button**.

server – (1) In the **client-server** model for file systems, the server is a machine with compute resources (and is sometimes called the *compute server*) and large memory capacity. Client machines can remotely access and make use of these resources. (2) In the client-server model for the X Window System, the server is a process that provides windowing services to an application, or *client process*.

Solaris – A UNIX-based operating environment developed by Sun Microsystems; includes the SunOS operating system and the X-based OpenWindows windowing environment.

SPARC – The 32-bit **S**calable **P**rocessor **ARC**hitecture from Sun Microsystems. SPARC is based on a reduced instruction set (**RISC**) concept. The architecture was designed by Sun and its suppliers in an effort to significantly improve price and performance. SPARC is now a registered trademark of SPARC International, Inc.

StaticColor – A class of **colormap** in which screen colors are rendered by using pixel values to index a predefined hardware colormap. The RGB values cannot be changed.

StaticGray – A class of **colormap** in which screen grays are rendered by using pixel values mapped to a predefined hardware monochrome map. The values cannot be changed.

stipple – A bitmap pattern used to tile a region that will serve as an additional clip mask for a fill operation with the current foreground color.

subnet – A working scheme that divides a single logical network into smaller physical networks to simplify routing.

subnet mask – A bit mask used to select bits from an Internet address for subnet addressing. The mask is 32 bits long and selects the network portion of the Internet address and one or more bits of the local portion. Synonymous with *address mask*.

SunOS – *See* **Solaris**.

swm – A character-based installation tool included with the Solaris 2.*x* environment; can sometimes be used instead of `pkgadd` (but not with Wabi software). `swm` is located by default in the `/usr/sbin` directory. *See also* **pkgadd**, **swmtool**.

swmtool – A graphical installation tool included with the Solaris 2.*x* environment; can sometimes be used instead of `pkgadd` (but not with Wabi software). `swmtool` is located by default in the `/usr/sbin` directory. *See also* **pkgadd**, **swm**.

TCP – *Transmission Control Protocol.* The major transport protocol in the Internet suite of protocols providing reliable, connection-oriented, full-duplex streams. Uses IP for delivery. *See also* **IP**, **TCP/IP**.

TCP/IP – *Transmission Control Protocol/Internet Protocol.* The protocol suite originally developed for the Internet. SunOS networks run on TCP/IP by default.

TCP window size – The maximum data packet (window) size that can be transmitted on the network. A data window has header and trailer "envelopes" with message data in between. Common window sizes are 512, 1024, or 2048 bytes, although other sizes are possible.

Telnet – The virtual terminal protocol in the Internet suite of protocols; enables users of one host to log in to a remote host and interact as normal terminal users of that host. When used as a verb, it means to log in to a system via Telnet.

TFTP – *Trivial File Transfer Protocol.* A simpler version of the FTP protocol that does not require a user name, account, or password. This protocol is used in some **RARP** processes.

ThickWire Ethernet – *See* **Ethernet**.

title bar – In most windowing environments, the band across the top of most windows; displays the window title.

twisted-pair Ethernet – *TPE. See* **Ethernet**.

UDP – *User Datagram Protocol.* A transport protocol in the Internet suite of protocols. UDP, like TCP, uses IP for delivery. Unlike TCP, UDP is *stateless*—that is, it exchanges datagrams without acknowledgments or guaranteed delivery, and makes no attempt to monitor the state, or condition, of the sending or receiving device. Furthermore, the server maintains no information about previous NFS requests or how various NFS requests may relate to each other. In the UDP scenario, the client program must keep track of all required information, including sorting data packets into the proper order and requesting the retransmission of lost or erroneous packets. *See also* **TCP/IP**, **protocol**.

umask – A template (or *mask*) that lets you specify default permissions to use when creating UNIX files and directories. By default, UNIX files and directories are created without read, write, or execute restrictions for the file's owner, group, or world. A umask can then be applied to provide increasing levels of restrictions—you can only restrict permissions with a umask, never increase them. Restrictions on individual files and directories can be removed later with any one of several UNIX commands. For example, you could specify a umask that allows read, write, and execute access to your files for yourself only, and not for members of your group, or the rest of the "world." You could then remove those restrictions, as needed, on a file-by-file basis. *See also* **file permissions**, **NFS**.

UNC – *Universal Naming Convention.* A means by which you can access files on a remote server without actually mounting the remote directory that contains those files. A common syntax is as follows:

> *\\servername\resource\dirpath\file(s)*

- *servername* is the name of the remote server on which the files you are interested in are located. This name is preceded by two backslashes (\\).

- *resource* is the name of a shared (exported) directory on the remote server.

- *dirpath* is the subdirectory, if any, containing the files in which you are interested.

- *file(s)* is the name of one or more files.

Wabi 2.0 and 2.1 software does not support UNC syntax; support is planned for future Wabi releases.

Unicode – An international 16-bit character-encoding standard that accommodates the characters in most of the languages in the world, including Japanese, Chinese, Korean, Cyrillic, Hebraic, Arabic, and Sanskrit. *See also* **file system**.

user ID – A unique number associated with each user name. Generally, a file server assigns your user ID to files that you create, and makes you the "owner" of those files. *See also* **user name**, **group ID**.

user name – The character string by which you identify yourself on the network. Generally, you must enter your user name and password when logging in to a network. Your user name is mapped to a user ID. For example, `tarzan` could be a user name that maps to user ID `123`. *See also* **user ID**, **group name**, **password**, **login**.

virtual disk drive – A drive letter assigned to an NFS **mount point**. For example, you could assign `H:` to represent a remote NFS directory named `/dev/home/josephine` to applications under Wabi. You could then refer to `H:` to access the files in `/dev/home/josephine`.

wabifs – The Wabi font server program; starts automatically if an available X11R5 server running the font service protocol is detected. Refer to "Wabi Font Server" on page 281 for more information. *See also* **font service protocol**.

wabiprog – The main Wabi program. All Windows applications running under Wabi software run within the `wabiprog` process.

window – In applications and graphical interfaces, a portion of the screen that can contain its own document or message. In window-based programs, the screen can be divided into several windows, each of which has its own boundaries and can contain a different document (or another view into the same document). Each window might also contain its own menu or other controls, and the user might be able to enlarge and shrink individual windows as desired.

window manager – An X Window program that handles the opening, closing, resizing, moving, and layering of windows on the screen for X client applications. As part of this process, a window manager handles all keyboard and mouse input, passing this input as appropriate to particular clients.

Workspace menu – The Solaris menu that is displayed when the MENU
mouse button is clicked anywhere in the *root window*. This menu
provides basic client programs and utilities, such as Lock Screen,
Refresh, and Exit. Also called the *root menu.*

wrapper – A script associated with one or more binary files; provides a
mechanism for accessing hardware- or version-specific binaries
without requiring modification of the execution path. With Wabi
software, the `wabi` command is a wrapper that calls, among other
things, the executables `wabiprog` and (usually) `wabifs`.

X11R5 – *X Window System Version 11 Release 5.* A version of the X
Window System; released in the Fall of 1991. Many significant
features were added to the X Window System in X11R5; in particular,
font service mechanisms (including support for the X **font service
protocol**), scalable fonts, internationalized text input and output,
device-independent color, and support for high-level 3-D graphics. *See
also* **X Window System**.

X11R6 – *X Window System Version 11 Release 6.* The latest version of the
X Window System; released in May or 1994. *See also* **X Window
System**.

X client – *See* **client application**.

X Consortium – The nonprofit organization of vendors and universities
responsible for maintaining the X Window core software and for
guiding the process of adapting X to different platforms and needs.
The X Consortium is chaired by the Massachusetts Institute of
Technology (MIT). The X Consortium general offices can be reached by
telephone at (617) 374–1000.

.Xdefaults – A common name for a resource file used by the `xrdb` client
on the X host or other client applications on any other host to build a
resource database upon startup. Like `.Xresources`, an `.Xdefaults`
file can be created for system-wide use, in a directory specified by the
system administrator, and for individual users, usually in a given
user's `home` directory. *See also* **resource**.

xdm – A client that automatically starts an **X server** and keeps it running;
provides a means by which users can log in and start other client
applications, regardless of the display server they are using. `xdm` is
usually run as a **daemon** on a host machine.

XDMCP – *X Display Manager Control Protocol.* A control protocol shared by the xdm client and X servers on the network; introduced in X11R4 to solve a number of problems with the version of xdm released in X11R3.

xdpyinfo – A client that determines the dimensions and resolution of any display server on which it is run.

xfd – The X Window font display utility; displays in a grid all characters of a particular font. *See also* **font**.

xfontsel – A utility that enables font selection; you can browse the complete character set of each available font in a window, and then click SELECT to choose the font. Note that this utility is available from the *X Consortium*, but is not included with the OpenWindows software package. *See also* **X Consortium**.

X host – The machine used to start an xterm program. *See also* xterm.

xlsfonts – A utility that lists all fonts available on the X server; display a lists of the font file names in the fonts directory.

.Xresources – *See* **.Xdefaults**.

X server – *See* **server**.

xset – A utility that enables users to change font paths while logged in to a host.

xterm – A basic terminal emulation program for X Window systems; provides a command interface for X display servers. xterm supports bitmapped, X-compliant applications and standard alphanumeric terminal emulations, in particular, VT100 and Tektronix® 4014.

X Window System – A network-based graphical windowing system and standard initially developed at the Massachusetts Institute of Technology. X Window (*X* for short) is based on a **client-server** model, in which application programs (*clients*) communicate with a display device indirectly via a display program (the *server*). Client programs do not need to run on the same machine as the server program, which makes the X Window System particularly suited for distributed computing environments. Many UNIX-based windowing systems—for example, OPEN LOOK and OpenVue—are derived from the X Window standard. *See also* **X11R5, X11R6**.

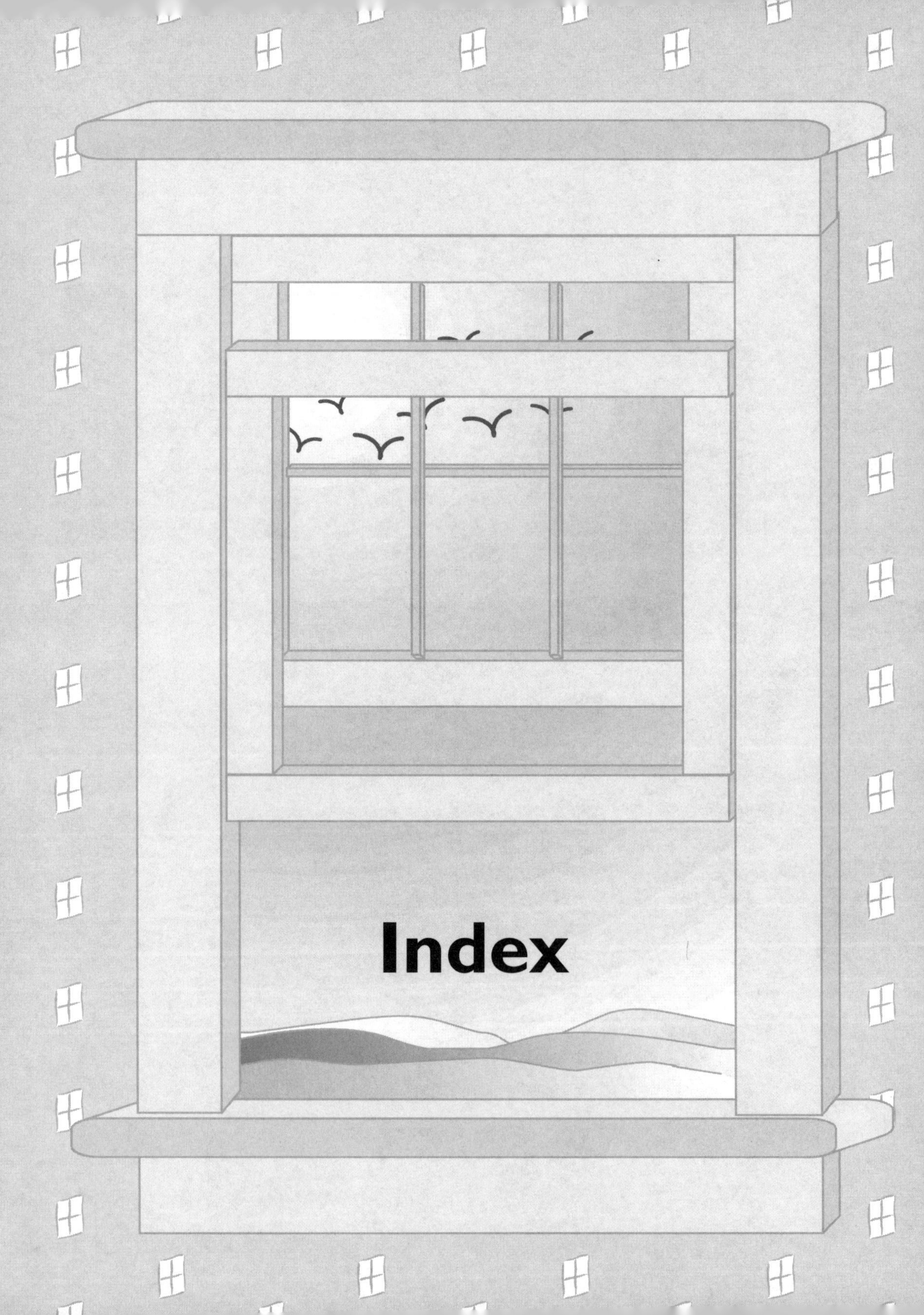

Index

Wabi 2: Opening Windows

Wabi 2: Opening Windows

Index

Wabi 2: Opening Windows